BlackBerry Enterprise Server for Microsoft® Exchange

Installation and Administration

Mitesh Desai

Dan Renfroe

BIRMINGHAM - MUMBAI

BlackBerry Enterprise Server for Microsoft® Exchange
Installation and Administration

First published: October 2007

Production Reference: 1151007

Published by Packt Publishing Ltd.
32 Lincoln Road
Olton
Birmingham, B27 6PA, UK.

ISBN 978-1-847192-46-2

www.packtpub.com

Cover Image by Vinayak Chittar (vinayak.chittar@gmail.com)

Credits

Author

Mitesh Desai

Co-author

Dan Renfroe

Reviewer

Dan Renfroe

Senior Acquisition Editor

David Barnes

Development Editor

Mithil Kulkarni

Technical Editor

Swapna. V. Verlekar

Editorial Manager

Dipali Chittar

Project Manager

Abhijeet Deobhakta

Project Coordinator

Sagara Naik

Indexer

Monica Ajmera

Proofreader

Damian Carvill

Production Coordinator

Shantanu Zagade

Cover Designer

Shantanu Zagade

About the Author

Mitesh Desai is a 29 year-old IT Consultant from London, UK. He has completed Blackberry projects for numerous clients in many different network infrastructures. He also operates an IT consultant company www.it-problems.co.uk

He enjoys a busy lifestyle supporting many prestigious companies in the heart of Central London, but makes time to enjoy sports and writing music.

He is also at hand on www.it-problems.co.uk to help budding Blackberry technicians.

About the Co-author

Dan Renfroe has been a technology professional for over ten years, working in diverse environments such as higher education, public safety, and federal government. He has a broad range of technical experience, including systems administration and analysis, multimedia development, technical writing, and quality assurance. He is currently a consultant for OST, Inc., a management consulting firm based in Washington, DC. He has authored multiple mobile and wireless technology articles for Network Computing magazine on topics ranging from mobile email servers and mobile VPN applications to WLAN infrastructure and analysis tools.

About the Reviewer

Dan Renfroe has been a technology professional for over ten years, working in diverse environments such as higher education, public safety, and federal government. He has a broad range of technical experience, including systems administration and analysis, multimedia development, technical writing, and quality assurance. He is currently a consultant for OST, Inc., a management consulting firm based in Washington, DC. He has authored multiple mobile and wireless technology articles for Network Computing magazine on topics ranging from mobile email servers and mobile VPN applications to WLAN infrastructure and analysis tools.

Table of Contents

Preface

Adopting and implementing new technologies can be a daunting task for IT professionals. Many times, we're already overwhelmed with the care and feeding of existing systems and networks and can hardly spare the time to properly plan, install, and configure a new system, to say nothing of the time required to learn about the underlying technology and architecture.

This book can't solve all of those problems... it can't give you more hours in a day or more money in your IT budget. When it comes to implementing a BlackBerry Enterprise Server environment for Microsoft Exchange, however, this book aims to provide the over-burdened IT administrator with some relief. We strive to provide you with the requisite knowledge to implement and administer a BlackBerry Enterprise Server. In addition to covering the basic administration and installation tasks, there are chapters devoted to the architecture and technical details of the BlackBerry environment.

This book is written for IT professionals and network administrators who are tasked with the implementation of a BlackBerry Enterprise Server. The text assumes basic familiarity with Microsoft Windows Server administration, but provides detailed instructions for administrators with varying levels of experience.

Each chapter is devoted to a specific implementation or administration topic, designed to provide readers with a technical introduction and, in the case of task-based chapters, detailed instructions on how to implement or configure settings within the BlackBerry environment. The book can be read cover-to-cover or readers may opt to jump around to gather specific information on topics of their interest.

We hope that you will find this book useful as you leap into the world of BlackBerry Enterprise Server!

What This Book Covers

Chapter 1, here readers will receive an introduction to the BlackBerry Enterprise Server, including the basic technological components and features.

Chapter 2 discusses the architecture in greater detail and the pre-requisites for an implementation.

Chapter 3 provides a walk-through on the steps required to satisfy installation pre-requisites, including Microsoft Windows and Exchange account creation and permissions.

Chapter 4, here the process for installing BlackBerry Enterprise Server is described in great detail.

Chapter 5, the creation of administrative users, provisioning of users and the methods of device activation are covered, including step-by-step instructions.

Chapter 6 details the IT policy capabilities of BlackBerry Enterprise Server and describes the process for deploying third-party applications and device software updates.

Chapter 7, readers are provided extensive background information on the settings that can be applied at the user, group and server-level to configure and enforce specific behaviors for the BlackBerry Enterprise Server.

Chapter 8 describes the security mechanisms that protect messages, data and devices within the BlackBerry environment and the approaches to disaster recovery and continuity of operations.

Who is This Book for

This book is written for IT professionals and network administrators that are tasked with implementation of a BlackBerry Enterprise Server. The text assumes basic familiarity with Microsoft Windows Server administration, but provides detailed instructions for administrators with varying levels of experience.

Conventions

In this book, you will find a number of styles of text that distinguish between different kinds of information. Here are some examples of these styles, and an explanation of their meaning.

New terms and **important words** are introduced in a bold-type font. Words that you see on the screen, in menus or dialog boxes for example, appear in our text like this: "clicking the **Next** button moves you to the next screen".

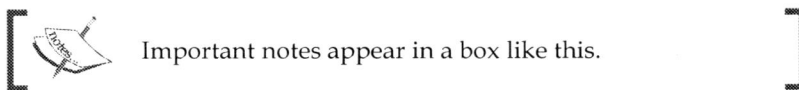 Important notes appear in a box like this.

Reader Feedback

Feedback from our readers is always welcome. Let us know what you think about this book, what you liked or may have disliked. Reader feedback is important for us to develop titles that you really get the most out of.

To send us general feedback, simply drop an email to feedback@packtpub.com, making sure to mention the book title in the subject of your message.

If there is a book that you need and would like to see us publish, please send us a note in the **SUGGEST A TITLE** form on www.packtpub.com or email suggest@packtpub.com.

If there is a topic that you have expertise in and you are interested in either writing or contributing to a book, see our author guide on www.packtpub.com/authors.

Customer Support

Now that you are the proud owner of a Packt book, we have a number of things to help you to get the most from your purchase.

Errata

Although we have taken every care to ensure the accuracy of our contents, mistakes do happen. If you find a mistake in one of our books—maybe a mistake in text or code—we would be grateful if you would report this to us. By doing this you can save other readers from frustration, and help to improve subsequent versions of this book. If you find any errata, report them by visiting http://www.packtpub.com/support, selecting your book, clicking on the **Submit Errata** link, and entering the details of your errata. Once your errata are verified, your submission will be accepted and the errata are added to the list of existing errata. The existing errata can be viewed by selecting your title from http://www.packtpub.com/support.

Questions

You can contact us at questions@packtpub.com if you are having a problem with some aspect of the book, and we will do our best to address it.

1
Introduction to the Blackberry World

In a world where decision makers demand information at their finger tips, the BlackBerry handheld device delivers it. It is rare to step into a corporate boardroom without seeing at least one person peering at a BlackBerry and several others with BlackBerries strapped to their hips. In fact, the constant use of these handheld devices is so prevalent that they have earned the nickname "Crackberry" due to the addictive behavior of their users.

For end users, with their ease of use and their access to push email, BlackBerries are a dream come true. For inexperienced IT administrators, the prospect of managing these high-end mobile devices loaded with sensitive corporate information can be a nightmare. As the demand for Blackberries grows within the corporate environment, the need for individuals who can expertly configure and administer the servers that support these devices will continue to expand. The BlackBerry Enterprise Server, or BES, provides the capability to deliver data to BlackBerry devices and to set and enforce security and management policies for these devices. In short, BES is the tool to ensure that you control the BlackBerries in your organization and not the other way around!

The installation and configuration of a Blackberry Enterprise Server can be far from easy, but with the help of this book you should be able to simplify the implementation of BES in your corporate environment. In this chapter, we will ease you into the world of BlackBerry Enterprise Servers by providing an overview of the components and capabilities of the BES, the security features of BES, and the data delivery mechanisms it provides.

BES Implementation Components

When tasked with implementing a BlackBerry Enterprise Server solution for their enterprise, many IT professionals may feel overwhelmed by the new technology and all that it entails. To make the task less daunting, we thought it would be helpful to describe the building blocks of a BES implementation. Preparing to install BES for your environment involves several components — the BlackBerry Enterprise Server, client devices, application servers, and networks.

BlackBerry Enterprise Server

There are many analogies that could be used to describe the BlackBerry Enterprise Server. In many ways, it's like an air traffic controller, managing the flow of traffic, or data in this case, directing it to its ultimate destination. The most common "traffic" is, of course, email messages; the BES serves as a conduit between the messaging server and the handheld device, ensuring consistent communications between the handheld and the email, or application server despite the sometimes-flaky nature of wireless networks.

The BES doesn't just serve as a traffic cop, however; it provides its own set of features and capabilities. The primary feature in the eyes of IT professionals is the device management capabilities that it offers. With a fleet of BlackBerry devices in the field, you'll want the capability to provision devices, de-activate, and wipe data from lost or stolen devices; and to enforce security policies. The BES delivers this and more, giving IT professionals the tools they need to effectively manage these highly-mobile corporate resources.

It's important to note that the BES is not a single service; it's actually made up of more than a dozen component services that combine to provide the functionality of BES. These components will be described in greater details in the next chapter, but the important thing to note is that they can be installed on a single server or distributed among several servers for greater scalability.

Clients

The clients in a BES implementation are BlackBerries, those ubiquitous wireless handheld devices strapped to the hips of top executives everywhere. Research in Motion (RIM), the manufacturer of the BlackBerry, has been producing wireless devices since the late 1990s. The capabilities of these devices have increased with each successive generation. The current generation of BlackBerries sports a rich array of features, including push email, mobile telephony, text messaging, Internet faxing, Web browsing, and myriad other wireless information services. RIM manufactures a range of BlackBerry models, providing consumers with options on the device from factor, size, and, of course, color.

It's also important to note that BlackBerries are not the only devices that can communicate with BlackBerry Enterprise Servers. RIM has licensed software known as BlackBerry Connect, which provides other device platforms with access to a similar set of capabilities with regard to BES access. Devices with BlackBerry Connect have push email, calendaring, and address lookup, similar to what's available on a BlackBerry. In addition, communication with these devices is secured in the same manner as a BlackBerry handheld. These devices are also subject to many of the administrative controls as a BlackBerry devices, making them easier for IT professionals to manage.

Application Servers

Like a stereo system without music, the BlackBerry Enterprise Server would be of little use without the support of third-party application servers. The array of third-party applications supported by BES runs the gamut from groupware and instant messaging to vertically-focused enterprise applications, including field force automation and Customer Relationship Management applications. The BES interfaces with these application servers, proxying information to and from the handheld client devices.

RIM doesn't play favorites when it comes to supporting these application servers. The list of groupware and instant messaging servers supported by BES is very solid.

Groupware Server Support	Instant Messaging Server Support
• Microsoft Exchange Server	• Microsoft Windows Messenger
• IBM Lotus Domino	• Microsoft Office Communicator
• Novell GroupWise	• IBM Lotus Sametime
	• Novell GroupWise Messenger

Networks

A BES implementation involves many different networks, some of which are entirely out of the control of the IT administrator. The handheld devices typically utilize the Wireless Wide Area Networks (WWANs) provided by the cellular operator, while the BES is usually housed on a corporate network behind the firewall where it can communicate with the various application servers. The BES initiates an outbound connection through the firewall to the BlackBerry Infrastructure operated by RIM; this infrastructure communicates with the BlackBerry handhelds, eliminating the need for the handhelds to connect directly to the BES. Alternatively, there is an implementation option, involving BlackBerry 7270 handhelds, in which the handheld devices use a corporate WLAN to communicate with BES, relying on SIP and IP telephony for voice services.

The typical BES architecture is depicted in the following figure:

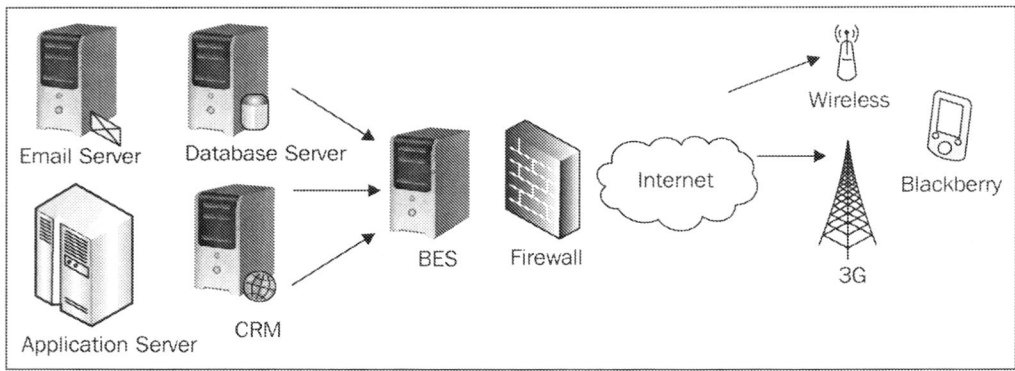

Pushing Data Down

There are two technical approaches to delivering data, especially email messages, to handheld devices. These approaches, known as **push** and **pull**, provide two different methods to achieve mobile data delivery. In a "pull" solution, the mobile device initiates the communication with the server on a frequent basis to check for new messages or other data. This is in contrast with a "push" solution, where the server pushes new data to the device as it is received. Both approaches have their merits, but most mobile messaging vendors, including RIM, have gravitated towards a push model for data delivery.

For BlackBerry users, the ultimate outcome of this push technology is that they don't have to lift a finger to receive their email. When new messages arrive for the user on the email server, the BES automatically sends a copy of the message to the user's handheld device. This is an improvement over previous mobile messaging products that would require the user to initiate the email synchronization activity, which made retrieving email a time-consuming process.

Blackberry Enterprise Solution Security

The topic of security weighs heavily on the minds of IT professionals, especially when they are planning to implement new services in their organization. RIM has developed a comprehensive approach to security for BlackBerry handhelds and their data. We will provide a brief overview of the security mechanisms built in to BES, including encryption, authentication, and security policies.

Encryption

Encryption is a key element of protecting the data that is managed by the BES. Encryption is applied in many ways.

- Data is encrypted while it is being transferred between the BES and the BlackBerry handheld.

- Data is encrypted on the BlackBerry handheld device.

- Data is encrypted in the BlackBerry configuration database, which is the database that stores information on the implementation.

BES utilizes symmetric key encryption algorithms to protect the data that is handled by the BlackBerry implementation. There are two industry-standard encryption algorithms used by BES, either Triple Data Encryption Standard (Triple DES or 3DES) or Advanced Encryption Standard (AES). 3DES uses 112-bit keys, while AES uses 256-bit keys, making AES the preferred encryption method. However, older BlackBerry devices may not support AES, which means that administrators must either use 3DES or a combination of AES and 3DES.

In addition to the standard encryption methods, BES provides the option to support several common desktop email encryption tools on your BlackBerry, including Secure Multipurpose Internet Mail Extensions (S/MIME) and OpenPGP. The S/MIME Support Package for BES provides the capability to install certificates on the BlackBerry device and allows users to send and receive S/MIME-encrypted messages. The PGP Support Package for BES provides the capability to install PGP keys on the BlackBerry device, allowing users to send and receive PGP-encrypted messages. These encryption methods may be used for emails and PIN messages, which are messages sent directly from one BlackBerry device to another.

In addition to the messaging security provided by the standard AES and 3DES encryption, as well as the S/MIME and OpenPGP options, BES encrypts the data traffic that is transmitted using the BlackBerry Mobile Data Service (MDS). MDS uses Hyper Text Transfer Protocol (HTTP) and Transport Control Protocol/Internet Protocol (TCP/IP) communications. These communications utilize Transport Layer Security/Secure Sockets Layer (TLS/SSL) to establish an HTTPS connection to the desired service.

Authentication

User authentication is a critical element for securing any service and BES is no exception. Authentication options are configurable by the BES administrator, but there are three basic user authentication methods.

1. Users are authenticated when activating a device for use with BES. A temporary device activation password is generated and communicated to the user; this ensures that only authorized users may add devices to the BlackBerry environment.

2. Administrators can require users to authenticate using a security password prior to using their handheld device. This ensures that only authorized users are able to access the data that is stored on the BlackBerry device. BES provides configurable options related to the password complexity and history.

3. Organizations that are highly security-conscious can implement two-factor authentication, using an optional BlackBerry Smart Card Reader, providing the security of a user password and the hardware token. BlackBerry MDS also supports the use of RSA SecurID® tokens to authenticate user access to MDS services.

Security Policies

BES provides a feature known as IT policies that allows administrators to configure a variety of aspects that govern BlackBerry device usage. While not all of them are security-specific, a subset of these policies provides options that secure BlackBerry devices. A sampling of the security-specific policies is listed below.

- Password policies, including enforcing device passwords, password complexity requirements, and device timeouts.

- Bluetooth policies, including data transfer options and device discoverability.

- Instant messenger policies, including availability of public IM services such as AIM and Google Talk.

- Application-specific policies, including application availability and audit reports.

In addition to a variety of security policies, a key security feature of the BES environment is the ability to remotely lock and wipe data from lost or stolen devices. This capability mitigates the risk that the data stored on BlackBerry handhelds might be accessed by unauthorized individuals.

Internet Browsing and Data Access

While most people only think of email when they think of BlackBerries, it is not the only service provided on BlackBerry handhelds. Access to Internet and intranet sites is a key feature of the BlackBerry and an area where the BES is preferable to standalone BlackBerry use. A standalone BlackBerry user, which is to say one that doesn't access a BES, has limitations in terms of access to Internet or intranet applications.

Non-BES BlackBerry users will typically use the BlackBerry Internet Service (BIS) or a Wireless Application Protocol (WAP) Gateway to access the Internet on their BlackBerry device. The BlackBerry Internet Service, hosted by RIM, provides users with access to Web pages that are converted into a format that is more suitable for viewing on a BlackBerry device. The WAP Gateway, hosted by the wireless operator, provides users with access to Web pages that are converted into a format that is suitable for a variety of mobile devices. Blackberry Internet Service communicates with the Blackberry Infrastructure using HTTP over the RIM IP Proxy Protocol (IPPP). This makes the delivery of HTML both faster and more efficient than HTTP over WAP in most current implementations.

BES implementations usually rely upon Mobile Data Services (MDS), a platform developed by RIM to enhance data delivery to BlackBerry devices. MDS provides functionality that is similar to the BIS, but also enhances the capability to access Internet and intranet sites, and provides a platform to deliver corporate applications and data on BlackBerry handhelds. With regard to Internet and intranet access, MDS provides enhanced security and data delivery features that are not found in the BIS. As previously mentioned, MDS provides TLS/SSL encryption capabilities, in addition to supporting AES and 3DES encryption. MDS enhances the data optimization and conversion, facilitating access to data by BlackBerry handhelds.

Following is a list of formats and standards supported by MDS.

Supported Image Formats	Graphics Interchange Format (GIF) Portable Network Graphics (PNG) Wireless Bitmap (WBMP) Joint Photographic Experts Group (JPEG)
Supported web scripting languages:	**WML**, WMLScript (1.2.1), **Compact HTML (cHTML)**, XHTML Mobile Profile (XHTML-MP), **HTML**, JavaScript™ (version 1.3 and subsets of 1.4 and 1.5), **Style Sheets (limited support)**

Summary

This chapter provided an overview of the BlackBerry Enterprise Server environment and the features and services that are available within that environment. In the next chapter, we will explore the architecture of a BlackBerry Enterprise Server implementation and discuss technical options related to the implementation.

2

BES Architecture and Implementation Planning

In the previous chapter, we provided you with a high-level overview of the BlackBerry Enterprise Server components and the capabilities that are delivered by BES. Planning is a key element of any IT implementation, but planning can only be accomplished with an understanding of the technical underpinnings of the proposed solution. In this chapter, we will delve more deeply into the technical architecture of BES in order to provide you with an understanding of what's under the hood. We will also cover the system requirements and pre-requisites for a BES implementation, including operating system, hardware, network, and database requirements.

BlackBerry Enterprise Server Components

As we mentioned in the first chapter, BlackBerry Enterprise Server is not a single service. Like many complex application servers, BES is comprised of a number of services and components that are integrated to deliver the full feature set. Below is a list of the components and a description of their function.

Component Name	Component Function
BlackBerry Attachment Service	The BlackBerry Attachment Service converts email attachments into a format that can be viewed on BlackBerry devices.
BlackBerry Collaboration Service	The BlackBerry Collaboration Service encrypts the communications between instant messaging servers and the instant messenger client on client on BlackBerry devices.

Component Name	Component Function
BlackBerry Configuration Database	The BlackBerry Configuration Database is a relational database that stores the configuration information for the BES components, using either Microsoft SQL Developer Edition (MSDE) or Microsoft SQL Server.
BlackBerry Controller	The BlackBerry Controller monitors BES components and restarts any stopped services.
BlackBerry Dispatcher	The BlackBerry Dispatcher handles compression and encryption for BlackBerry data.
BlackBerry Manager	The BlackBerry Manager is used for administration of the BES.
BlackBerry MDS Connection Service	The BlackBerry MDS Connection Service is used to connect BlackBerry devices to online content and applications.
BlackBerry MDS Services	The BlackBerry MDS Services provide connectivity between BlackBerry MDS Studio Applications on BlackBerry devices and enterprise applications.
BlackBerry MDS Studio Application Repository	The BlackBerry MDS Studio Application Repository stores and manages BlackBerry MDS Studio Applications.
BlackBerry Messaging Agent	The BlackBerry Messaging Agent serves as the connection between the email server and the other BES components.
BlackBerry Policy Service	The BlackBerry Policy Service manages the IT policies for the BlackBerry devices.
BlackBerry Router	The BlackBerry Router connects to the BlackBerry Infrastructure and communicates with the BlackBerry devices.
BlackBerry Synchronization Service	The BlackBerry Synchronization Service syncs organizer data (tasks, calendar, etc.) between the email server and the BlackBerry devices.

The component-based design of BES provides flexibility and scalability as you plan your implementation. This is due to the fact that the components can be installed on a single server or distributed among several servers based on your needs. The BlackBerry Enterprise Server components are integrated to deliver the desired services to your handheld clients.

BlackBerry Enterprise Server Requirements and Prerequisites

The BlackBerry Enterprise Server system requirements vary based on the number of users supported. Below are the recommended minimum requirements for a BlackBerry Enterprise Server v4.1 for Microsoft Exchange that supports 500 users. Refer to the BlackBerry Enterprise Server Version 4.1 for Microsoft Exchange Server Capacity Calculator at the BlackBerry Technical Solution Center (`http://www.blackberry.com/btsc/`) to calculate the system requirements for your environment.

- Intel® Pentium® IV, 2 GHz or better.
- 1.5GB RAM.

BES supports specific Microsoft Windows and Exchange environments. Following are the basic software requirements.

- Microsoft Windows 2000 Server or Windows Server 2003.
- Microsoft Exchange 5.5 (SP4 or better), Microsoft Exchange 2000 (SP2 or better), Microsoft Exchange 2003, Microsoft Exchange 2007.
- Microsoft Internet Explorer 6.0 or better.

In addition to the basic hardware and software requirements, there are a number of prerequisites for BES. Some of the prerequisites are installed as a part of the BES setup program, but others must be installed prior to starting the BES installation. Below is the list of prerequisites.

Prerequisite	Required/ Optional	Notes
Microsoft Messaging Queue (MSMQ) Version 3.0	Optional	This is required for installations that will use Microsoft Windows Messenger.
Microsoft .NET Framework Version 1.1	Required	This may be installed during BES installation. SP1 is required to use Microsoft Windows Messenger.
Microsoft Data Access Components (MDAC) Version 2.8	Required	This requires either Security Patch MS04-003 (Version 2000.85.1025.00) or SP2 (Version 2000.86.1830.00) for Microsoft Windows Server 2003 SP1.
Java® 2 Platform, Standard Edition (J2SE™) Runtime Environment Version 5.0 update 9	Required	This may be installed during BES installation.

Prerequisite	Required/ Optional	Notes
Internet Service Manager for Internet Information Services	Optional	This is required for Microsoft Exchange 2007 support.
Microsoft Exchange administration tools	Required	The appropriate tools for your Exchange version should be installed.
		Microsoft Exchange Version 5.5 Administrator
		Microsoft Exchange 2000 System Manager
		Microsoft Exchange 2003 System Manager
		Microsoft Exchange Server MAPI Client and Collaboration Data Objects 1.2.1
		For Exchange 2007, Microsoft Exchange Server MAPI Client and Collaboration Data Objects 1.2.1, or Microsoft Exchange Server 2003 System Manager with SP2

Refer to the BlackBerry Enterprise Server for Microsoft Exchange Installation Guide for your version of BES for an up-to-date list of system requirements, especially if you are planning to implement additional services above and beyond the basic messaging and collaboration.

BlackBerry Enterprise Server Network Requirements

The network requirements for a typical BES implementation are relatively simple. The BlackBerry Enterprise Server should be installed in a high-speed, switched network environment. The number of hops between the BES and the messaging servers should be minimized in order to ensure optimal performance. The other basic requirement is that the BES should be able to initiate outbound connections to the BlackBerry Infrastructure on TCP port 3101. Chances are that you won't need to modify your network configuration, as most firewalls are configured to allow this type of connection by default.

RIM recommends that BlackBerry Enterprise Servers should be installed behind the corporate firewall; this placement typically doesn't require any changes to the network, while still ensuring the security of your BES implementation. Placing BES in a demilitarized zone (DMZ) is not advisable, as it may require numerous changes to your firewall and other network configurations to establish connectivity between BES and the servers behind the firewall, including messaging and collaboration, application servers, etc.

However, RIM does provide options if your network environment that requires traffic from the BES passes through a host in your DMZ before being routed to the BlackBerry Infrastructure and onward to the client device. As previously discussed, RIM has divided BES into functional components, one of which is the BlackBerry Router. The BlackBerry Router is the component that manages the communication between the other BES components and the BlackBerry Infrastructure, and the client devices. Security is maintained even though the BlackBerry Router is placed in the DMZ because all communications with the BlackBerry Router component are encrypted. For more information on this configuration, refer to RIM's documentation titled *Placing the BlackBerry Router in the DMZ*.

BlackBerry Enterprise Server Database Requirements

The BlackBerry Enterprise Server stores information in a component known as the BlackBerry Configuration Database. This component relies upon a relational database management system (RDBMS) for storage and retrieval of configuration data. BES 4.1 supports the following RDBMS applications.

- Microsoft SQL Server 2000 Desktop Engine (MSDE 2000).
- Microsoft SQL Server 2000 SP3a.
- Microsoft SQL Server 2005 Standard, Enterprise, or Express editions.

The RDBMS selection will have an impact on the future growth and scalability of your BES environment. MSDE is a lightweight version of Microsoft SQL Server that can be installed during the BES installation process. The ease of implementation makes it a popular option, especially for small BES implementations. The database size for MSDE is limited to 2GB, which will limit the number of users you can effectively support. The rule of thumb is that the base Configuration Database is approximately 100MB and each additional user requires 1MB, restricting BES implementations with MSDE to less than 2000 users. You are not locked in if you opt to use the MSDE for your initial BlackBerry Configuration Database, as RIM provides detailed instructions on switching from MSDE to the SQL Server.

Using Microsoft SQL Server to house your BlackBerry Configuration Database provides greater flexibility and scalability, especially in the area of disaster recovery. RIM does not support MSDE for standby Configuration Databases, which means that you'll need to be more proactive about backing up the Configuration Database. Also, SQL Server is typically installed on a different server than BES, which frees up the system resources to support BES.

Summary

In this chapter, we have discussed the components that make up the BlackBerry Enterprise Server. In addition, we have provided an overview of the system requirements for installing BES, including the hardware, software, network, and database requirements. In the next chapter, we will roll up our sleeves and walk through the process of installing the BlackBerry Enterprise Server.

3

Preparing for the BES Installation

The majority of prerequisites for the BlackBerry Enterprise Server can be met simply by installing the required software specified in the previous chapter. Not all of the prerequisites are so easy to satisfy, because the key components require some additional configuration and preparation prior to starting the BES installation. Specifically, we will need to configure the Microsoft Exchange environment, the Windows server that will host BES and the desired SQL Server database environment. These configuration steps include the creation of an administrative account and associated mailbox, as well as the delegation of the necessary security privileges for these environments. This chapter provides information on how to perform each of these configurations, but you will need to select the appropriate configurations based on your desired BES environment. We will be performing our installation using Microsoft Exchange 2007, so the steps may vary if you use a different version of Exchange.

Enabling the Messaging Environment to Communicate with the BES

BlackBerry Enterprise Server uses a service account for administrative tasks and to communicate with the Microsoft Exchange messaging environment. This account, and an associated Exchange mailbox, is created within the Active Directory and granted the necessary permissions to operate effectively. The account must be created prior to the installation of BES using the Active Directory and Exchange administrative tools.

Create Service Account and Mailbox

1. On an administrator workstation, click **Start | Programs | Administrative Tools | Active Directory Users and Computers**.

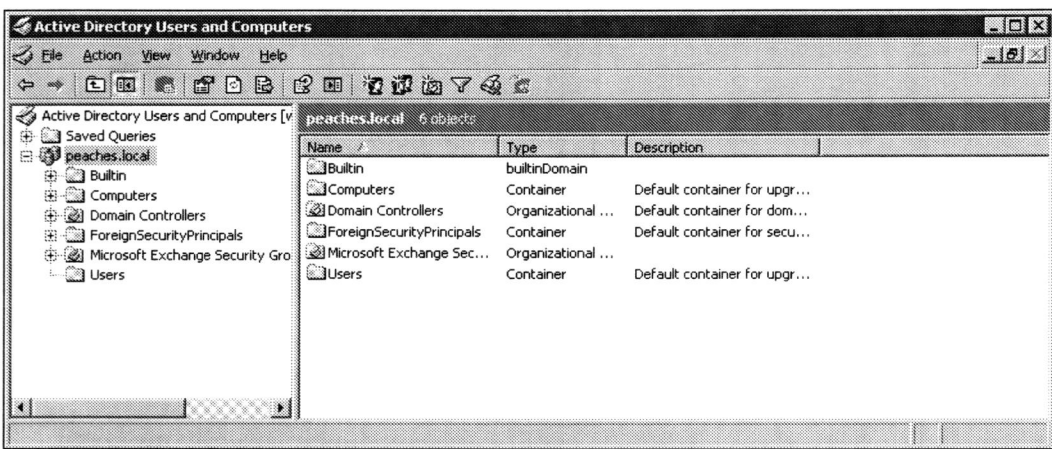

2. Right-click on the organizational unit (OU) or user container where you want to create the service account user and select **New User**.

3. Enter a username in the **First Name:** and **User logon name:** fields.

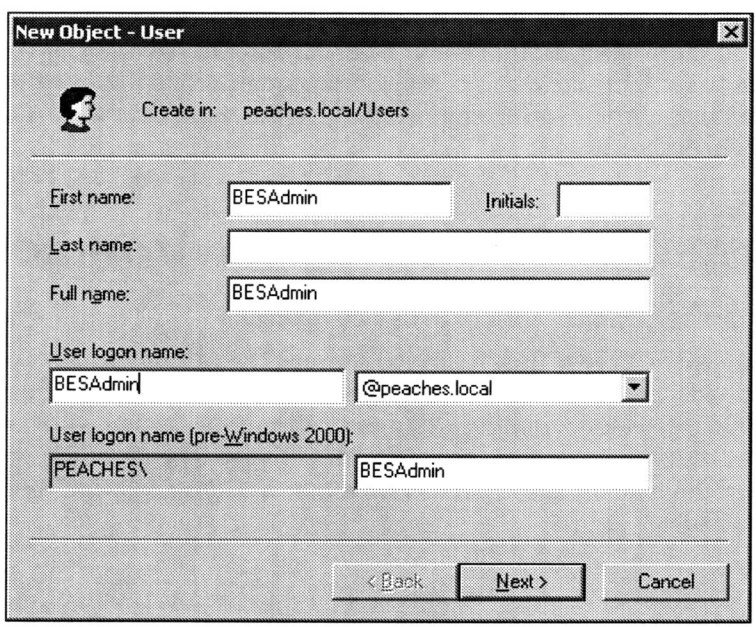

BESAdmin is the default service account username recommended by RIM, but you may choose a different username that fits with your naming conventions or standard operating procedures.

4. Enter a strong password in the **Password:** and **Confirm password:** fields. Check the **Password never expires** check box.

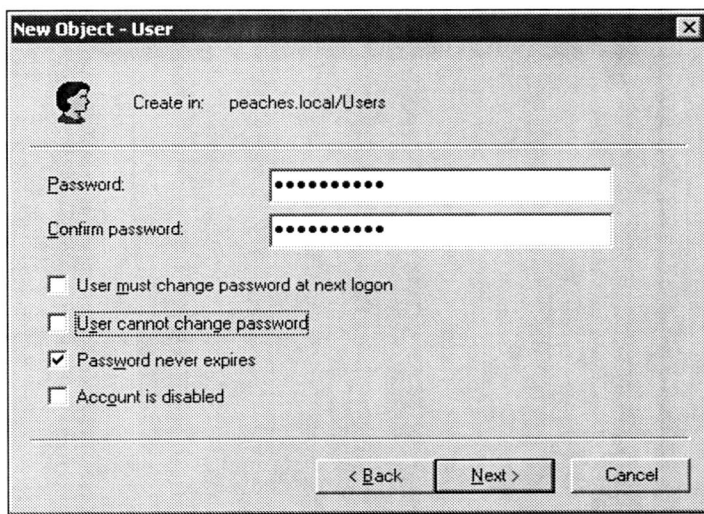

5. Click **Finish** to create the user account.

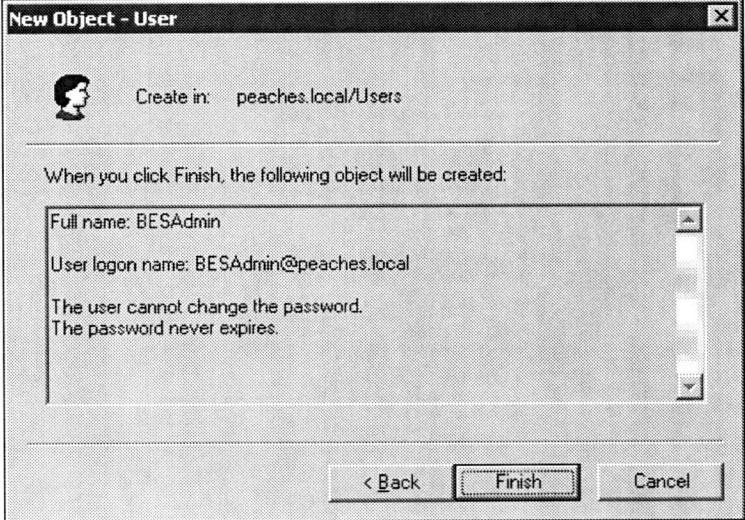

6. Click **Start | Programs | Microsoft Exchange Server 2007 | Exchange Management Console**.

7. Select **Recipient Configuration** and click the **New Mailbox...** action.

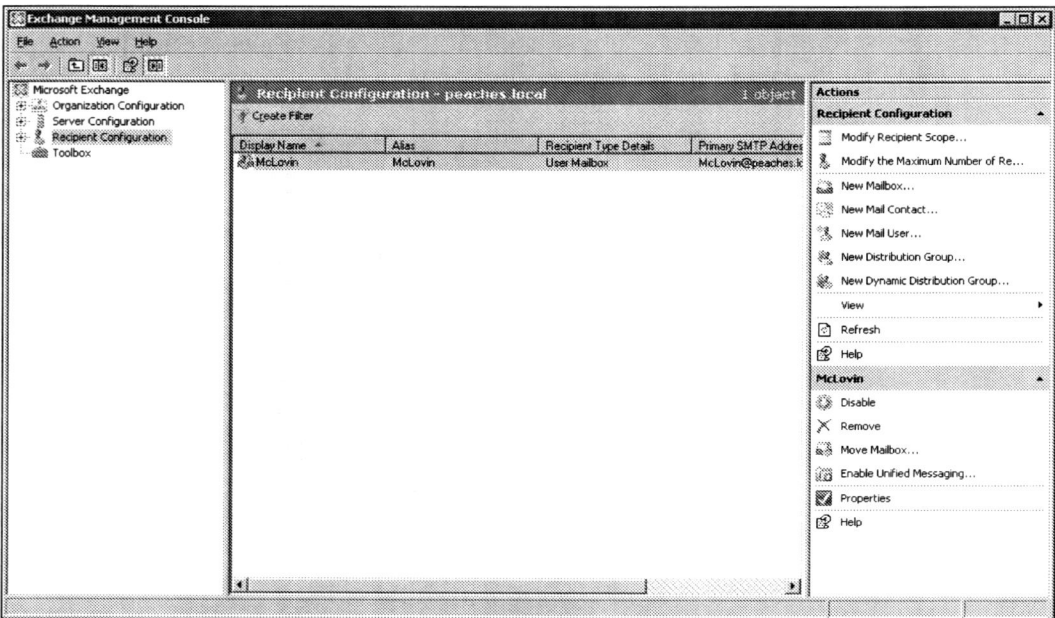

8. Select the **User Mailbox** radio button and click **Next**.

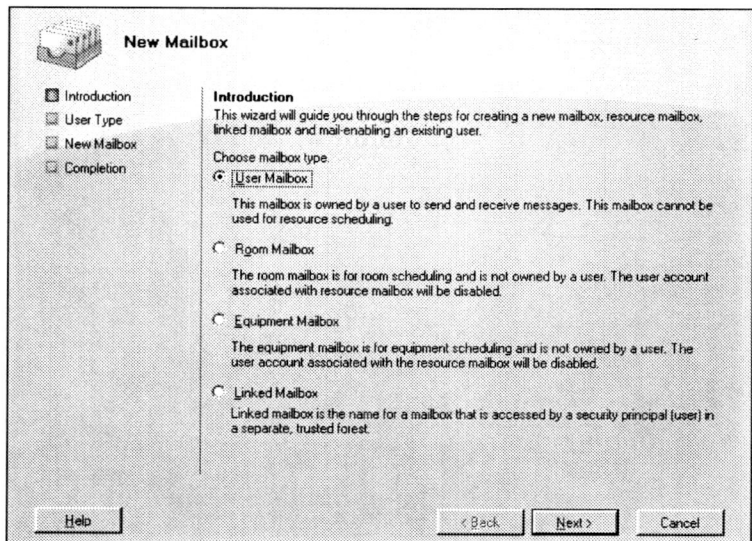

9. Select the **Existing user:** radio button and click the **Browse** button.

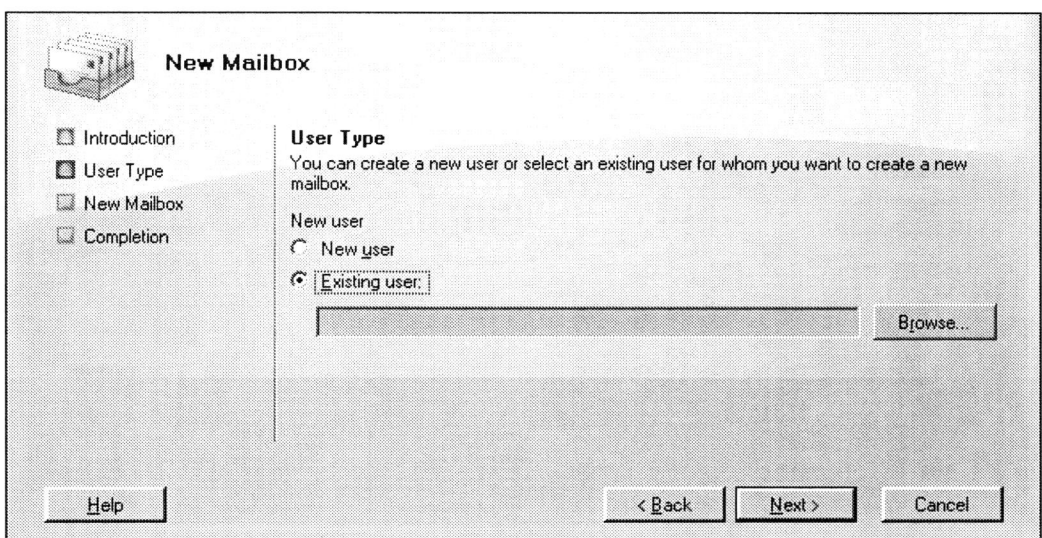

10. Select the username of the service account and click **OK**.

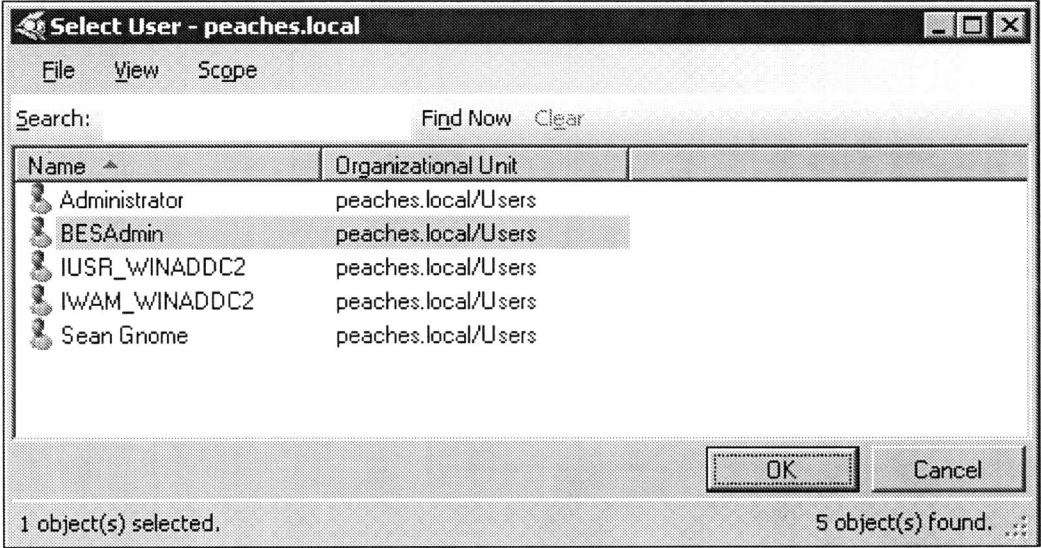

11. Click **Next** to continue mailbox creation.

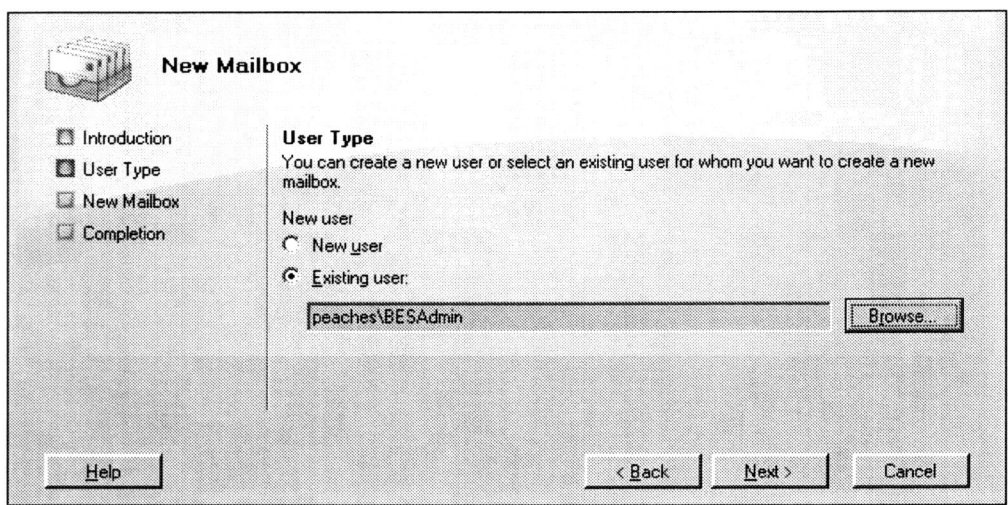

12. Modify the mailbox settings as desired and click **Next**.

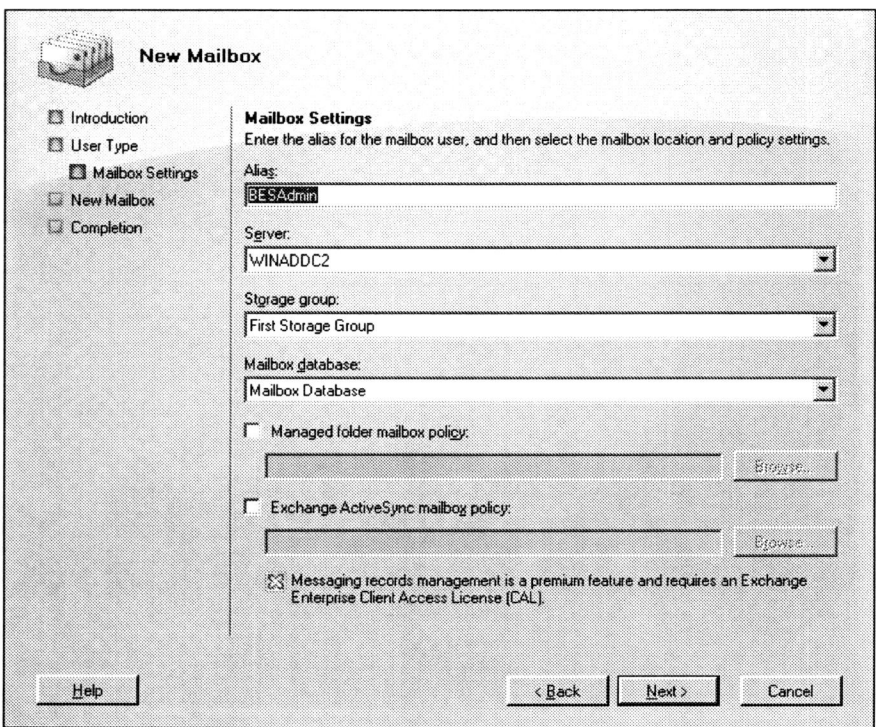

13. Click **New** to confirm the creation of the new mailbox.

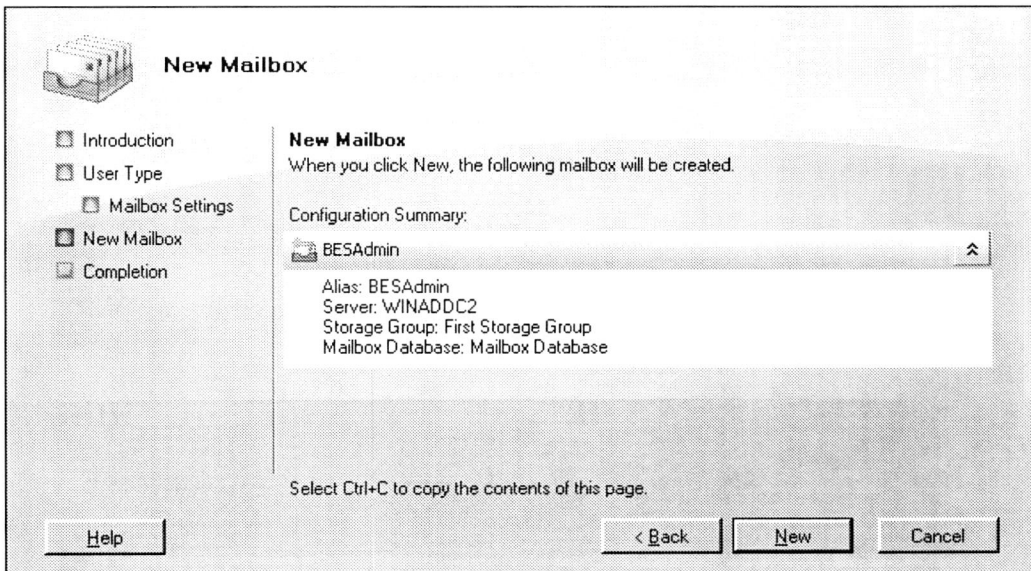

14. Click **Finish** after the mailbox has been successfully created.

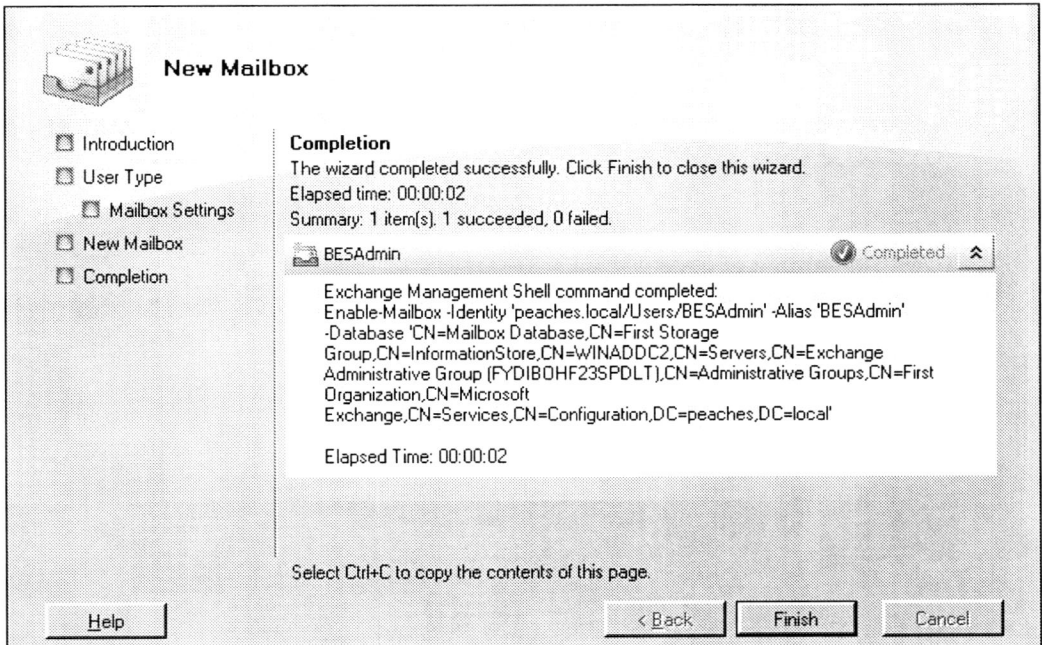

Assigning Microsoft Exchange Permissions to the Service Account

The service account must be granted specific Microsoft Exchange permissions in order to function, including the ability to send messages on behalf of the users in your Microsoft Exchange organization. The following procedure describes how to assign these permissions.

1. On an administrator workstation, click **Start | Programs | Administrative Tools | Active Directory Users and Computers**.

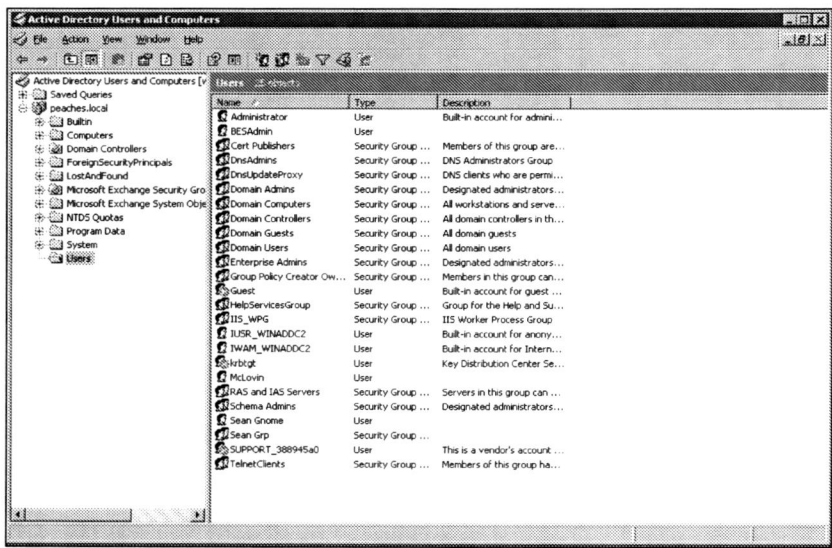

2. Click the **View** menu and select **Advanced Features**, if it isn't already enabled.

3. Right-click on the organizational unit or user container and select **Properties**.

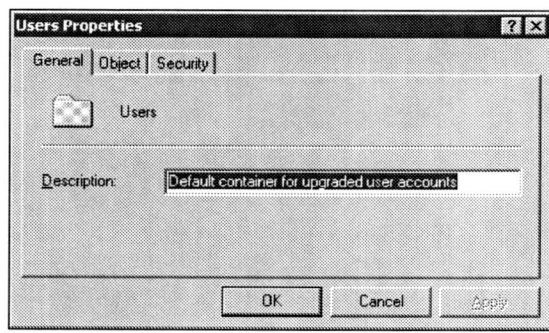

4. Click on the **Security** tab.

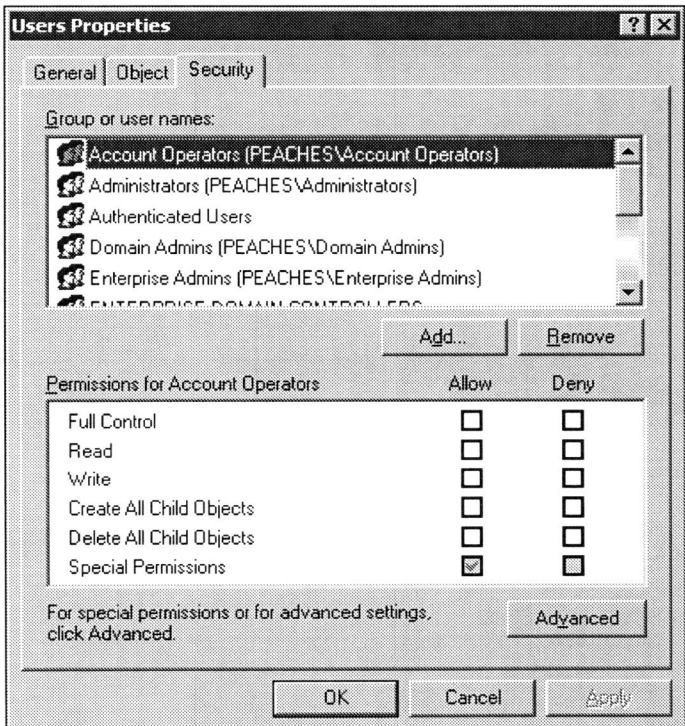

5. Click the **Add** button.

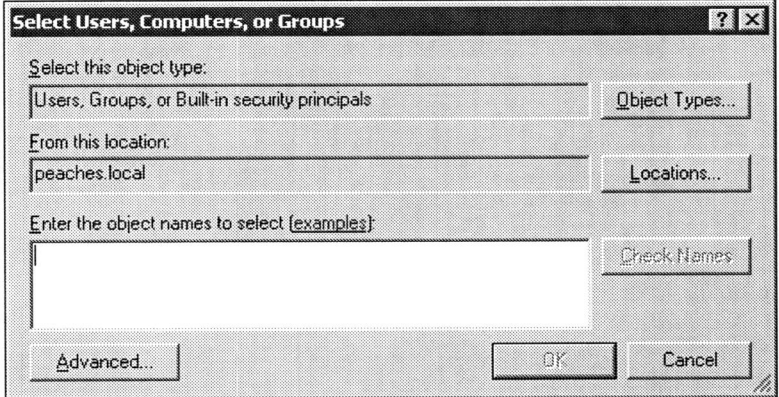

6. Enter the name of the service account in the **Enter the object names to select:** field and click **OK**.

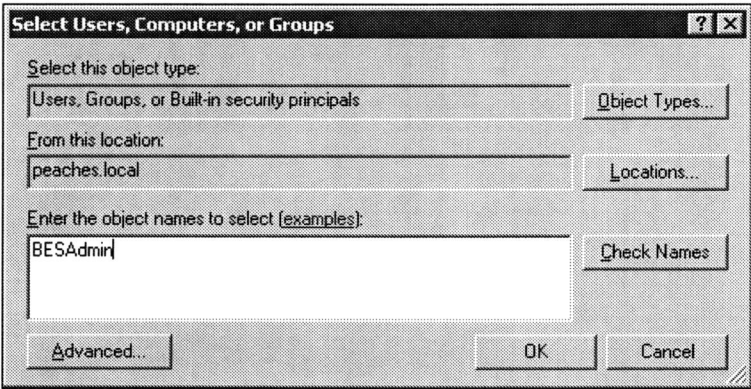

7. Click the **Advanced** button.

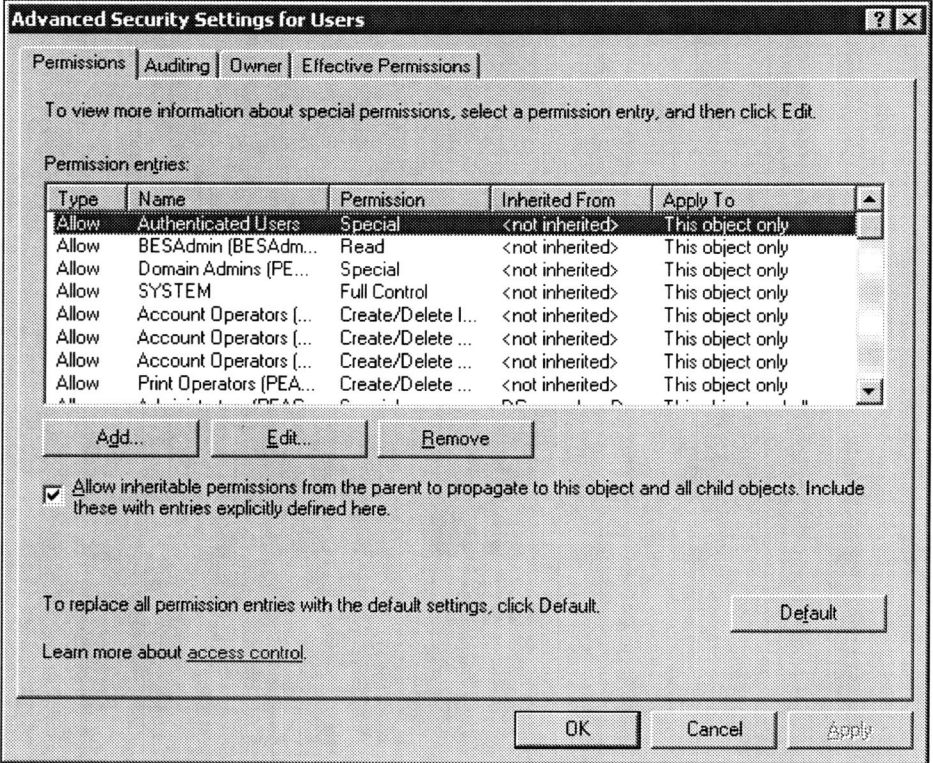

8. Select the service account from the **Permission entries:** list and click the **Edit** button.

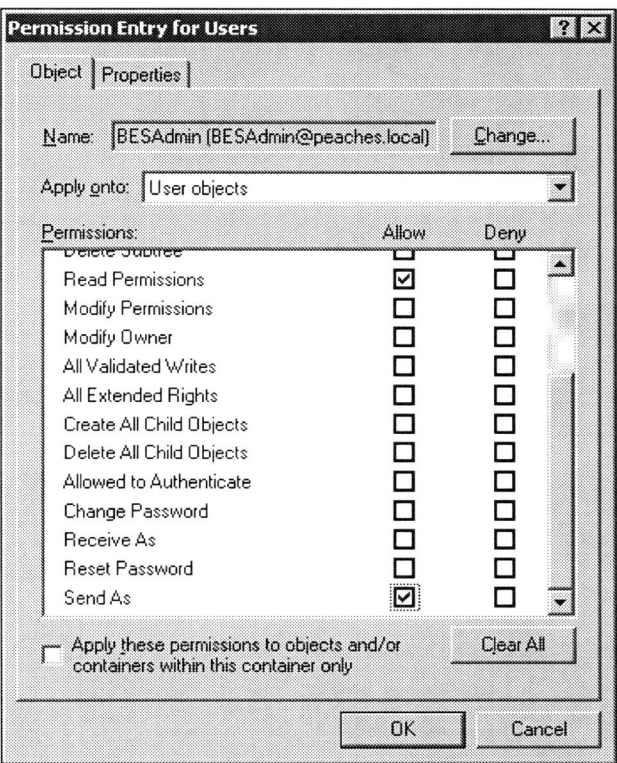

9. Verify that the service account is listed in the **Name:** field and that the **User objects** is selected in the **Apply onto:** field. Check the **Allow** box for the **Send As** permission and click **OK**.

Assigning Microsoft Windows Permissions to the Service Account

The service account must be granted specific permissions on the Microsoft Windows server that will serve as your BES, including local administrator privileges and the ability to log on locally and as a service. If you will be distributing the BES components among multiple servers, then these permissions must be granted on every server on which BES components will be installed. The following procedure describes how to assign these permissions.

1. On the Microsoft Windows server, click **Start | Programs | Administrative Tools | Local Security Policy**.

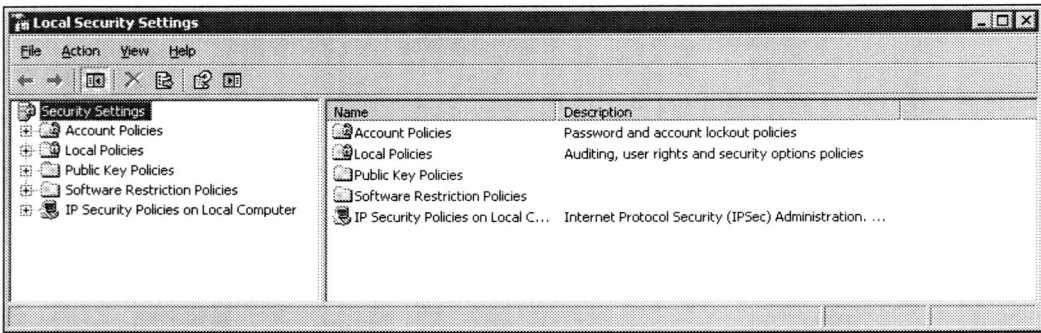

2. Expand the **Local Policies** folder and select the **User Rights Assignment** folder.

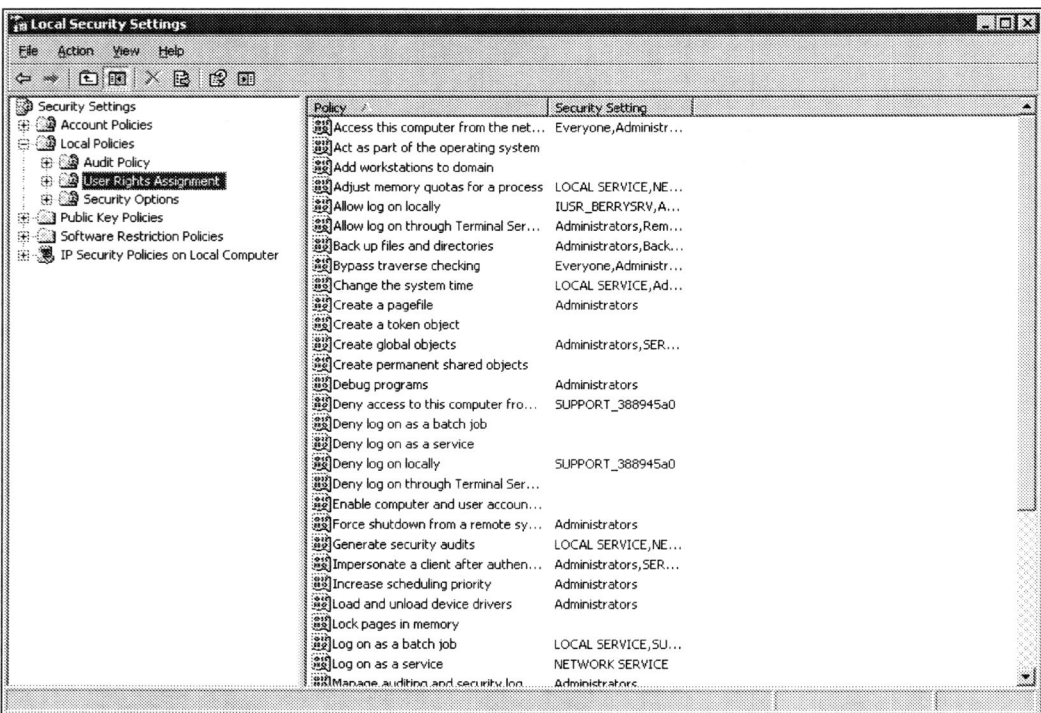

3. Right-click **Log on as a service** and select **Properties**.

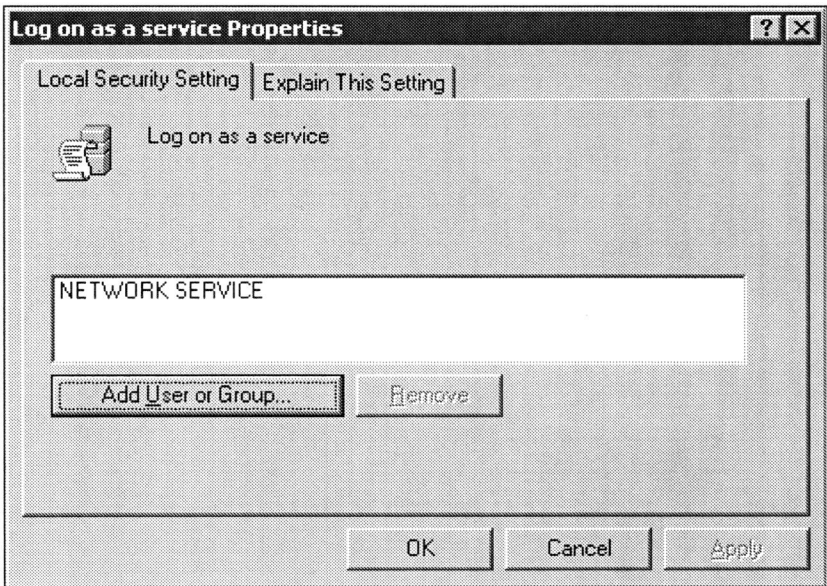

4. Click the **Add User or Group** button.

5. Enter the name of the service account in the **Enter the object names to select:** field and click **OK**.

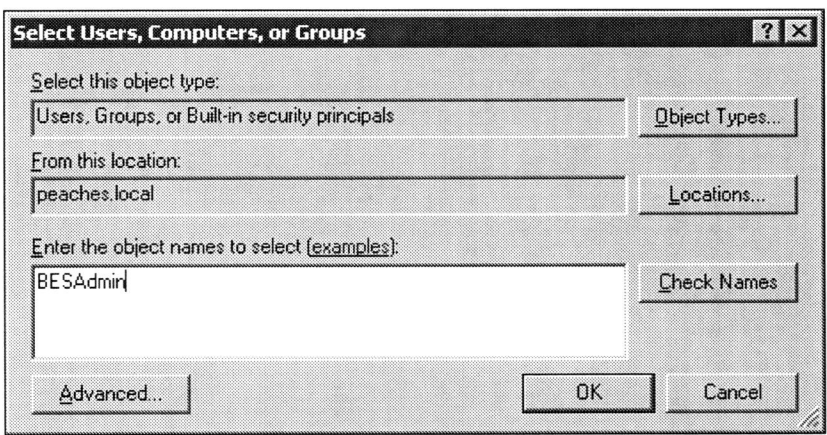

6. Click **OK** to close the **Logon as a service Properties** window.

7. Right-click **Allow log on locally** and select **Properties**.

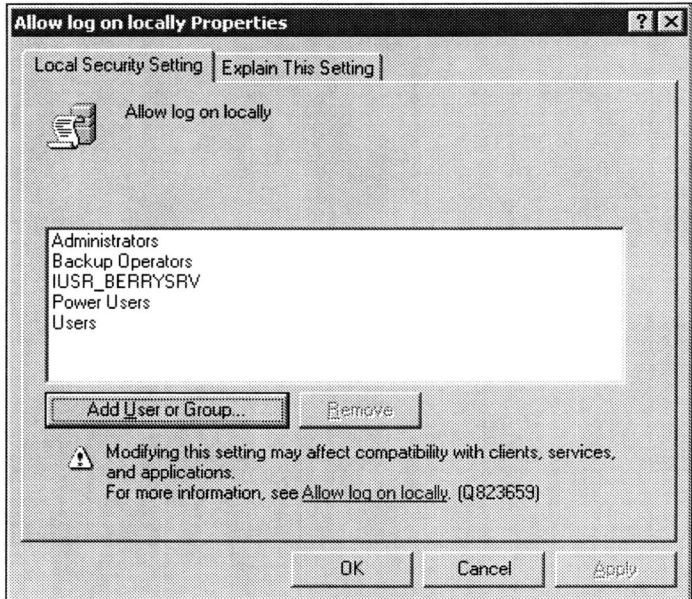

8. Click the **Add User or Group** button.

9. Enter the name of the service account in the **Enter the object names to select:** field and click **OK**.

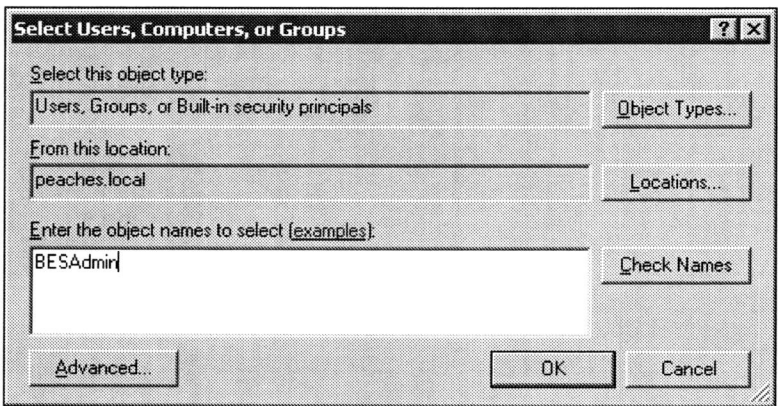

10. Click **OK** to close the **Allow logon locally Properties** window.

11. Exit the **Local Security Policy** application.

12. Click **Start | Programs | Administrative Tools | Computer Management**.

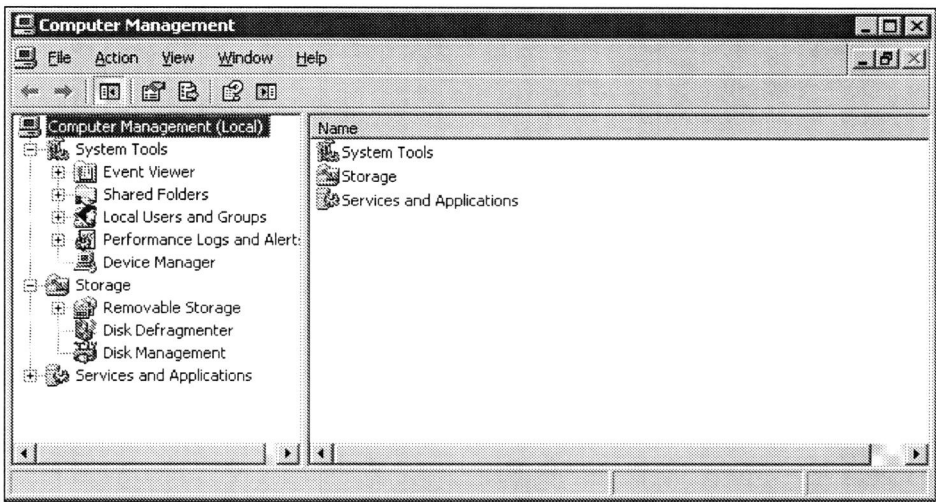

13. Expand the **Local Users and Groups** folder and select **Groups**.

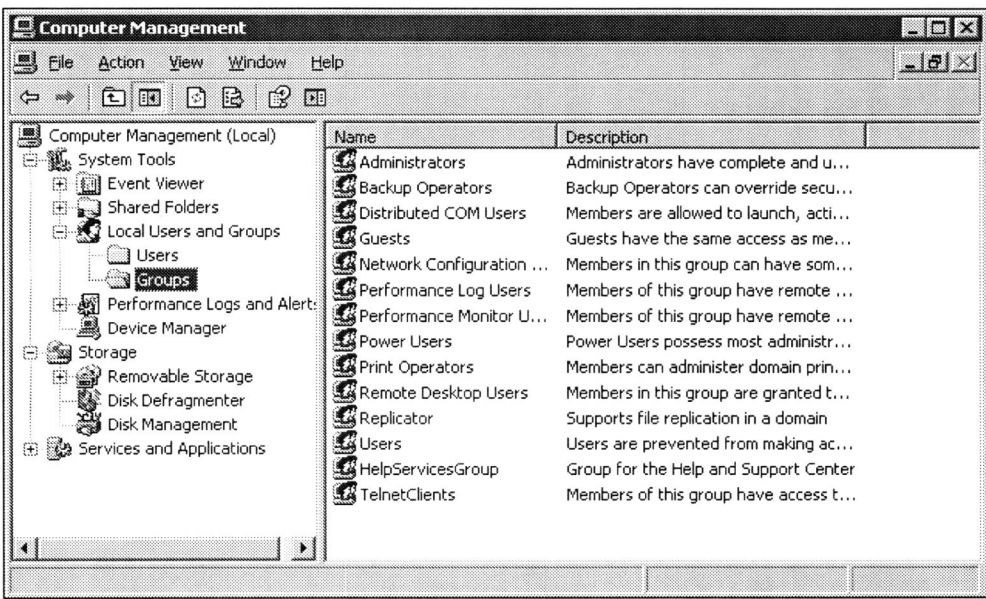

14. Right-click on the **Administrators** group and select **Add to Group**.

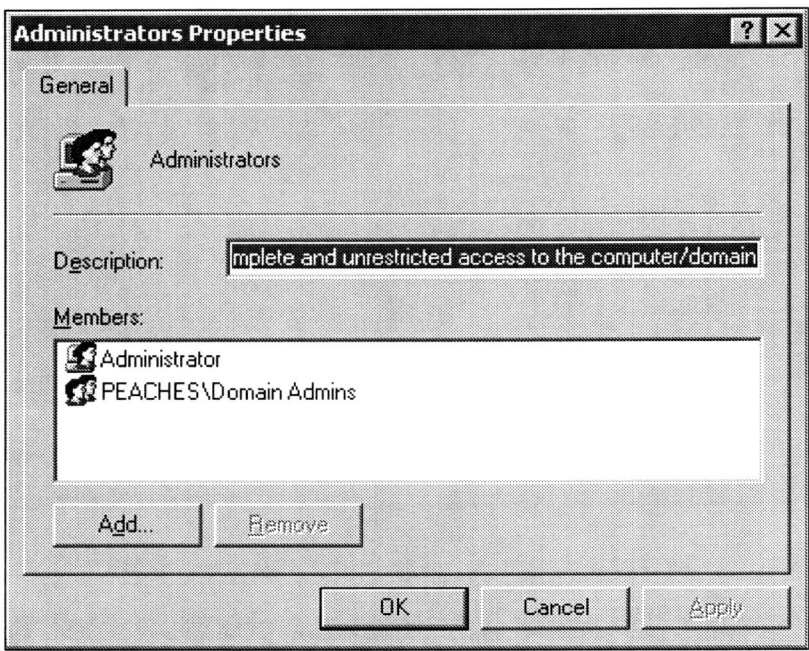

15. Click the **Add** button.

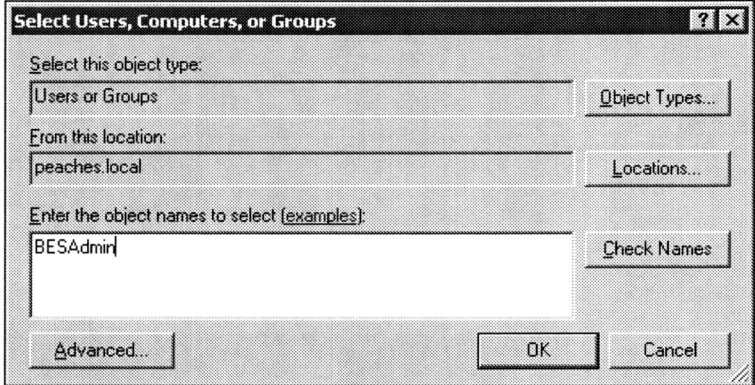

16. Enter the name of the service account in the **Enter the object names to select:** field and click **OK**.

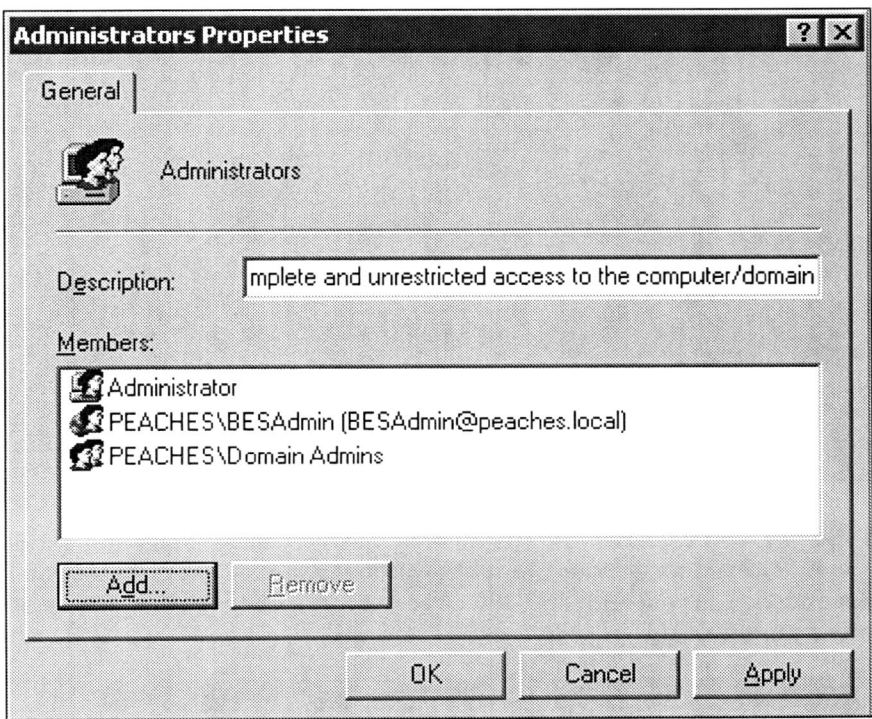

17. Click **OK** to close the **Administrators Properties** window.

Configuring Microsoft Exchange Permissions for the Service Account

The service account must be granted additional Microsoft Exchange permissions in order to send and receive messages as other users and to administer the Exchange Information Store. The following procedure describes how to assign these permissions for Microsoft Exchange Server 2007.

1. On an administrator workstation, or the Microsoft Exchange Server, click **Start | Programs | Microsoft Exchange Server 2007 | Exchange Management Shell**.

2. Type add-exchangeadministrator "*Service Account Name*" -role
   ViewOnly Admin and press <Enter>.

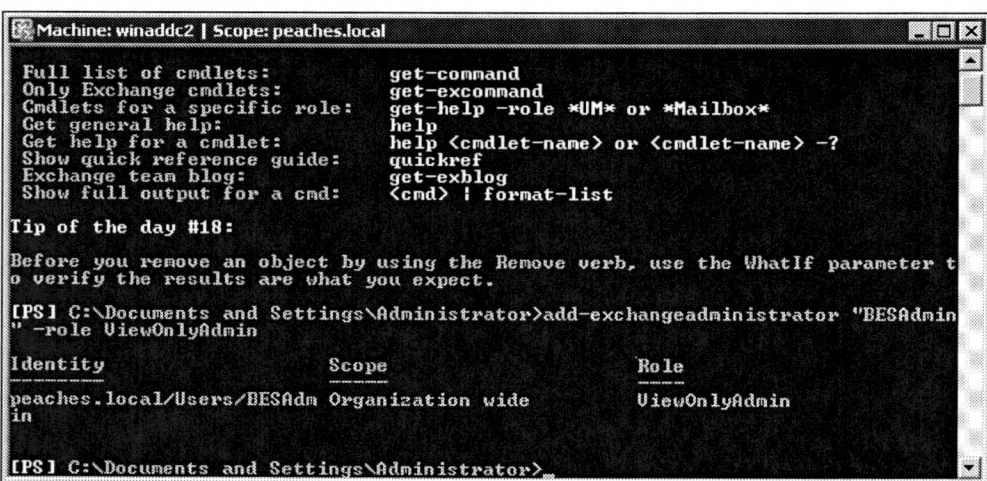

3. Type set-mailboxserver "*Exchange Server Name*"|add-adpermission
   -user "*Service Account Name*" -accessrights ExtendedRight -
   extendedrights Send-As, Receive-As, ms-Exch-Store-Admin and
   press <Enter>.

Enabling the Database Server to Communicate with BES

In addition to the permissions for Active Directory and Microsoft Exchange, we must configure specific permissions for the database that supports the Blackberry Configuration Database. As we discussed in the previous chapter, the BlackBerry Configuration Database can be hosted on the Microsoft SQL Server 2000 Desktop Engine (MSDE), Microsoft SQL Server 2000 SP3a, or Microsoft SQL Server 2005. The permissions requirement will vary based on which version of SQL Server you choose and whether it is installed locally on the BES or remotely.

There are two methods for authenticating with the BlackBerry Configuration Database, either a Windows (Trusted) login using the service account or a designated SQL login. The database user account must have the following roles to create and manage the BlackBerry Configuration Database.

- Database Creators Role (db_create) — this role is required to create the Blackberry Configuration Database.

- SQL Server (serveradmin) — this role is necessary to create tasks in the Blackberry Configuration Database. The service account does not need access to the SQL System Administrator account.

To update and maintain the Blackberry Configuration Database the database user account requires the following roles:

- SQL Server (serveradmin)
- Database Role (db_owner)

If you choose to use a local MSDE 2000 installation to host your Blackberry Configuration Database, the required roles are automatically assigned when the service account is assigned local Administrator privileges on the Windows server — no additional actions are required to assign database permissions. Selecting the Windows Trusted authentication option during BES installation also assigns the required permissions to the user account that executes the installation program.

Configuring Microsoft SQL Server 2005

If you opt to use Microsoft SQL Server 2005, you must perform the following actions to assign the appropriate database permissions and privileges. There are two methods to assign permissions; permissions may either be assigned to a Windows account or to an SQL login account. Follow the appropriate instructions below based on your preference.

Assigning a Server Role to the Service Account for Windows (Trusted) Authentication

1. On a workstation with Microsoft SQL Server Management Studio, click **Start | Programs | Microsoft SQL Server 2005 | SQL Server Management Studio**.

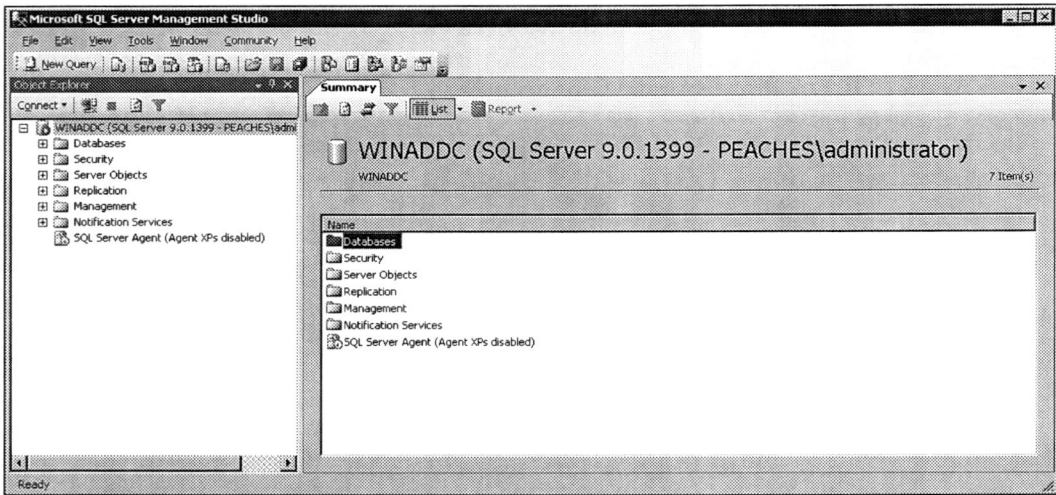

2. Expand the **Security** option.

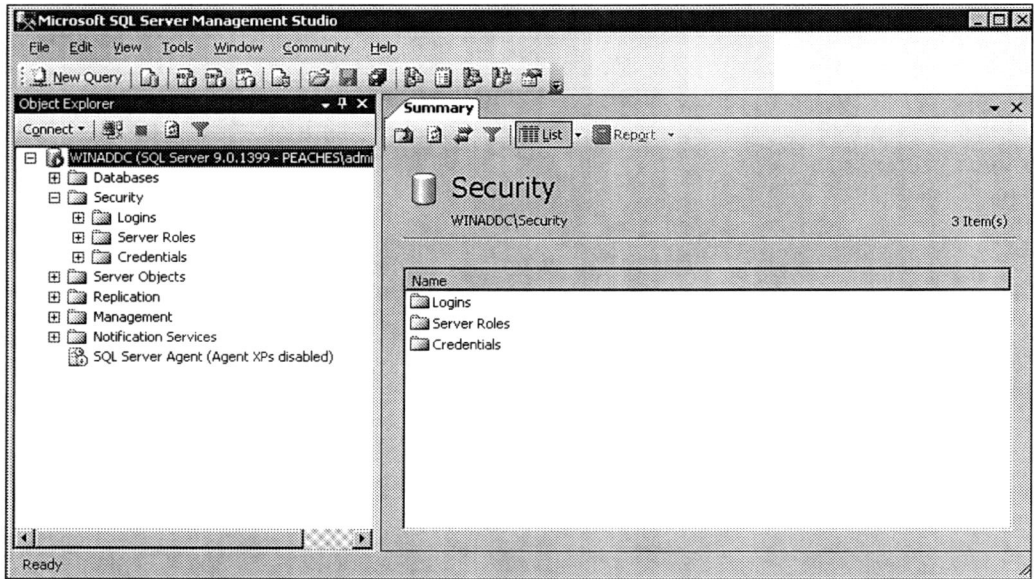

3. Right-click on **Logins** and select **New Login**.

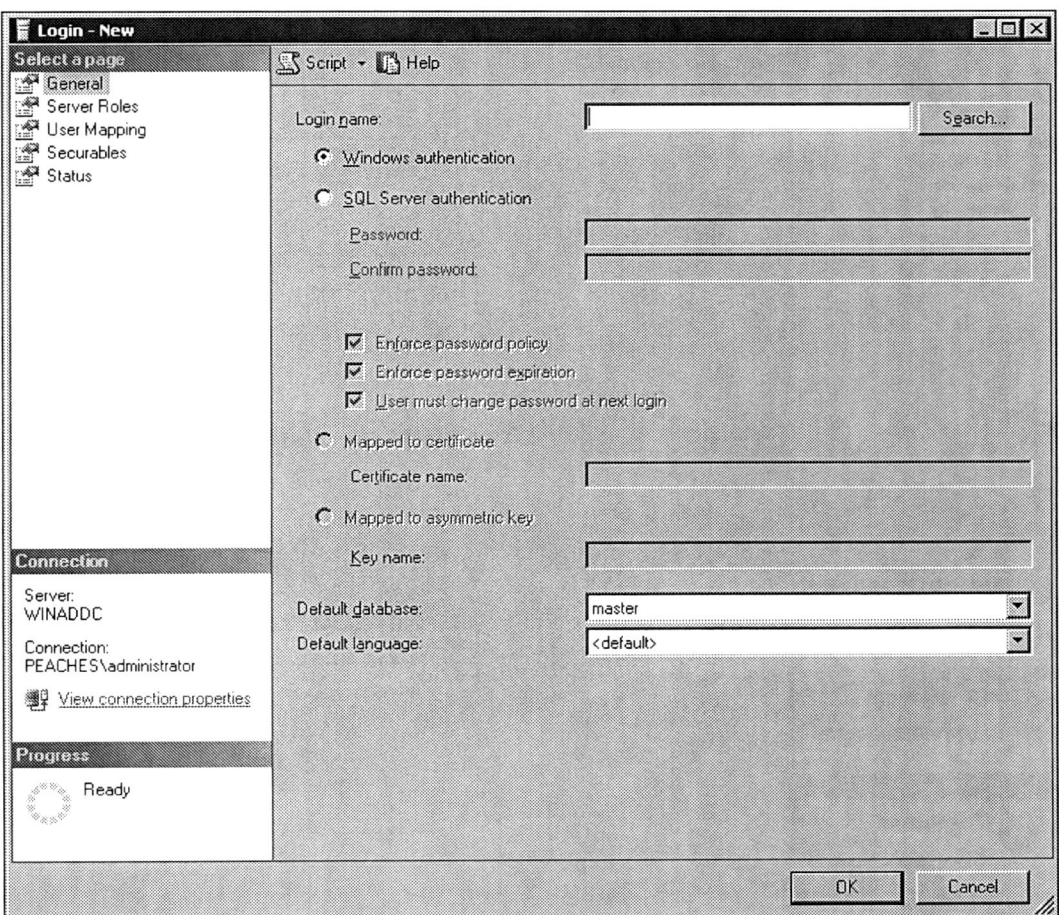

4. Enter the service account username in the **Login name**: field as **DOMAIN\username**.

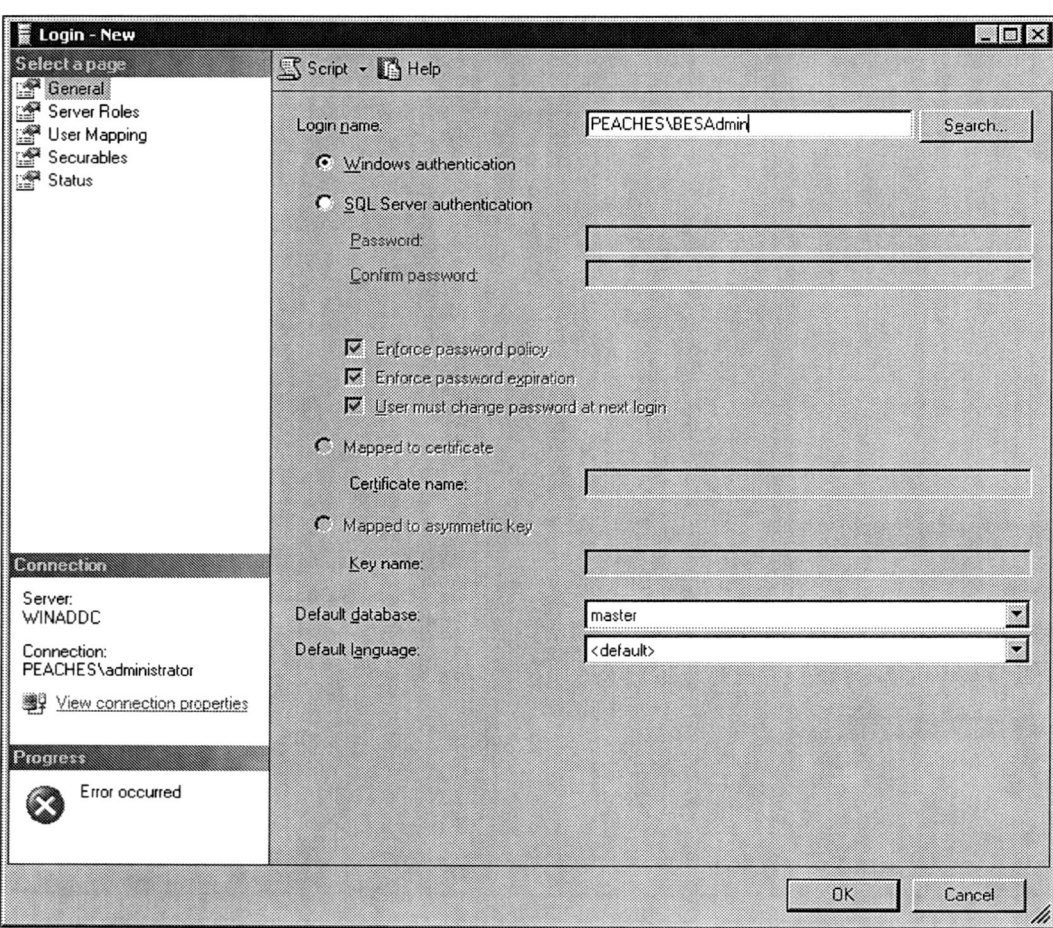

5. Select **Server Roles** from the **Select a page** section, click the check box for the following roles and click **OK**.

   ◦ **dbcreator**

   ◦ **serveradmin**

   ◦ **sysadmin**

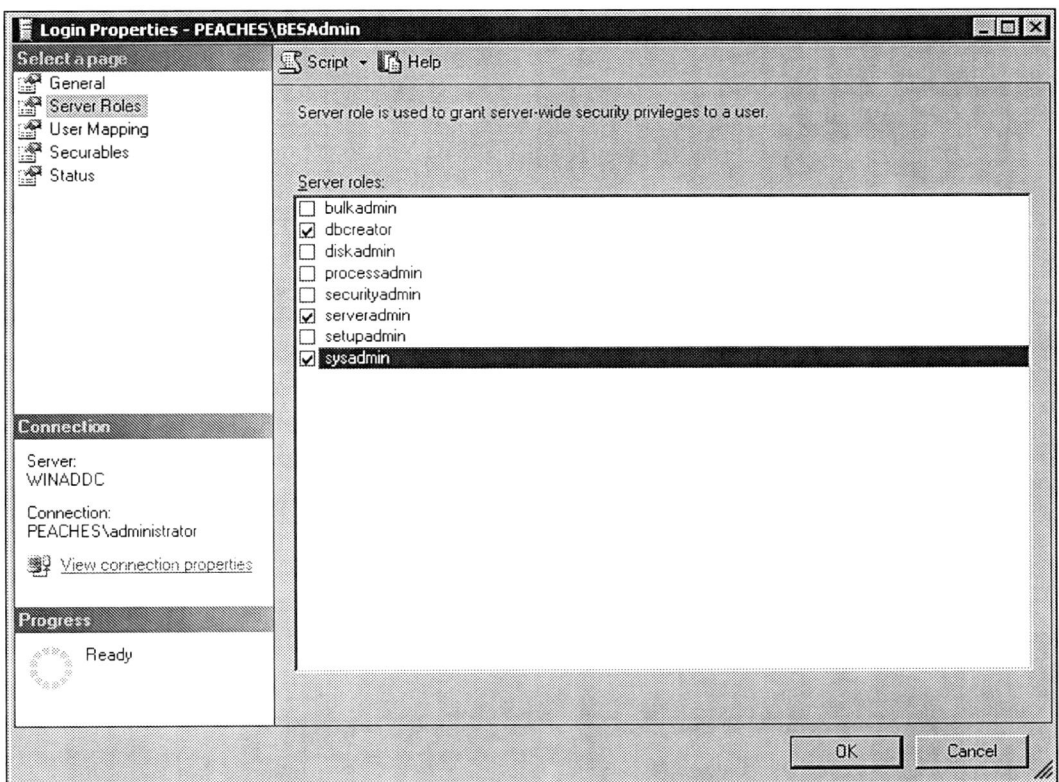

Assigning a Server Role to a SQL Login for SQL authentication

1. On a workstation with Microsoft SQL Server Management Studio, click **Start | Programs | Microsoft SQL Server 2005 | SQL Server Management Studio**.

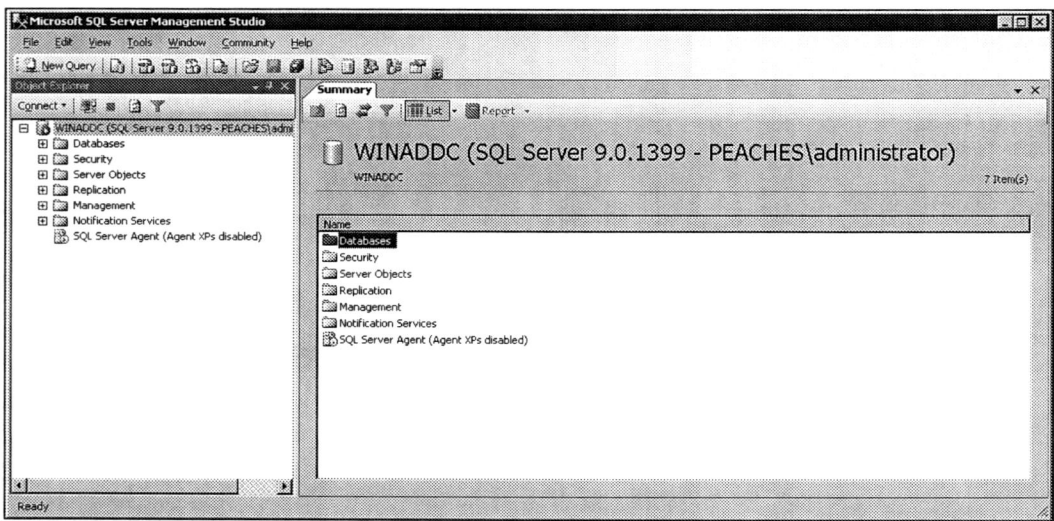

2. Expand the **Security** option.

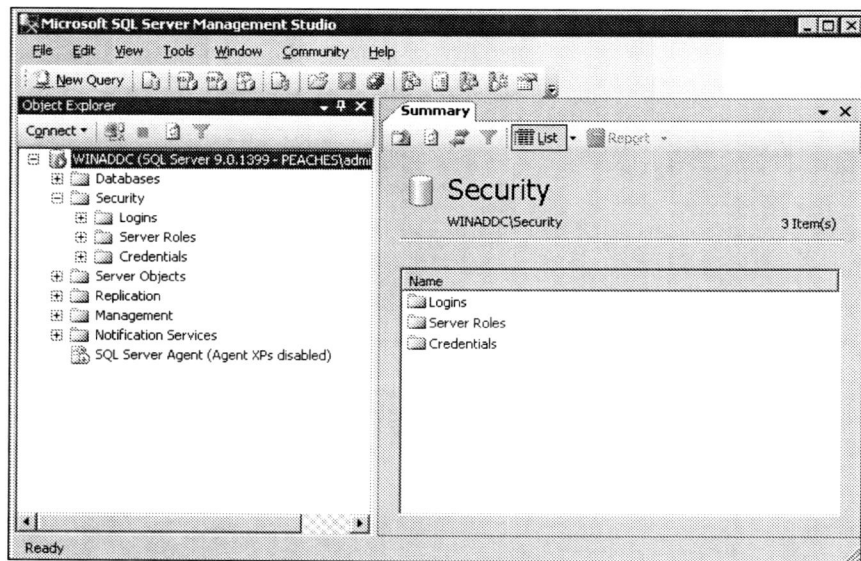

3. Right-click on **Logins** and select **New Login**.

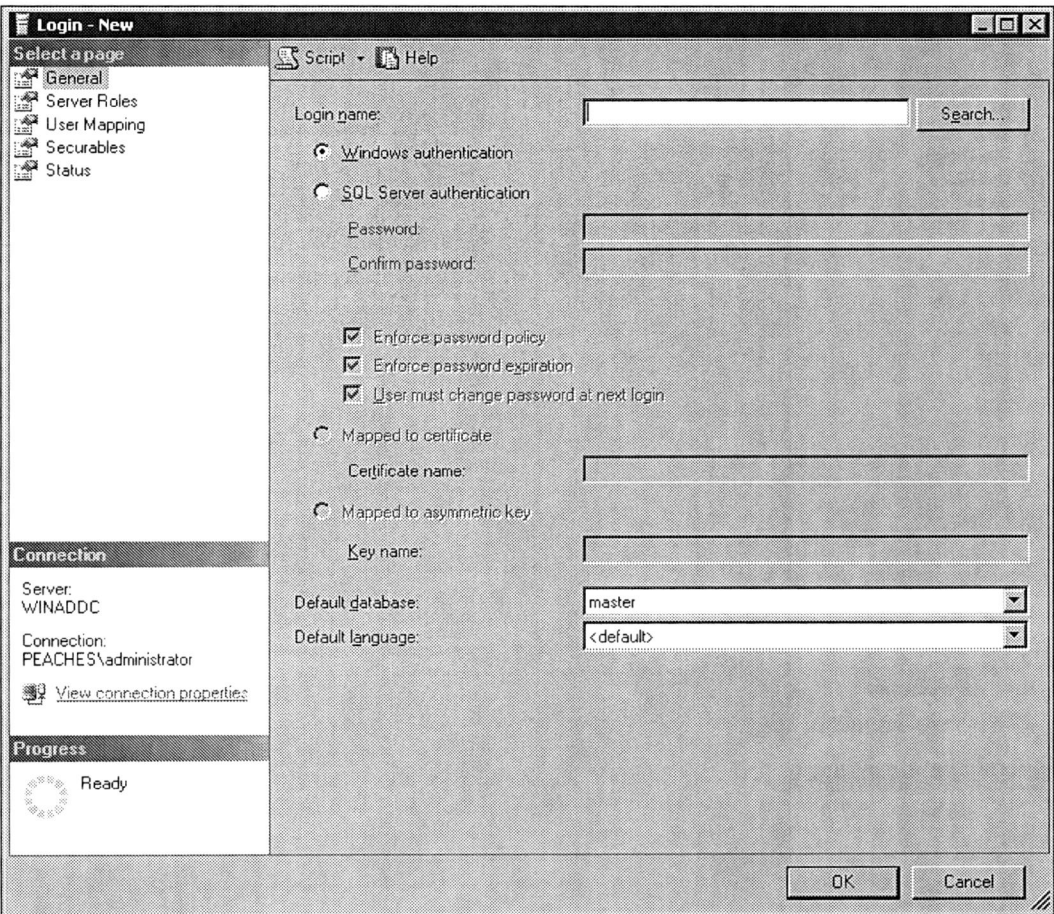

4. Select the **SQL Server authentication** radio button, enter the account name in the **Login name:** field, and un-check **Enforce password expiration**.

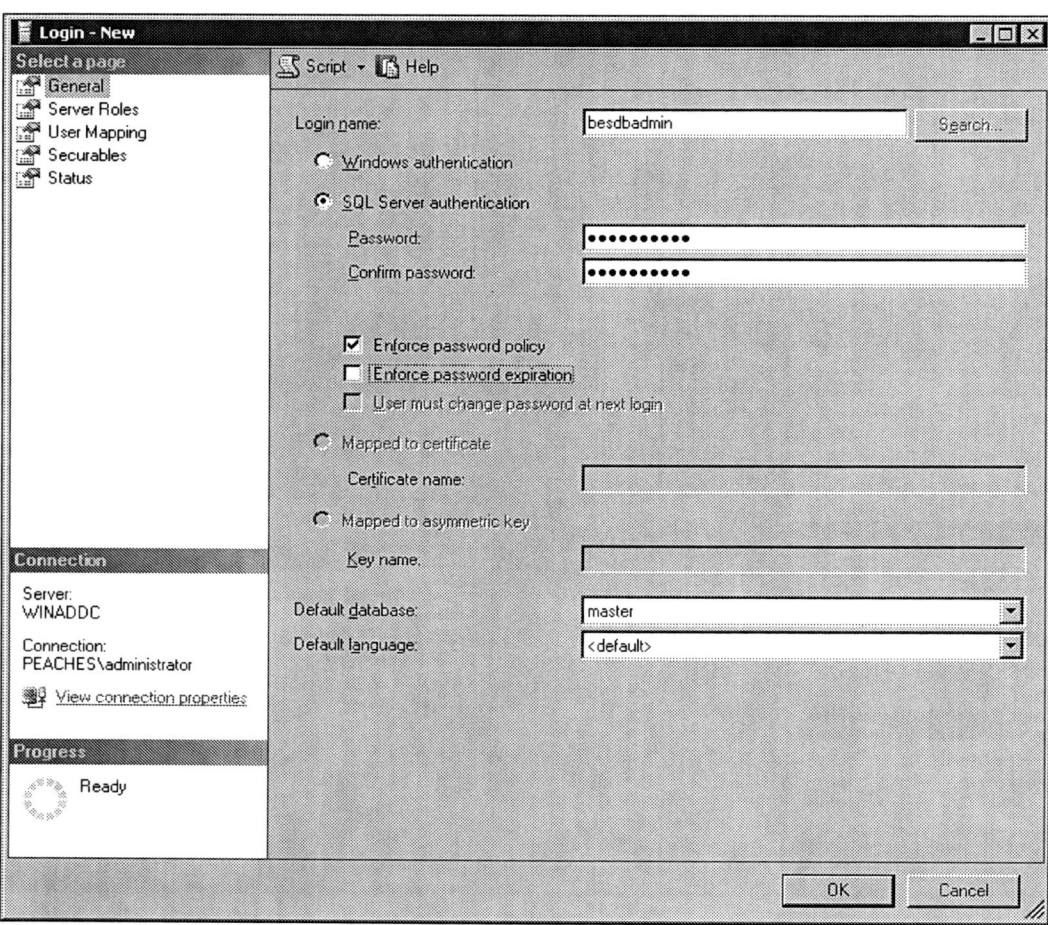

5. Select **Server Roles** from the **Select a page** section, click the check box for the following roles and click **OK**.

    °   **dbcreator**

    °   **serveradmin**

    °   **sysadmin**

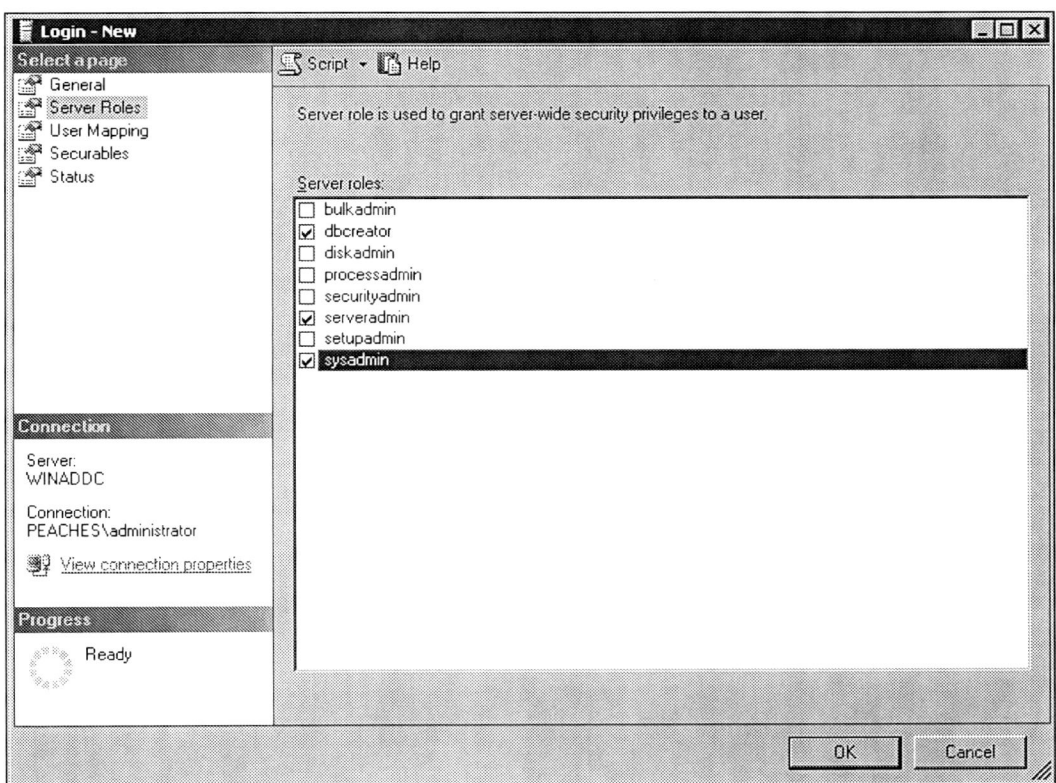

Summary

In this chapter, we have completed the prerequisite configurations for Active Directory, Microsoft Exchange, and SQL Server. We have created the service account that will be used to administer the BlackBerry Enterprise Server and assigned the necessary administrative, messaging, and database permissions. In the next chapter, we will dive into the installation of the BlackBerry Enterprise Server.

4

Installing BES for Microsoft Exchange

Now that we've completed all of the pre-requisite tasks, we are ready to install the BlackBerry Enterprise Server. This chapter will cover the installation process step-by-step, providing the information you need to deploy BES within your corporate environment. The installation process should be performed using the service account we created in the previous chapter, as it has the necessary permissions to complete the installation.

The Installation Process

Prior to beginning the installation, it's important to ensure that you have all of the information you will need. You should have the installation files, provided on CD or downloaded on the server that will host BES, as well as the license key and SRP information for your server.

Log on to the server using the service account.

Launch the installation program either from the Blackberry Enterprise Server Installation CD or the downloaded files.

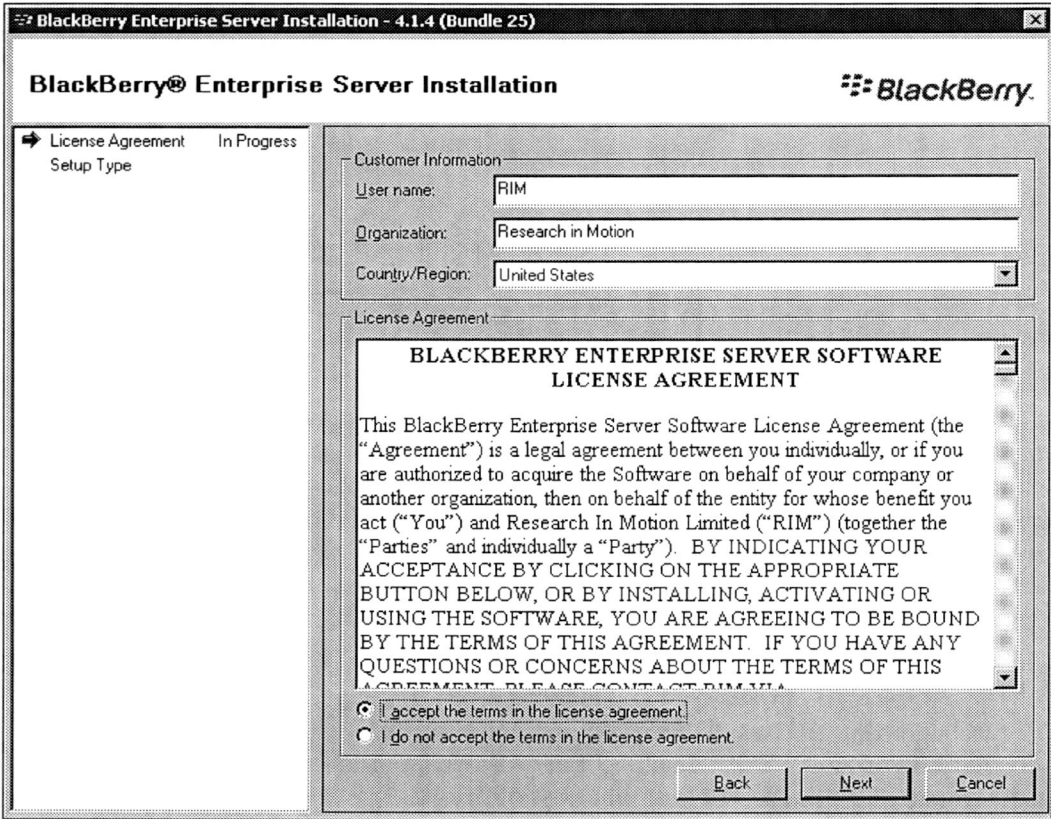

The **License Agreement** screen is used to enter your organization's information and to confirm your acceptance of the software license agreement.

Enter a name in the **User name:** field. This is not the service account name; rather it is a name that will be used to identify your installation.

Enter the name of your company in the **Organization:** field.

Select your country and region in the **Country/Region:** pull-down.

Click the **I accept the terms in the license agreement** radio button and click **Next**.

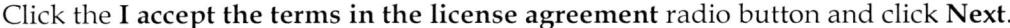

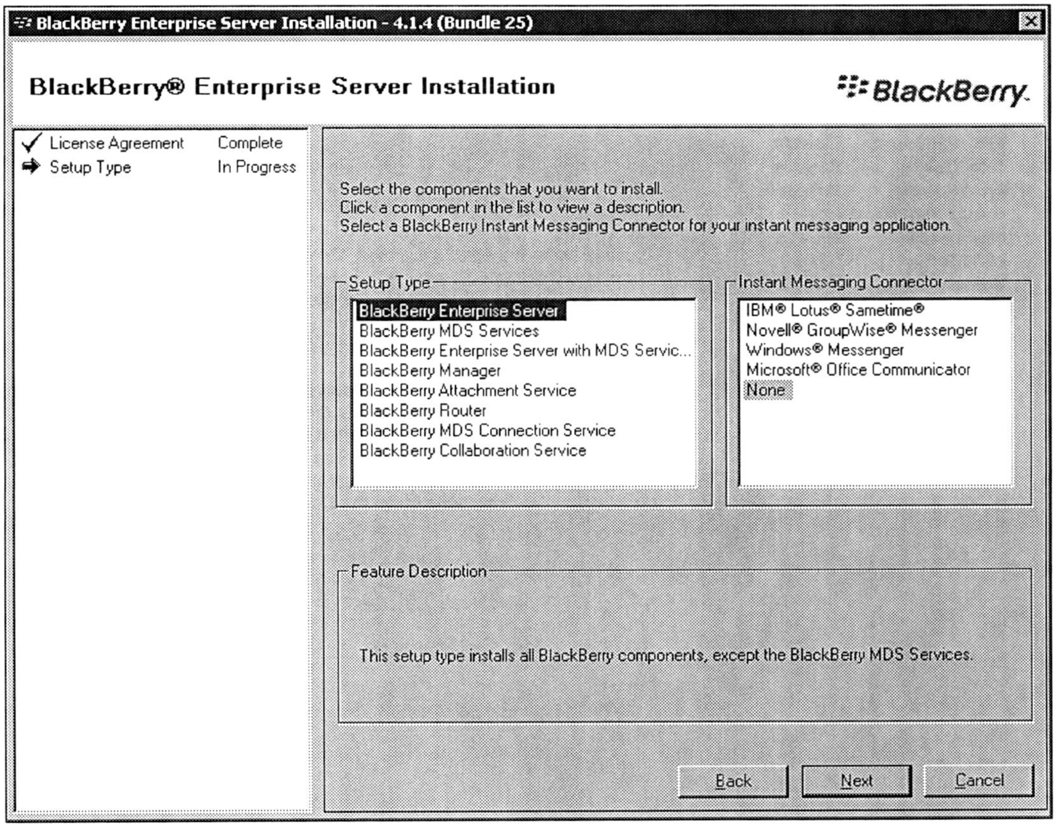

The **Setup Type** screen allows you to customize the BES components that will be installed on the server.

Select your installation type from the **Setup Type** field. Refer to the **Feature Description** field for a description of the components that will be installed for the selected **Setup Type**.

Select the type of instant messaging server you wish to install, if any, from the **Instant Messaging Connector** field.

Click **Next** to continue.

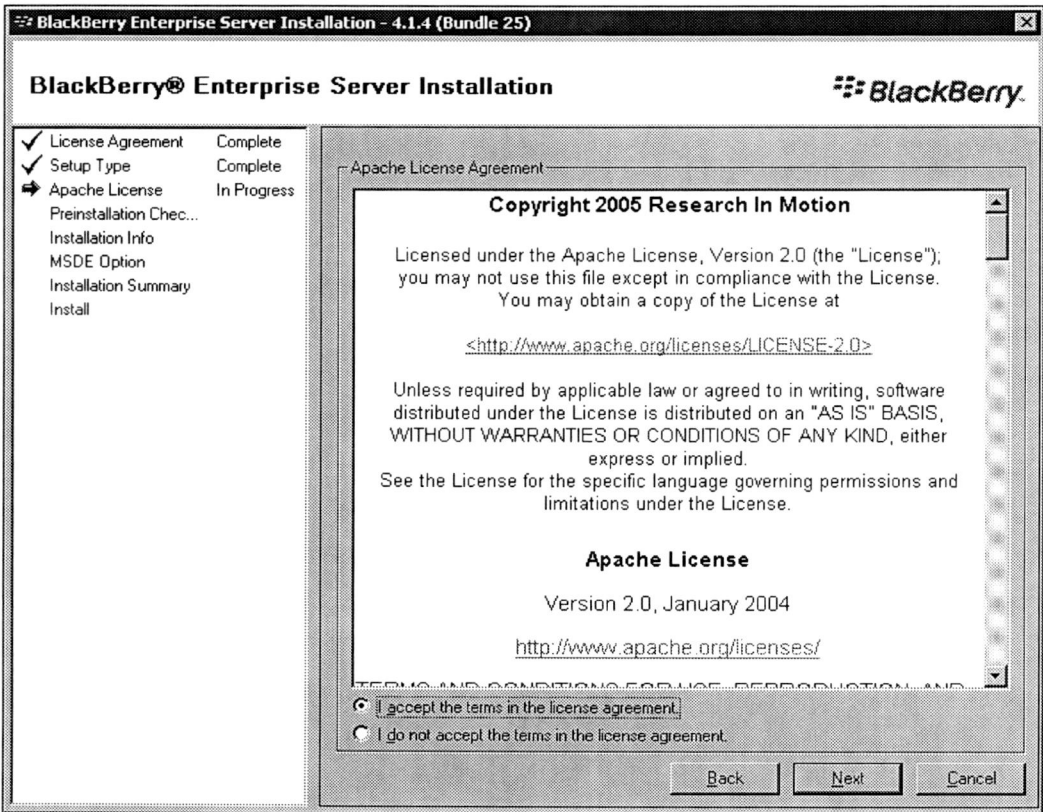

The **Apache License** screen is used to confirm your acceptance of the Apache License that governs several of the components that are bundled with BES.

Click the, **I accept the terms in the license agreement** radio button to accept the Apache License.

Click **Next** to continue.

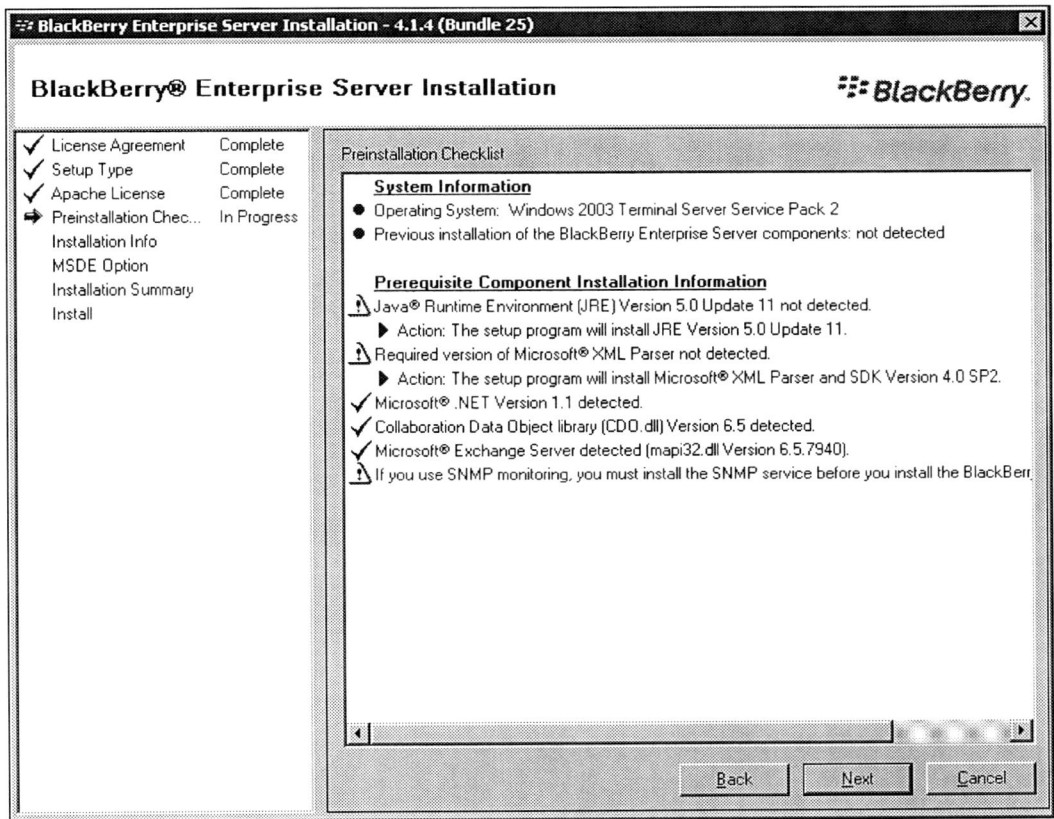

The **Pre-Install Check List** screen displays a summary of the pre-requisite components detected by the installation program. At this point, the installation program will install specific components if they are missing, including the Java Runtime Environment and the MSXML Parser and SDK. The installation program will also confirm the version information for the Collaboration Data Objects and MAPI subsystem.

Click **Next** to continue.

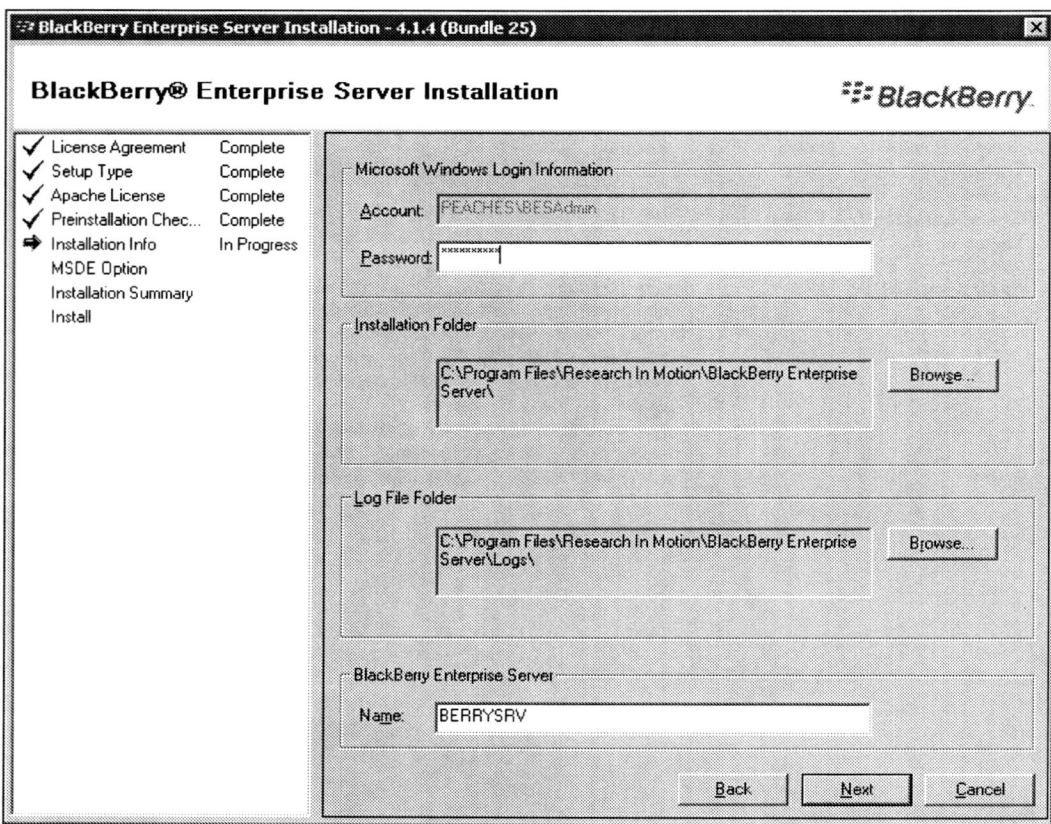

The **Installation Info** screen displays the basic installation configuration details for the BES installation.

Enter the password for the service account in the **Password:** field.

If desired, change the install location by clicking the **Browse** button in the **Installation folder** section and selecting a different location.

If desired, change the log file location by clicking the **Browse** button in the **Log file folder** section and selecting a different location.

Enter the hostname of the BlackBerry Enterprise Server in the **Name:** field of the **BlackBerry Enterprise Server** section.

Click **Next** to continue.

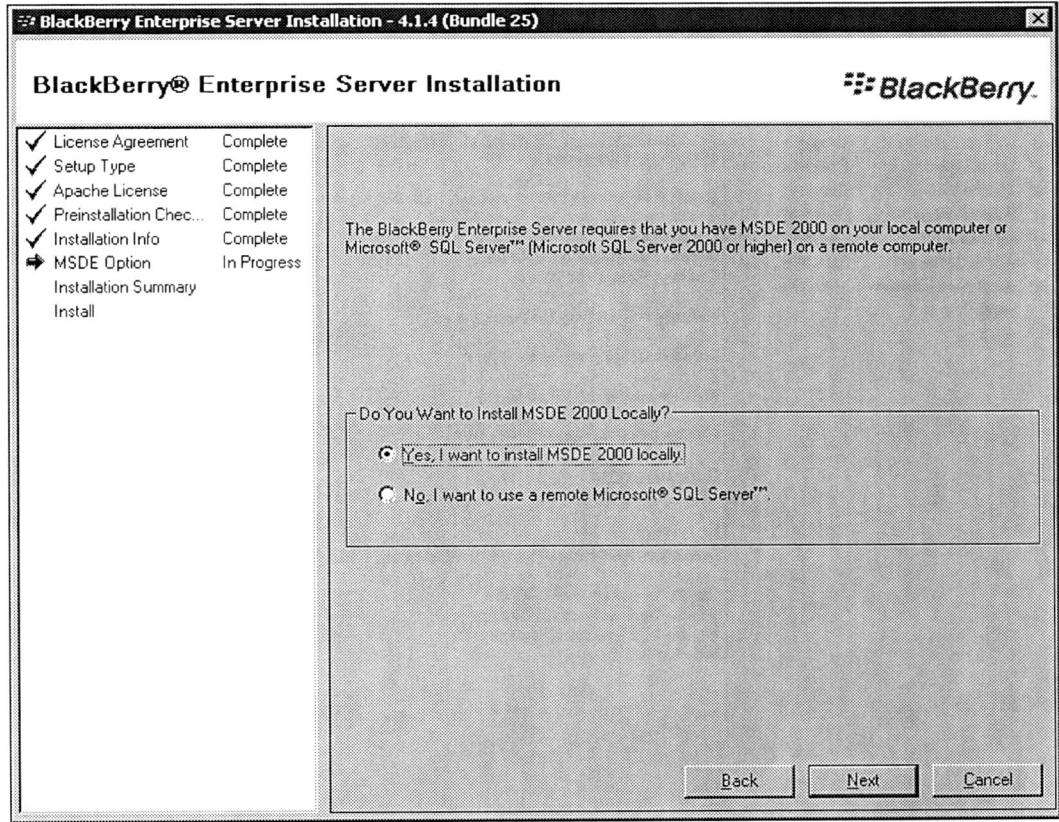

The **MSDE Option** screen provides the option to install the Microsoft SQL Server 2000 Desktop Engine, if desired.

Select the desired SQL server from the **Do You Want to Install MSDE 2000 Locally?** section.

Click **Next** to continue.

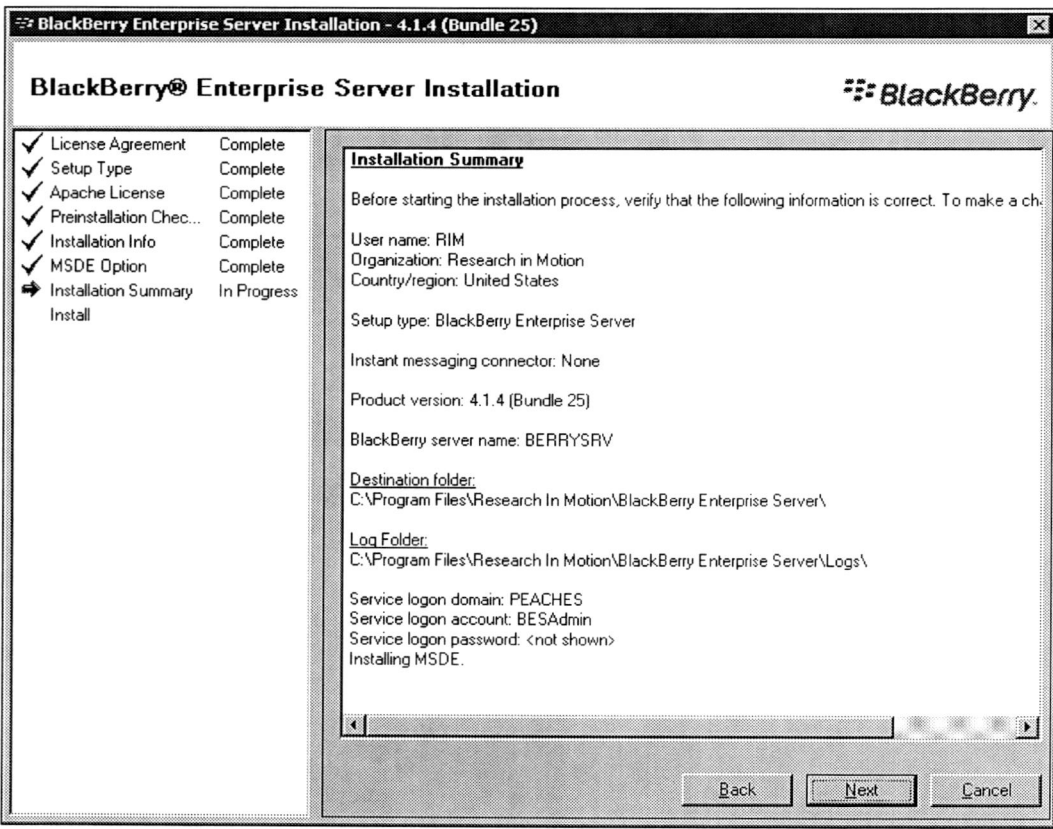

The **Installation Summary** screen displays a summary of all of the installation options selected up to this point. Review the summary and, if necessary, return to the previous screens to make any desired corrections.

Click **Next** to begin the installation.

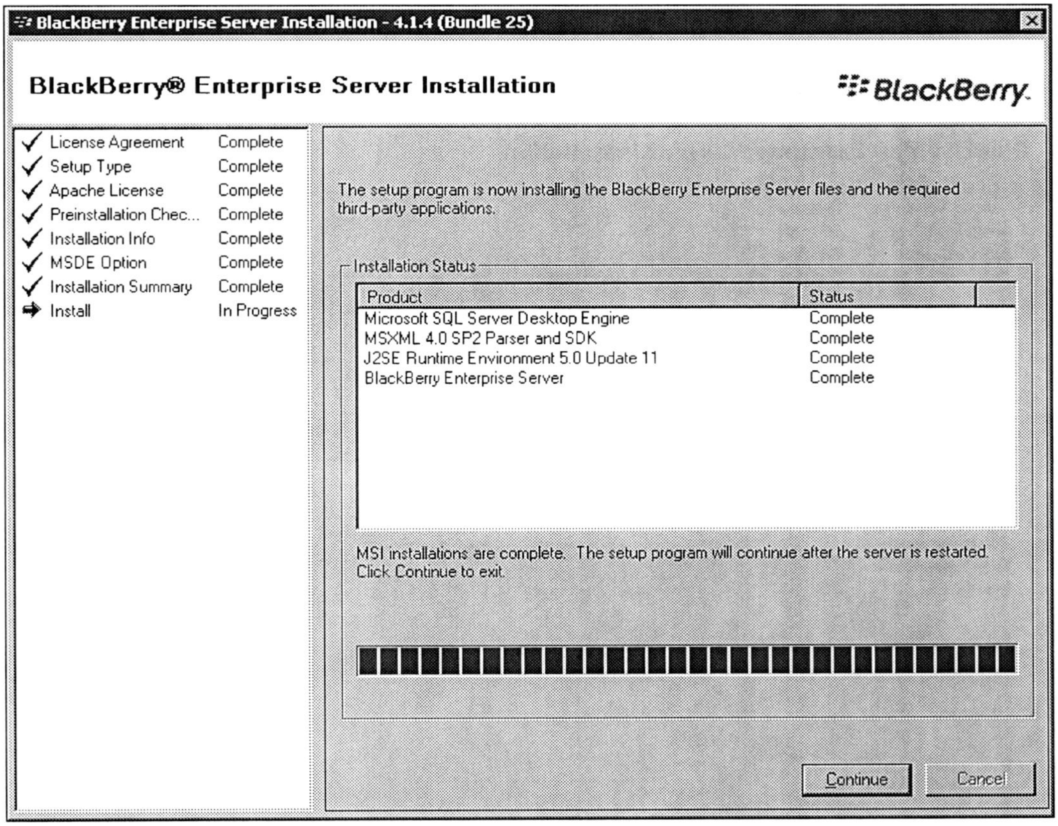

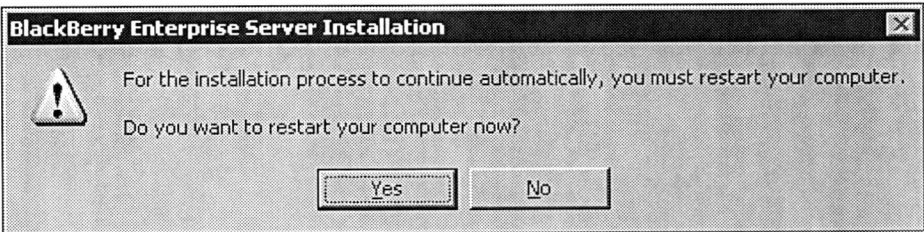

The **Install** screen displays the installation progress for the selected components. Once the initial installation is complete, the installation program will prompt you to restart the server.

Click **Continue** once the **Installation status** field displays **Complete** for all products.

Click **Yes** on the BlackBerry Enterprise Server Installation dialog box to restart the server; after the server has restarted, login using the service account. The installation program will start automatically with additional installation activities.

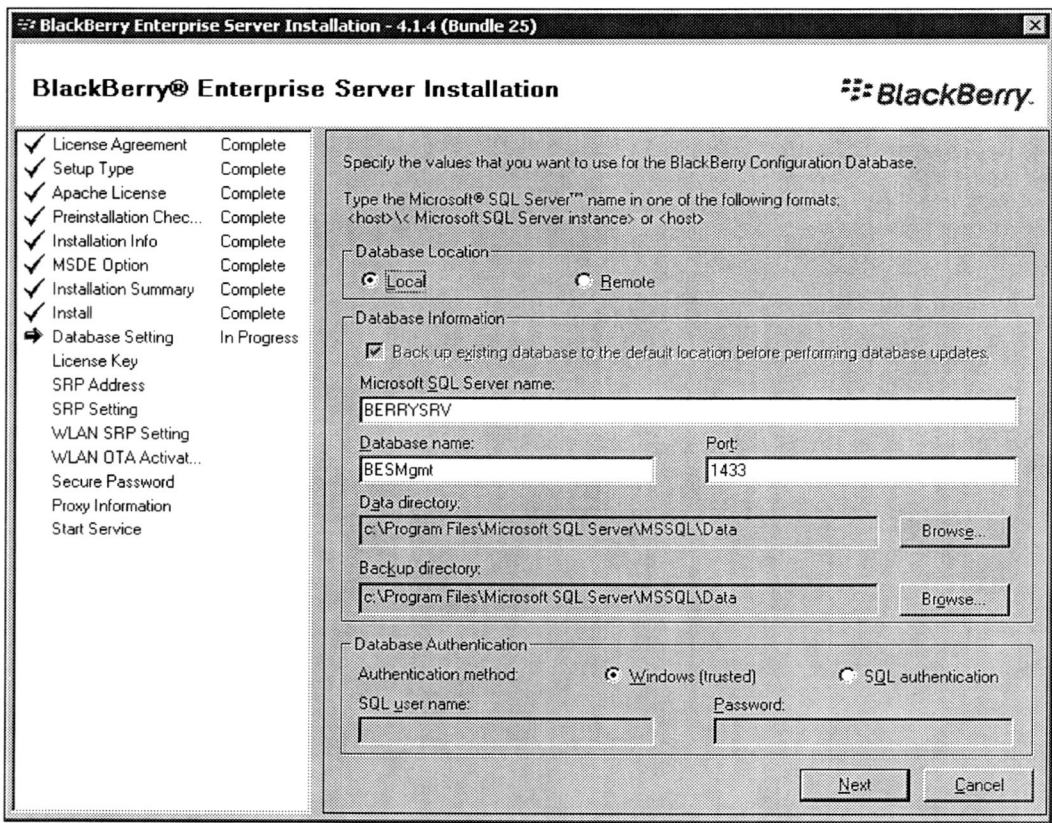

The **Database Setting** screen is used to record the BlackBerry Configuration Database settings.

Select the appropriate radio button in the **Database location** section.

Enter the name of the database server in the **Microsoft SQL server name:** field.

Enter the name of the database instance in the **Database name:** field, or accept the default of **BESMgmt**.

Enter the network port in the **Port:** field, or accept the default of **1433**.

If desired, change the data directory or backup directory locations by clicking the **Browse** button in the appropriate section and selecting a different location.

Select the appropriate database authentication method based on whether you assigned privileges to the service account or created an SQL login. If you created an SQL login, enter the username and password in the **SQL user name:** and **Password:** fields.

Click **Next** to continue.

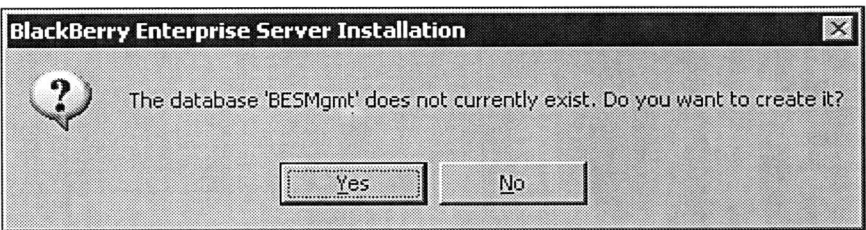

The installation program will verify the settings you enter on this page by attempting to connect to the specified database. If you receive an error after clicking **Next**, you must correct your configuration settings before proceeding. If the database settings are correct, the installation program will prompt you to create the BlackBerry Configuration Database in the specified instance. Click **Yes** to initiate the database setup.

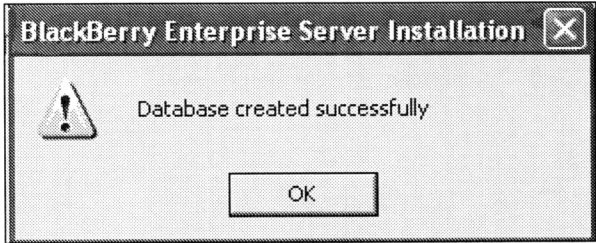

The installation program will provide you with a confirmation that the database was successfully created. Click **OK** to close the confirmation dialog box.

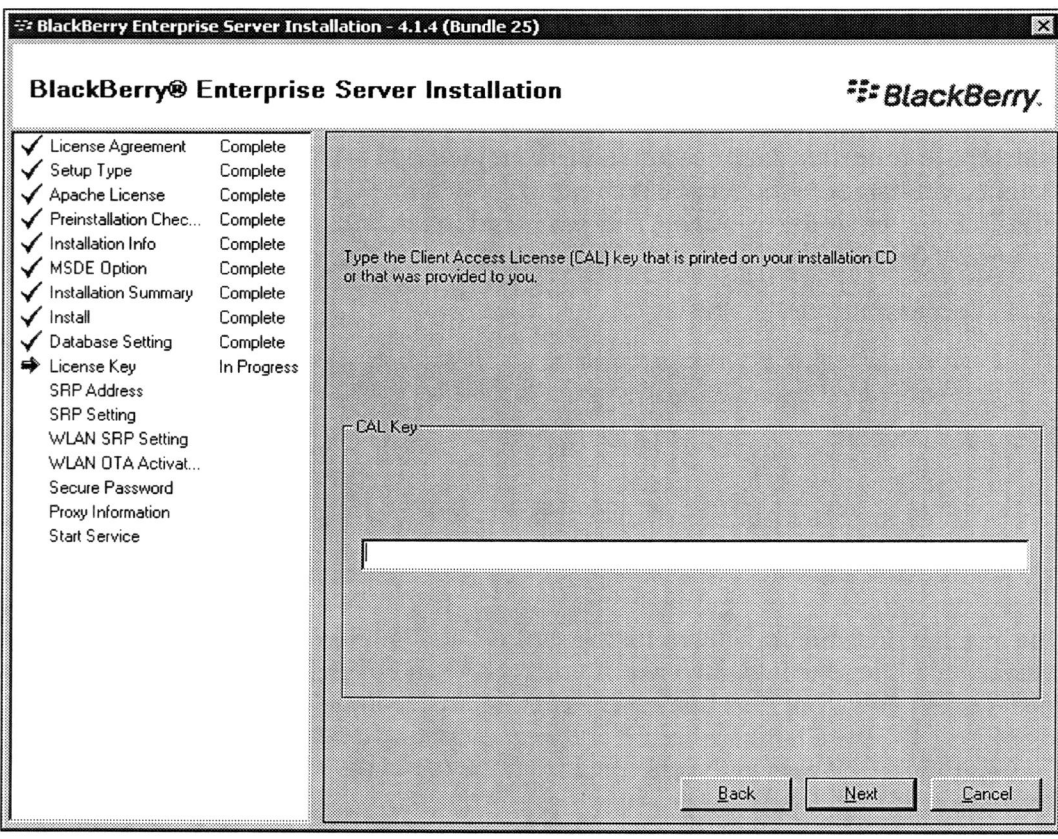

The **License Key** screen is used to enter the license key provided when you purchased the BlackBerry Enterprise Server software.

Enter the license key in the **CAL Key** field and click **Next**.

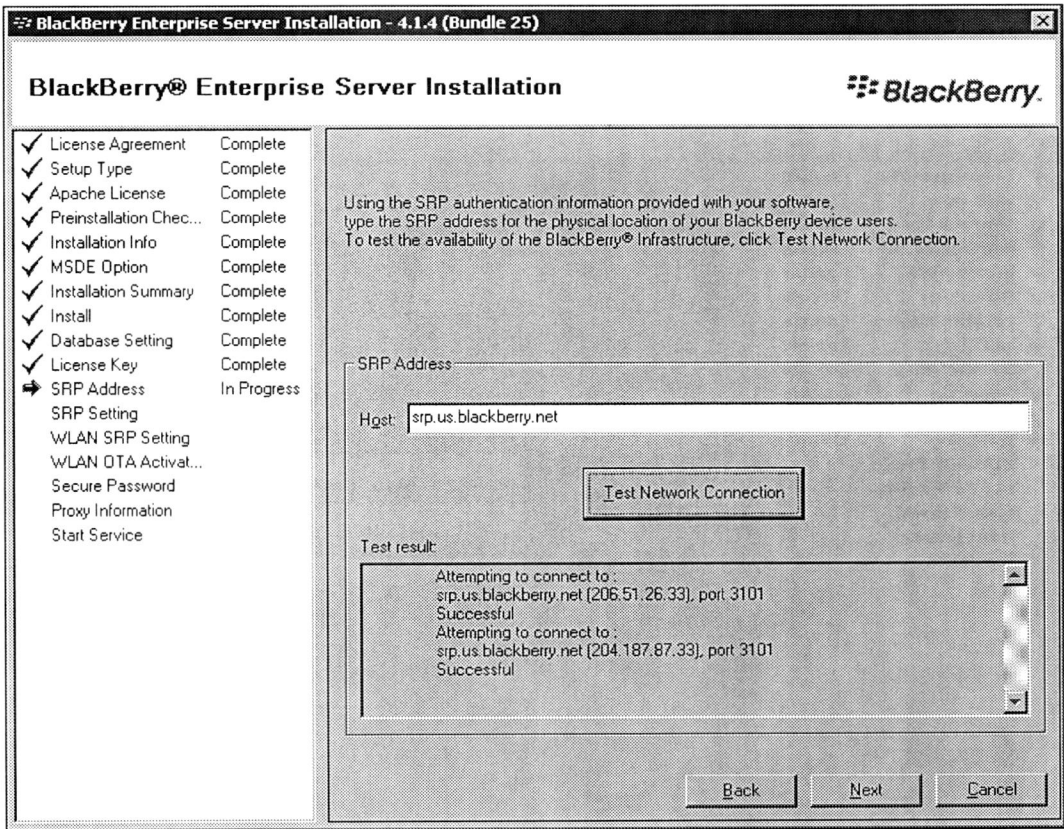

The **SRP Address** screen is used to enter the address for the appropriate BlackBerry Infrastructure site, based on the geographic location of your BlackBerry users and your BlackBerry Enterprise Server.

Enter the SRP address in the **Host:** field and click **Test Network Connection**. If successful, click **Next** to continue.

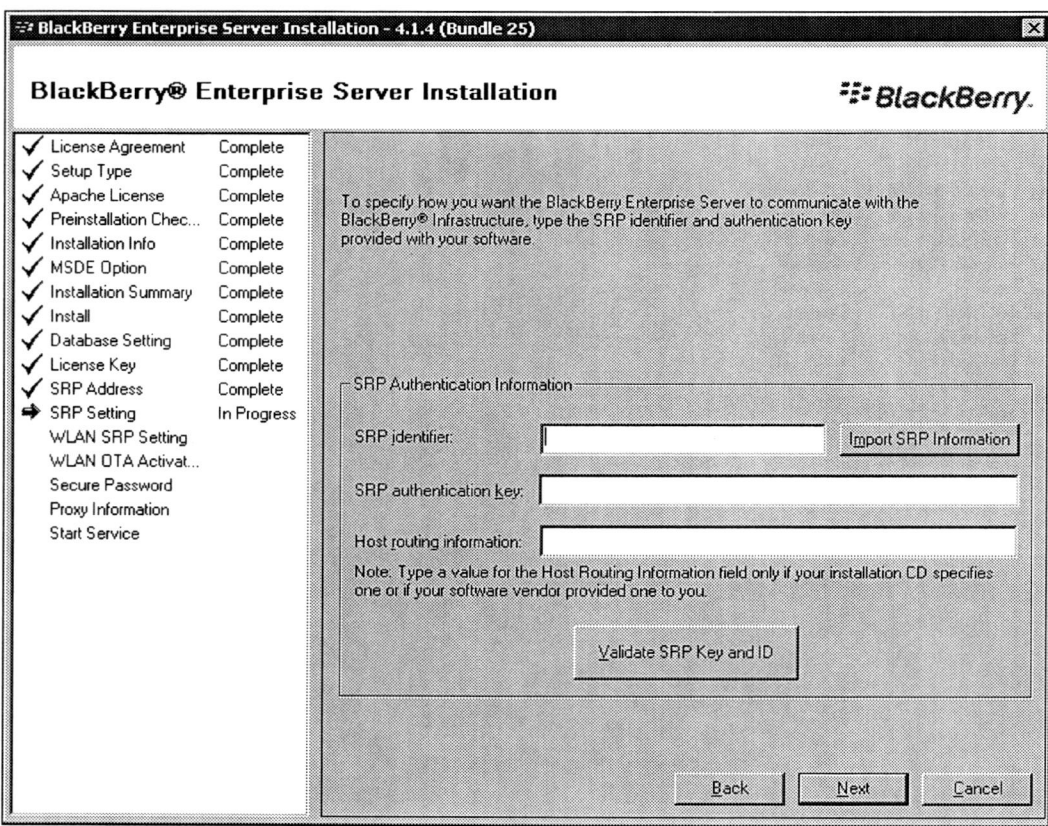

The **SRP Setting** screen is used to specify the Service Routing Protocol information for your BES.

Enter the SRP information provided with your BlackBerry software in the **SRP Identifier:** and **SRP Authentication Key:** fields. If your SRP information has been provided electronically, click the **Import SRP Information** button to import this information. If applicable, complete the **Host Routing Information:** field.

Click the **Validate SRP Key and ID** button to confirm the information you have entered.

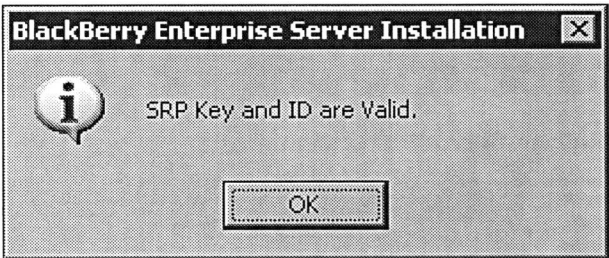

Click **OK** to close the confirmation dialog box and click **Next** on the **SRP Setting** screen to continue.

The **Microsoft Exchange Server** screen confirms the Microsoft Exchange credentials and settings for the BlackBerry Enterprise Server service account.

Enter your Exchange server hostname in the **Microsoft Exchange server:** field.

Enter the mailbox name for your service account in the **Mailbox:** field. This is typically the same as the username for the service account.

Click the **Check Name** button and click **OK** to continue.

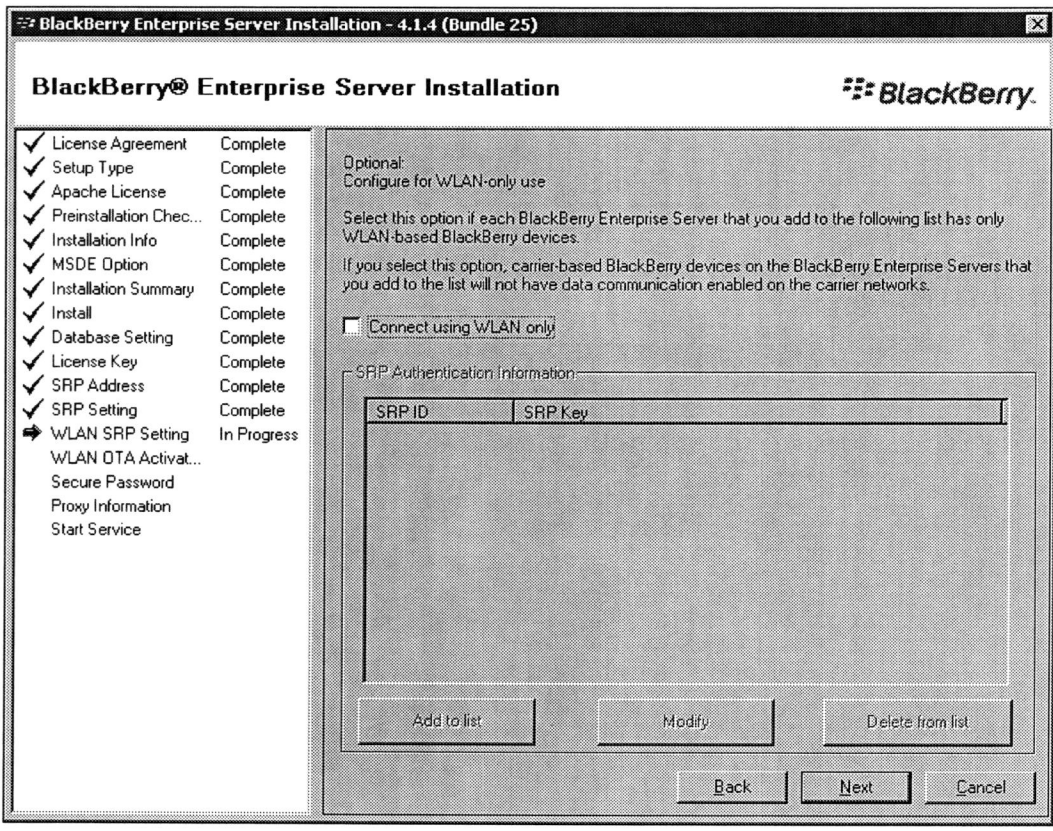

The **WLAN SRP Setting** screen is used for WLAN-only implementations of BlackBerry Enterprise Server. This is an implementation option used by enterprises that deploy BlackBerries that rely on WLAN for data access and utilize SIP-based IP telephony for voice services. This method will not be described in this book.

Click **Next** to continue.

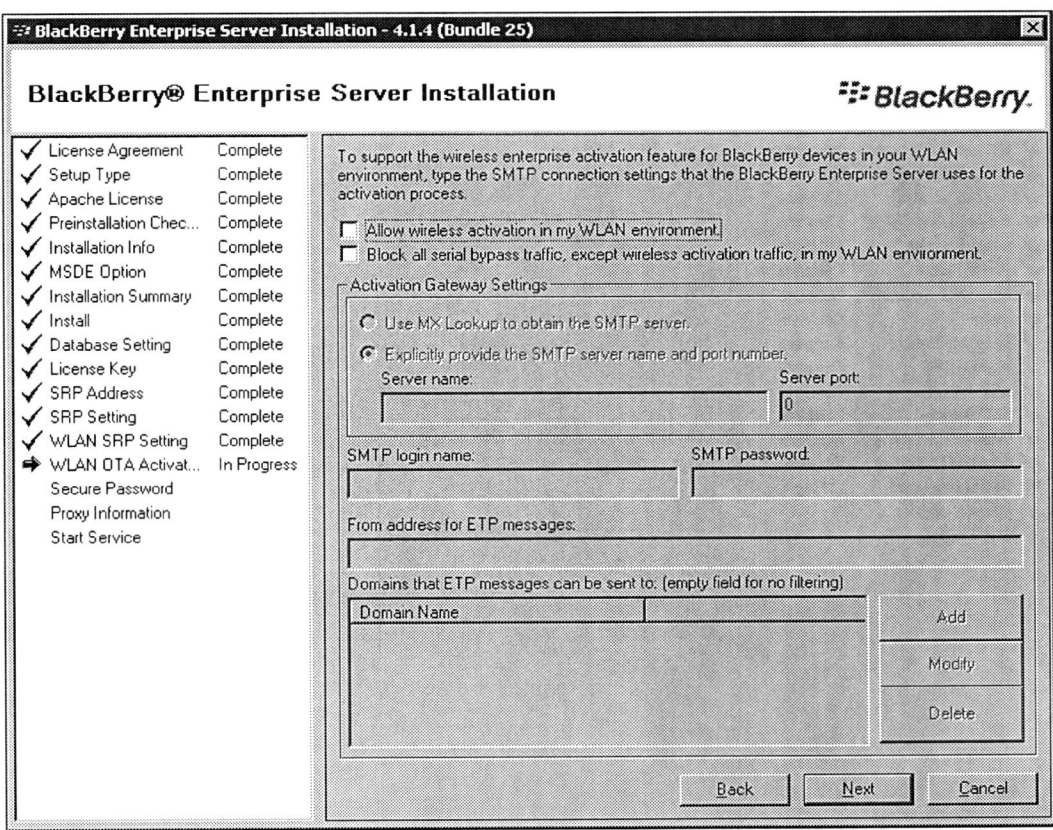

The **WLAN OTA Activation** screen is also used for WLAN-only implementations of BlackBerry Enterprise Server to configure wireless enterprise activation.

Click **Next** to continue.

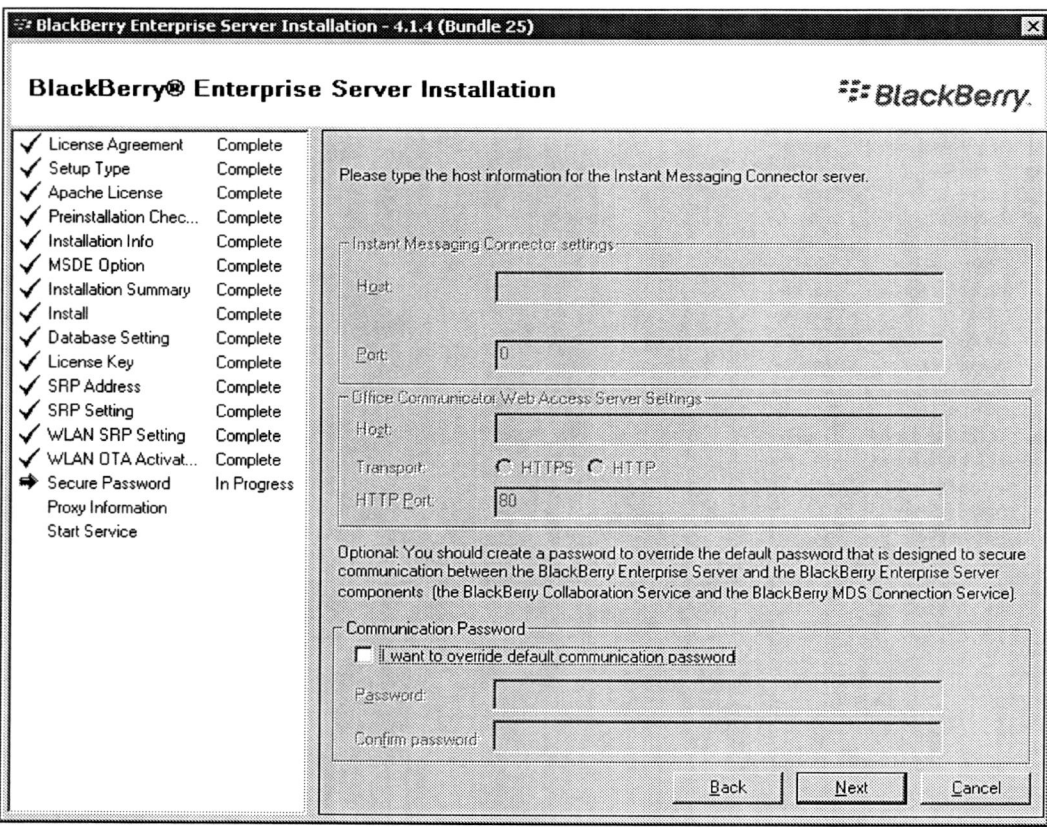

The **Secure Password** screen is used to configure enterprise instant messenger settings and the default secure password setting. The secure password is used for authentication and communication between BlackBerry Enterprise Server and the distributed components. Our implementation will not be using instant messaging services and we don't want to change the default password, so there is no need to modify the settings on this page.

Click **Next** to continue.

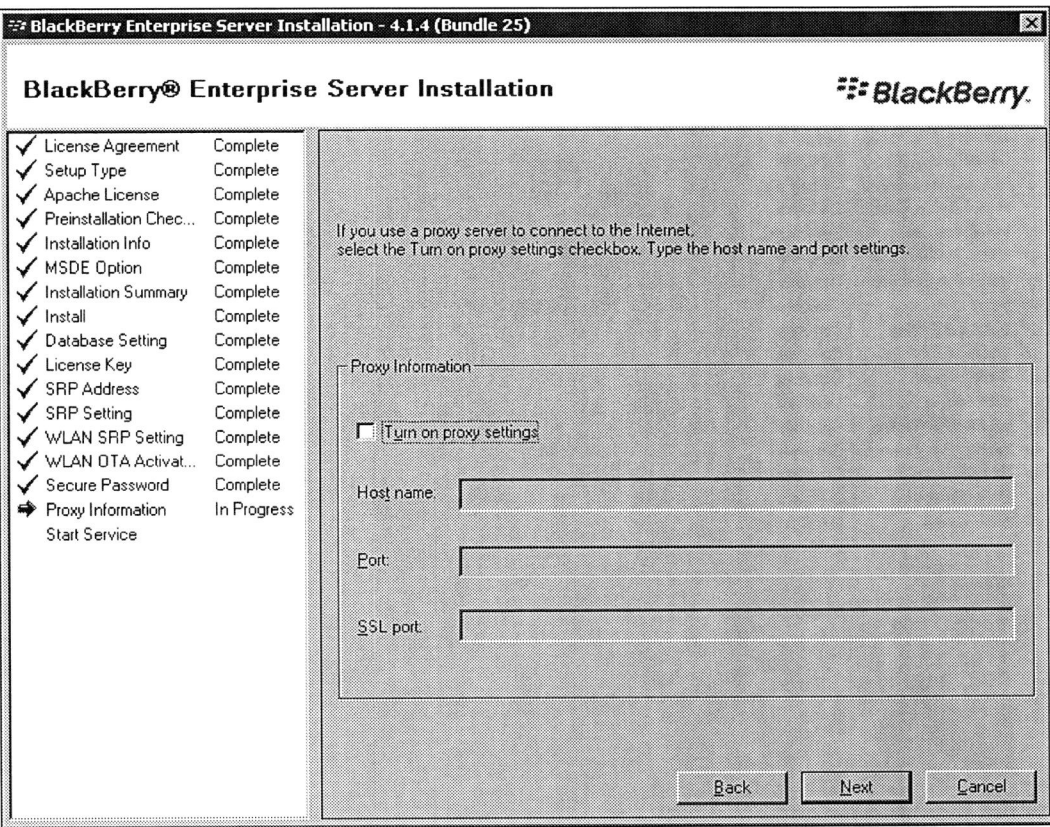

The **Proxy Information** screen is used to configure proxy server settings. If your BES must connect to a proxy server in order to access the Internet, this screen is used to enter that information. If this is necessary, click the **Turn on proxy settings** check box and enter your proxy server information in the fields below.

Click **Next** to continue.

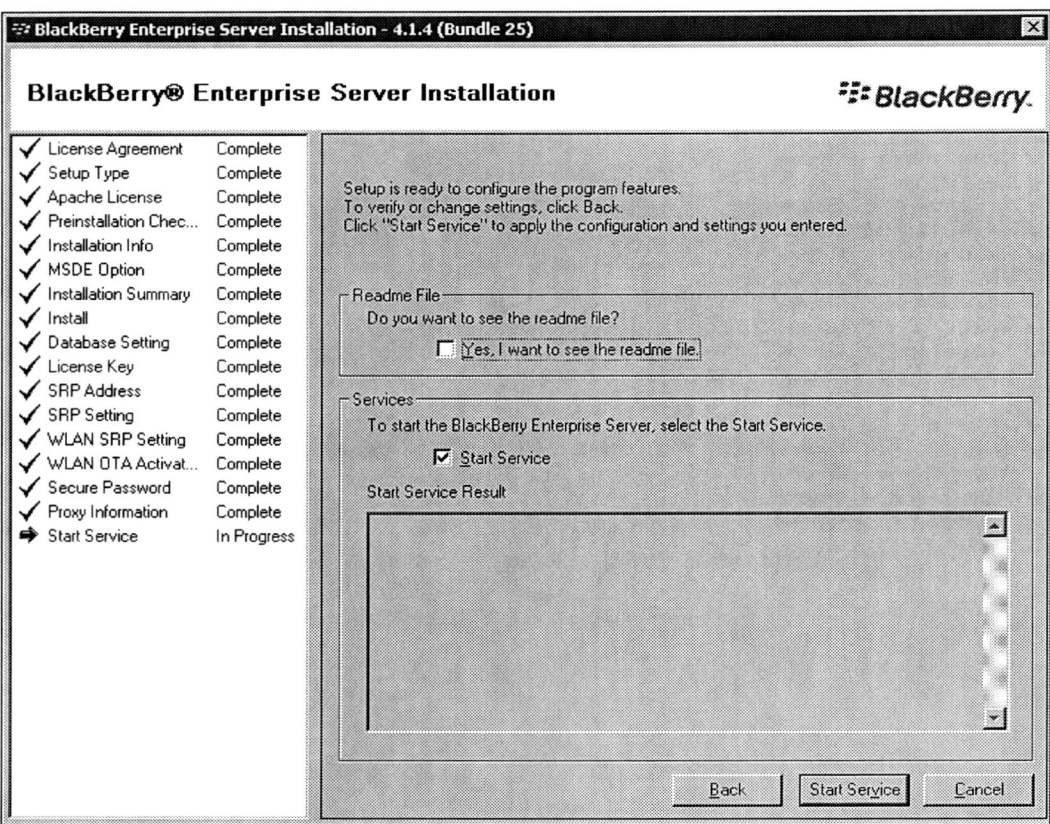

The **Start Service** screen is the last screen in the installation process, allowing you to start the services that have been installed.

If desired, check the **Yes, I want to see the readme file.** check box to read the release notes.

Click the **Start Service** check box to start the BlackBerry Enterprise Server services and click the **Start Service** button.

Click the **Finish** button when the services have successfully started.

Summary

Congratulations! You have successfully completed the installation of BlackBerry Enterprise Server, created the BlackBerry Configuration Database, and validated your connection to the BlackBerry Infrastructure. The job is far from over, though. In the next chapter, we will be covering the process of configuring your BES environment and provisioning users.

5

Provisioning BlackBerry Users and Devices

In the previous chapter, we successfully completed our installation of Blackberry Enterprise Server. This chapter will provide you with the information you need to get your users started on BES. Specifically, we are going to cover administrative user roles, the steps to provision user accounts on BES and the methods that can be used to activate BlackBerry handhelds.

Administrative Roles

Now that you have BES installed, you will have to start dealing with the day-to-day tasks of managing those mobile users and their associated devices. Hopefully all of that work won't fall on the shoulders of one person, especially if you're planning a large BlackBerry rollout. RIM has developed BES with the assumption that enterprises have many different roles in their IT organization, ranging from help desk personnel to application server administrators. To support complex IT organizations, BES includes role-based administration, with six pre-defined administrative roles, each with a specific set of permissions and capabilities. The table below lists the default administrative roles and a description of their capabilities.

Administrative Role	Description
Security Administrator rim_db_admin_security	This is the overarching administrative role, with the permissions to administer all aspects of the BES environment, including security settings (role membership, licensing, and encryption settings) that are not available to other administrators.
Enterprise Administrator rim_db_admin_enterprise	This is the most privileged role after the Security Administrator, who is delegated the ability to perform most administrative functions, except for the security settings that are limited to the Security Administrator.
Device Administrator rim_db_admin_handheld	This administrative role is focused on the capabilities required to manage user accounts and mobile devices. This includes the ability to set configurations for software, third-party applications, and other settings that are sent out to the BlackBerry devices.
Senior Helpdesk Administrator rim_db_admin_sr_helpdesk	This administrative role has the permission to perform all user management tasks, as well as managing IT policies, and IT administration commands (such as remote device wipe).
Junior Helpdesk Administrator rim_db_admin_jr_helpdesk	Aside from the Audit roles, this is the least privileged administrative account, with the ability to perform basic user management (such as wireless activation) and re-sending IT policies and service books.
Audit rim_db_admin_audit_ <role>	The Audit roles are "read-only" versions of the other administrative roles, providing the ability to train new administrators without allowing them to make any changes to BES.

Assigning Administrative Roles

Administrative roles are assigned to database users, which can be associated with either Microsoft Windows users or groups, or SQL logins. This provides some flexibility in the way administrators are provisioned for BES. It is recommended that you assign administrative roles to Windows groups, as this reduces the number of locations to manage administrative users. Administrative roles may be assigned to existing database users or new database users. The following sections describe both methods for assigning administrative roles.

Assigning Administrative Roles to Existing Database Users

1. On a workstation with BlackBerry Manager installed, click **Start | Programs | BlackBerry Enterprise Server | BlackBerry Manager**.

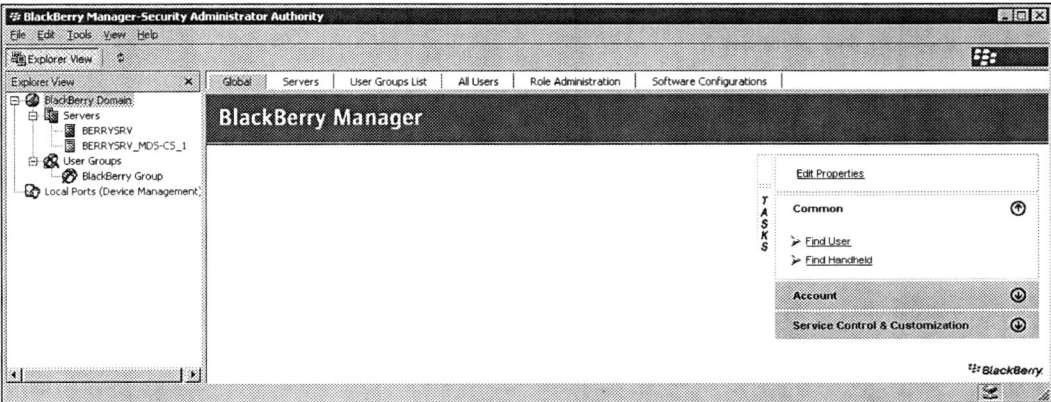

2. Select **BlackBerry Domain** from the left-hand window.

3. Select the **Role Administration** tab and select the role that you want to assign.

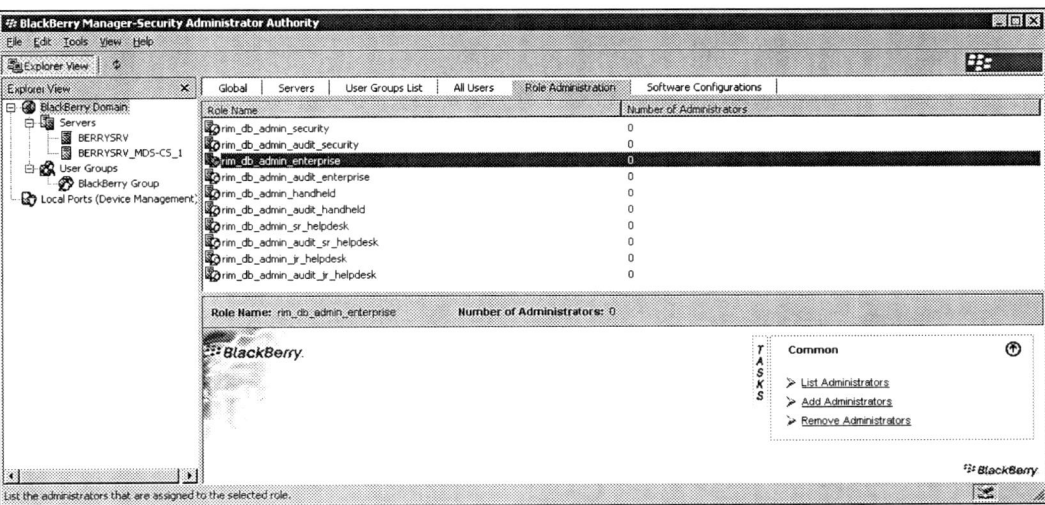

4.   Select **List Administrators**.

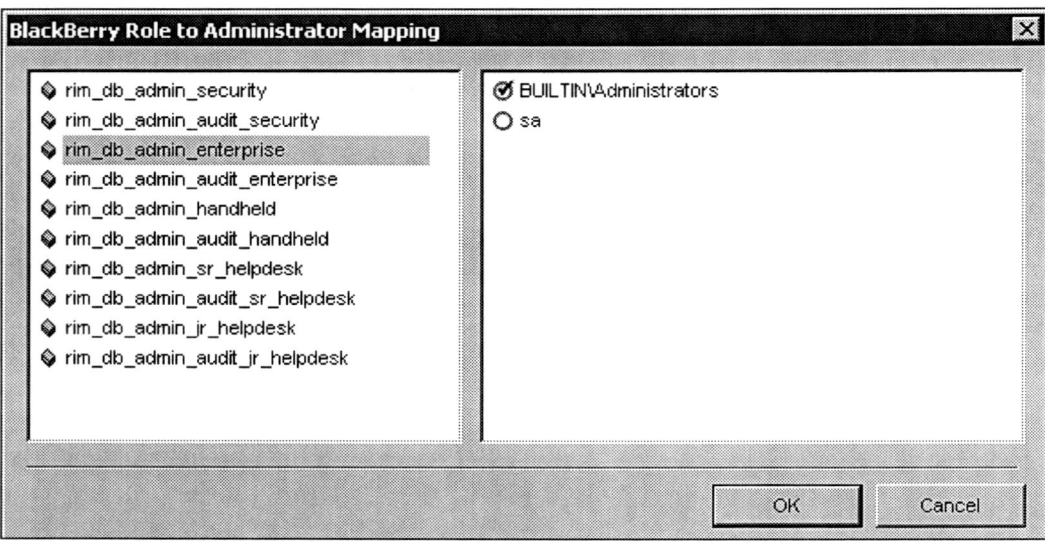

5.   Select the database user that you want to assign to the role and click **OK**.

Assigning Administrative Roles to New Database Users

1.   On a workstation with BlackBerry Manager installed, click **Start | Programs | BlackBerry Enterprise Server | BlackBerry Manager**.

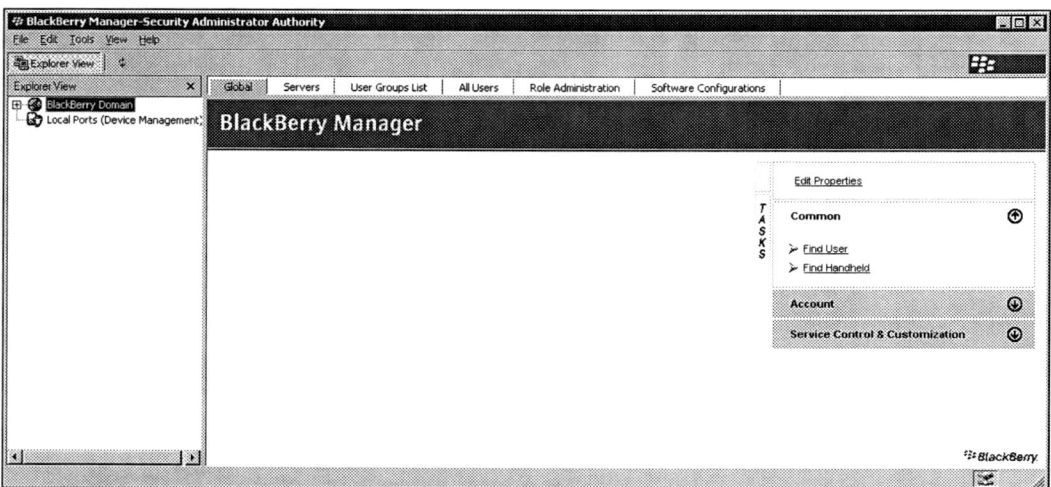

2. Select **BlackBerry Domain** from the left-hand window.

3. Select the **Role Administration** tab and select the role that you want to assign.

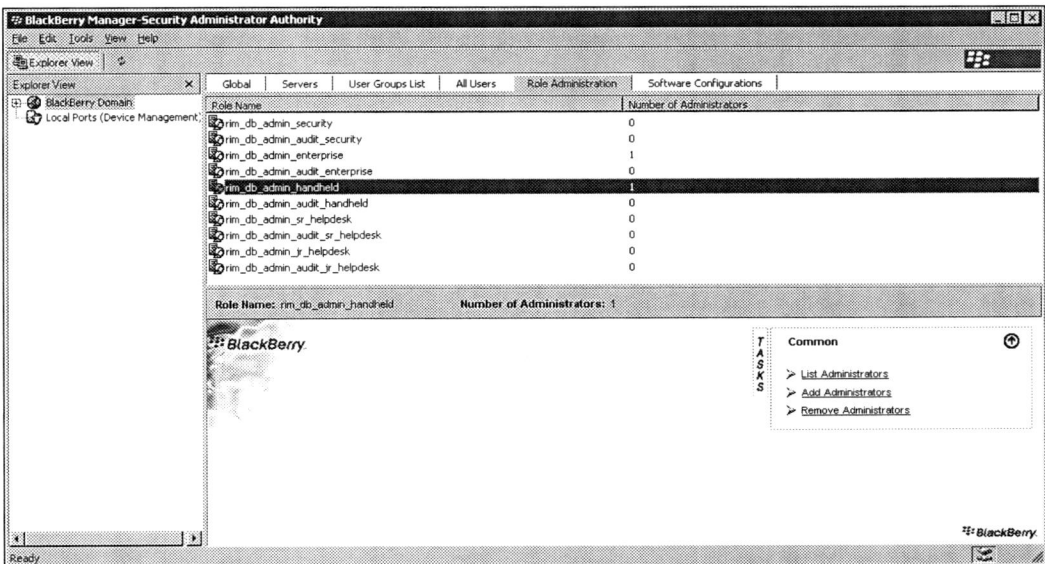

4. Select **Add Administrators**.

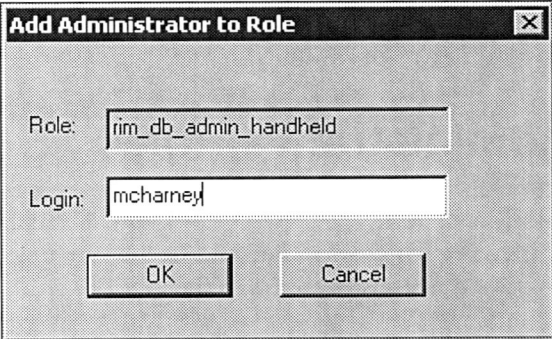

5. Enter the login name of the user in the **User Name:** field and click **OK**.

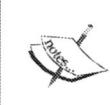 If you want to assign the administrative role to a Microsoft Windows-authenticated database user, enter the Windows username in the username field using the DOMAIN\Username convention. You will not be prompted to enter a password, since the Windows password will be used for authentication.

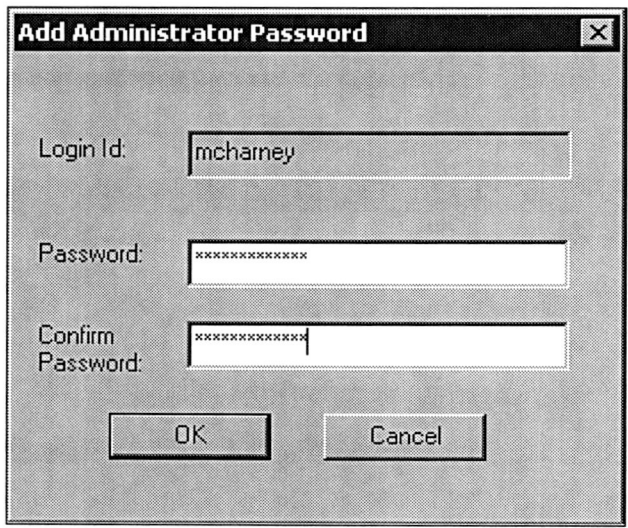

6. Enter the password in the **Password:** field and the **Confirm Password:** field and click **OK**.

Managing Administrative Roles

Due to reorganizations within your IT organization, you may need to alter previously-assigned administrative roles. BES provides the capability to move users from one administrative role to another and to remove users from roles. The following sections describe the steps to perform these actions.

Changing Administrative Roles

1. On a workstation with BlackBerry Manager installed, click **Start | Programs | BlackBerry Enterprise Server | BlackBerry Manager**.

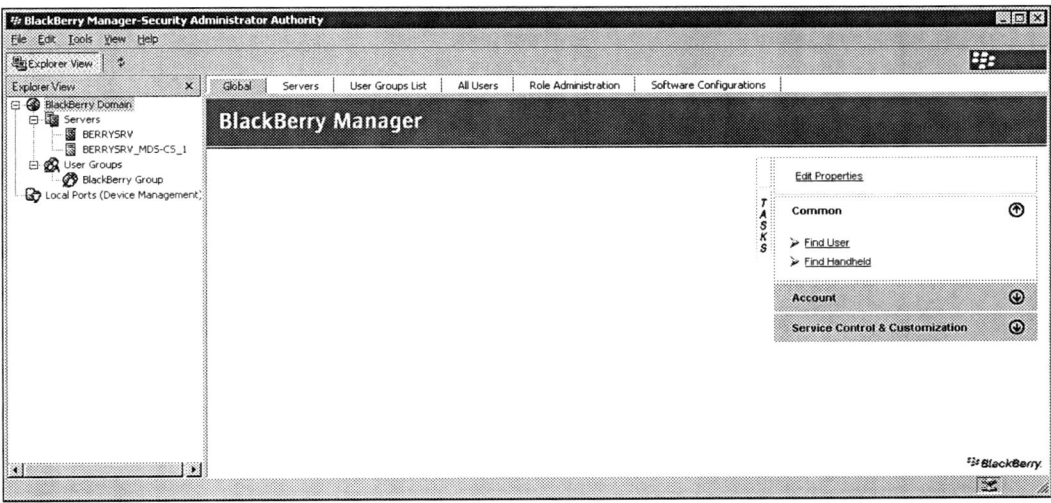

2. Select **BlackBerry Domain** from the left-hand window.

3. Select the **Role Administration** tab and select the role to which the user is currently assigned.

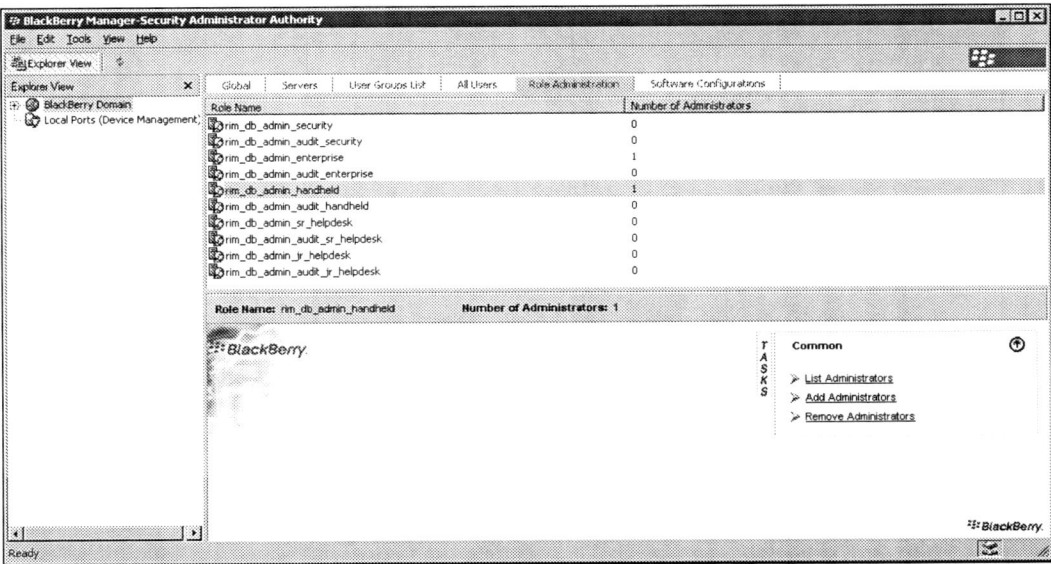

4. Select **List Administrators**.

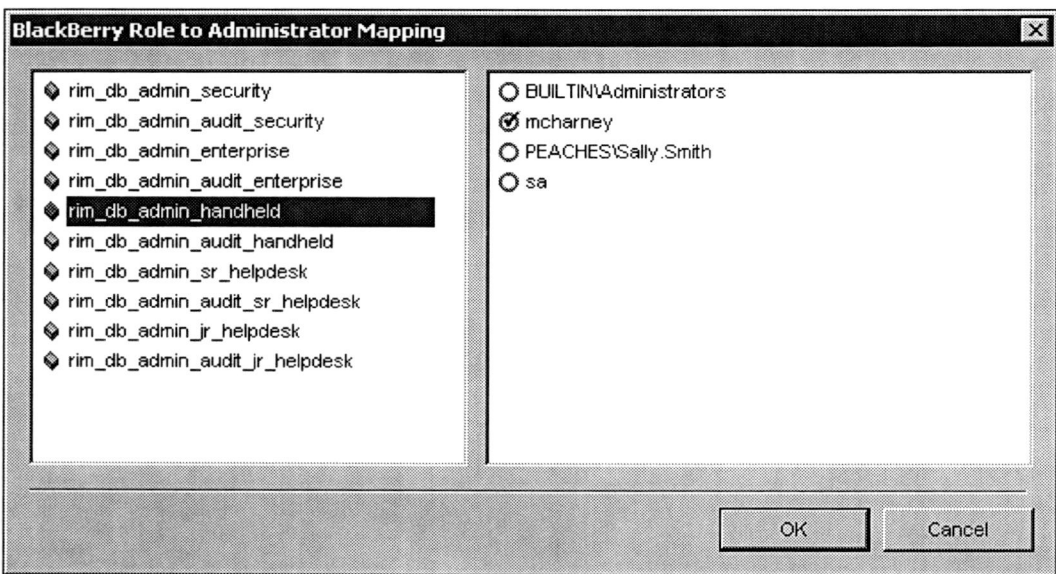

5. Uncheck the circle to the left of the username.

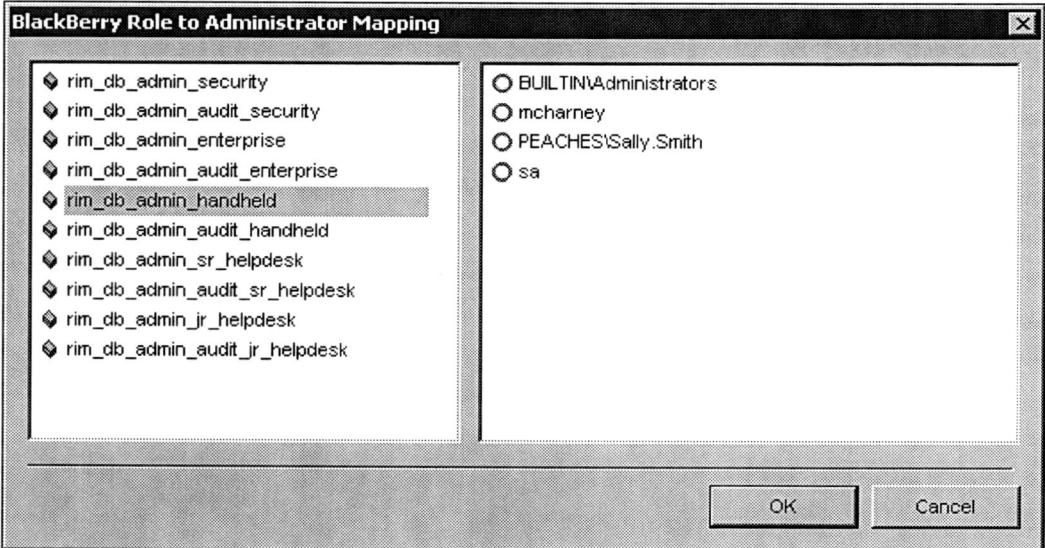

6. Select the new administrative role for the user on the left-hand pane and check the circle to the left of the username.

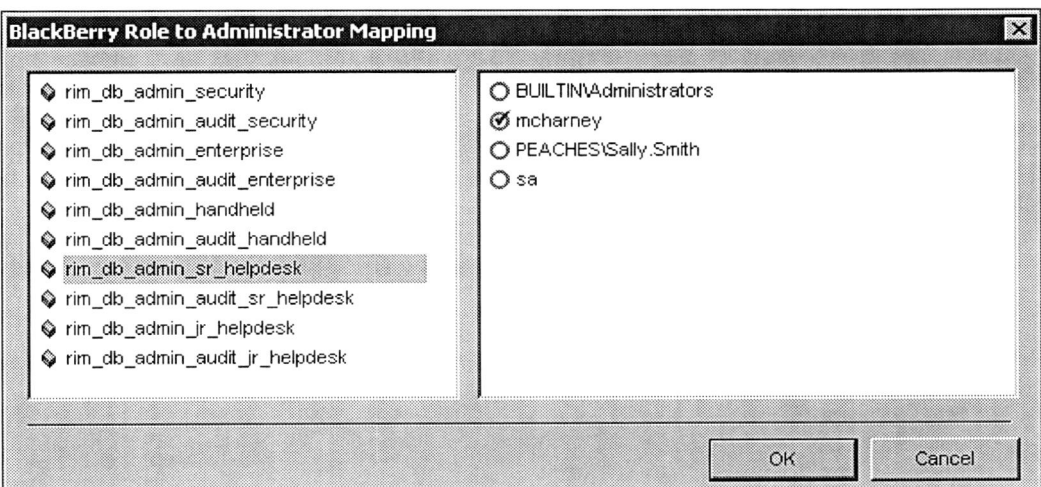

7. Click **OK**.

  A user's administrative role is checked only when BlackBerry Manager is opened, so the application may need to be restarted in order for the new role to take effect.

Removing Administrative Roles

1. On a workstation with BlackBerry Manager installed, click **Start | Programs | BlackBerry Enterprise Server | BlackBerry Manager**.

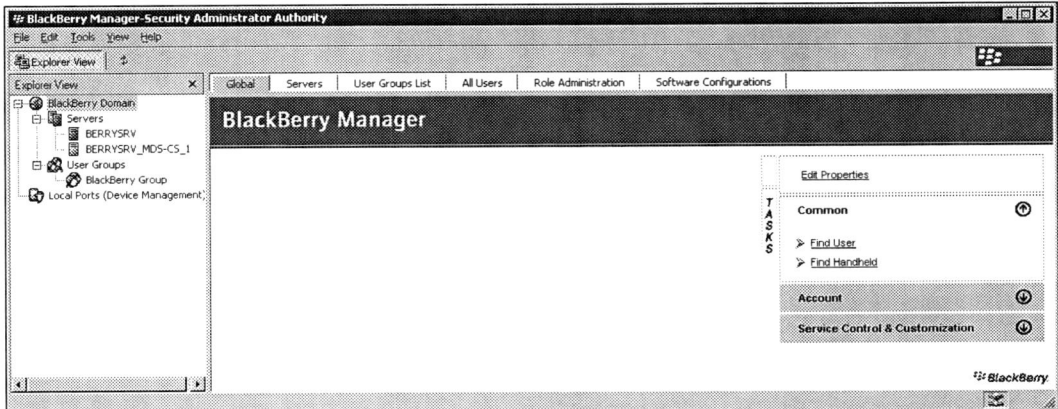

2. Select **BlackBerry Domain** from the left-hand window.

3. Select the **Role Administration** tab and select the role from which you want to remove a user.

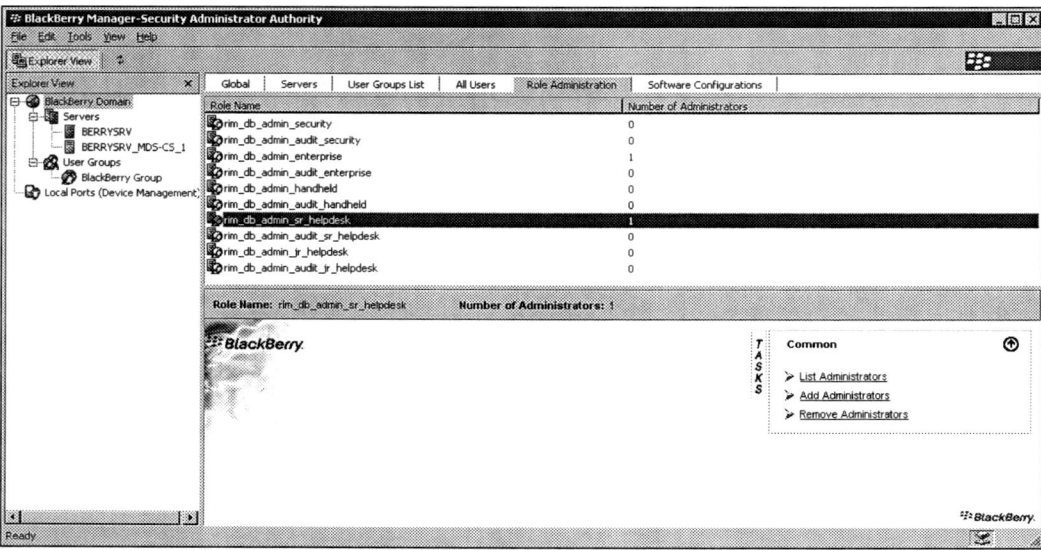

4. Select **Remove Administrators**.

5. Select the database user that you want to remove from the **Login:** pull-down and click **OK**.

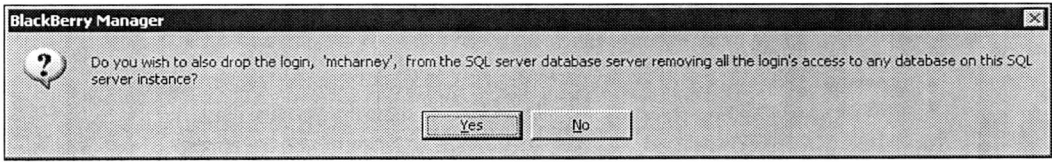

6. If desired, click **Yes** to delete the SQL login from the database server.

Configuring BlackBerry Manager for SQL Login Authentication

BlackBerry Manager uses Windows authentication credentials by default. If you have assigned administrative roles to SQL logins, you must change the authentication method for BlackBerry Manager. The following steps describe the process for changing the authentication method.

1. On a workstation with BlackBerry Manager installed, click **Start | Programs | BlackBerry Enterprise Server | BlackBerry Manager**.

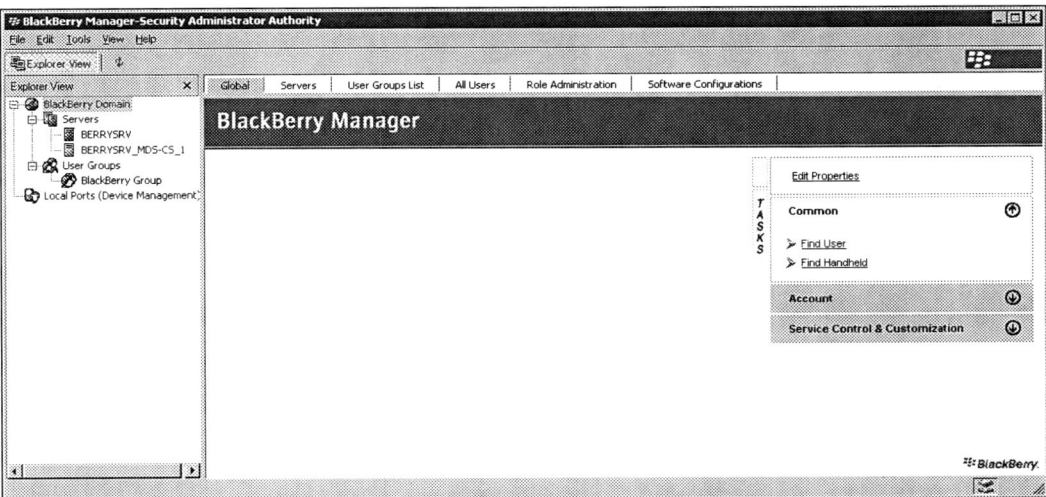

2. Click the **Tools** menu and select **Options**.

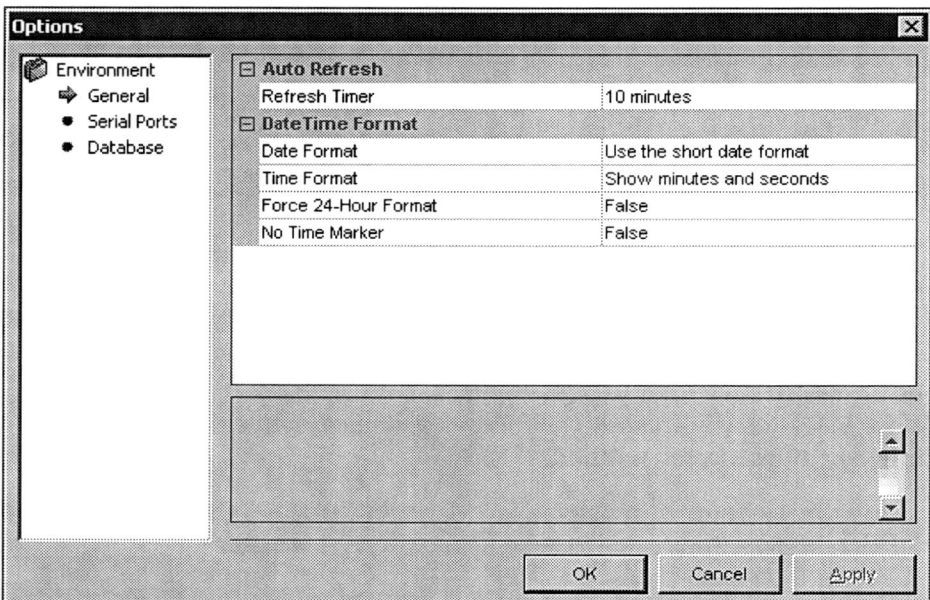

2. Select the **Database** option and select **Database Authentication** in the **Authentication** drop-down list.

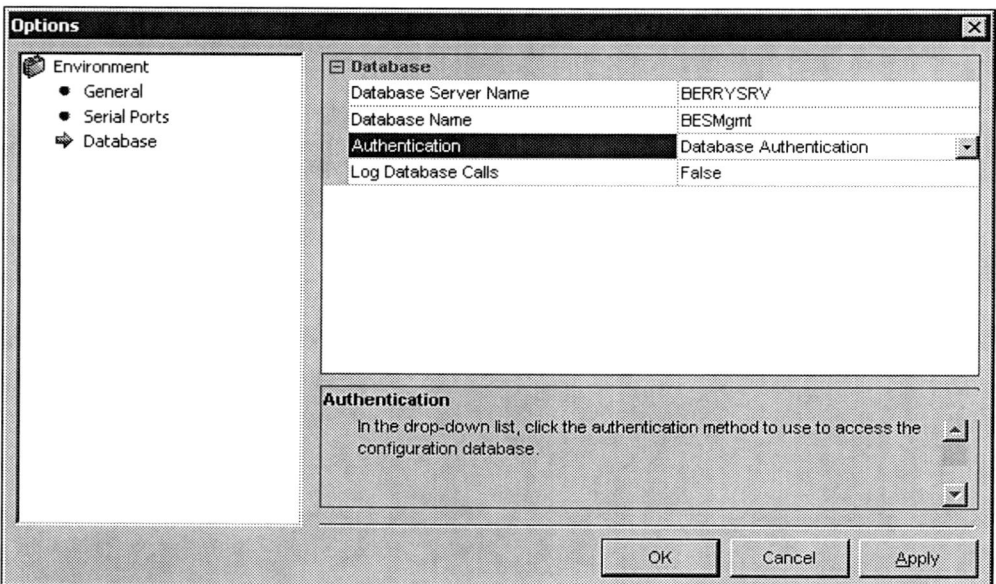

3. Click **OK** and close and re-open **BlackBerry Manager** for the changes to take effect.

Provisioning Users

Now that we have established the administrative roles for our BlackBerry Enterprise Server, we're ready to provide our Microsoft Exchange users access to the BES. Users may only be provisioned on a single BES at a time; if you add a user that was previously using BlackBerry Desktop Redirector or was part of a different BlackBerry Domain, you will need to reconfigure the BlackBerry device. For more information on this process, refer to the Provisioning Devices section later in this chapter. The following steps detail the process for adding a user to the BES.

1. On a workstation with BlackBerry Manager installed, click **Start | Programs | BlackBerry Enterprise Server | BlackBerry Manager**.

2.   Select your BlackBerry Enterprise Server from the left-hand window.

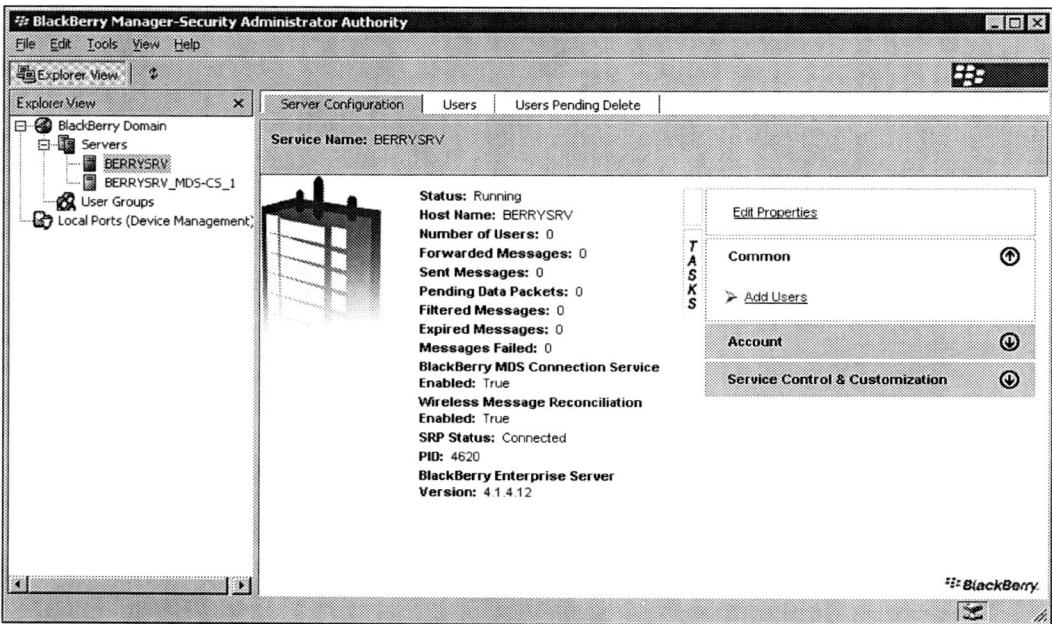

3.   Select the **Server Configuration** tab and select the **Common** group.

4.   Select the **Add Users** option.

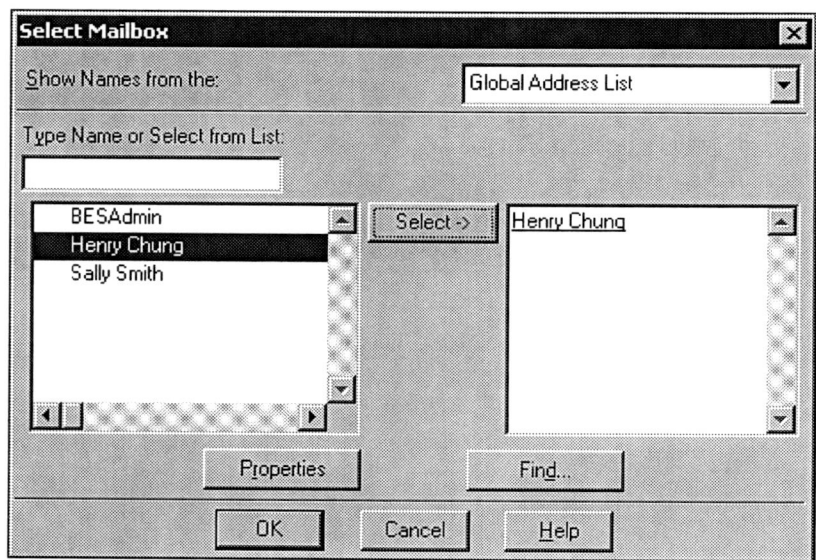

5. Select an address group from the **Show names from the:** drop-down list, select the user that you wish to add from the user list, and click the **Select** button.

6. Click **OK**.

User Groups

In order to facilitate administration, BES provides the ability to create user groups. You can apply configuration settings and perform administrative tasks on individuals or on user groups. Users automatically inherit any settings for a user group when they are added to that group. The following steps detail the process for creating a group, configuring the common settings and adding a user to the group.

1. On a workstation with BlackBerry Manager installed, click **Start | Programs | BlackBerry Enterprise Server | BlackBerry Manager**.

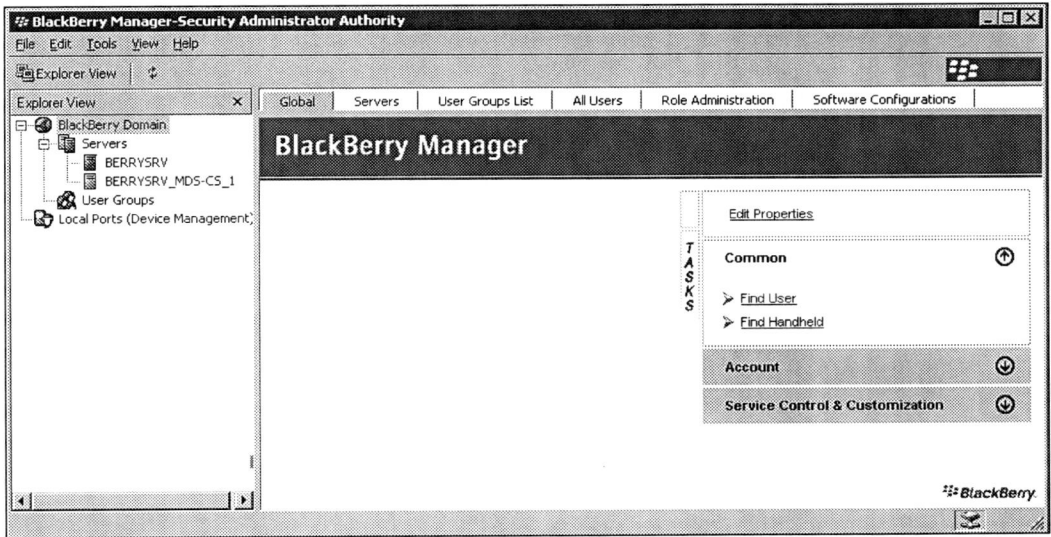

2. Select **User Groups** from the left-hand window.

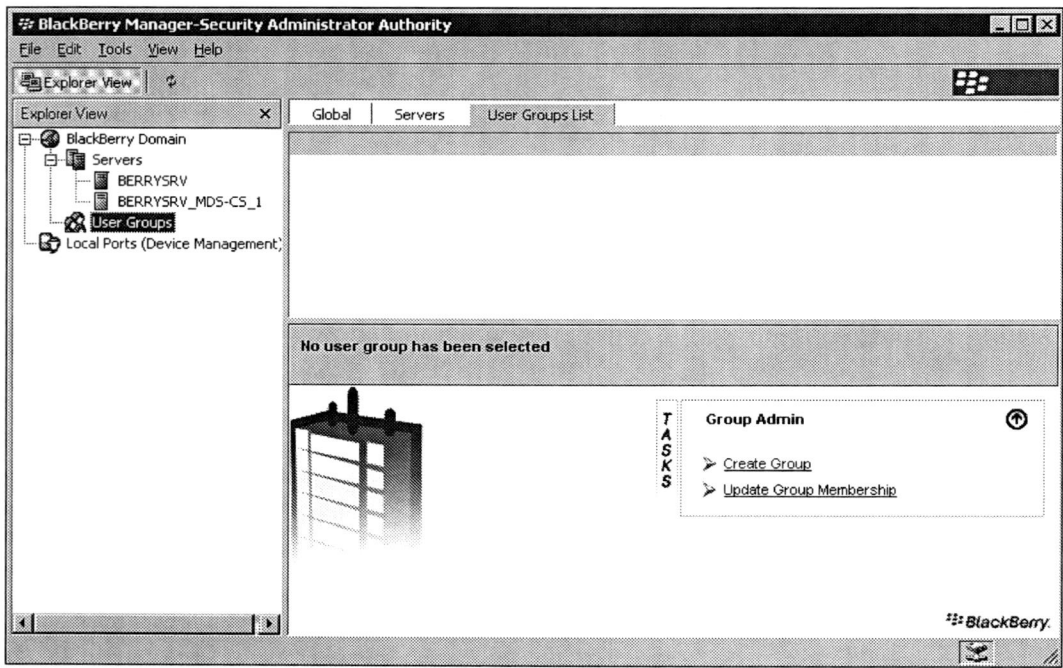

3. Select the **Create Group** option.

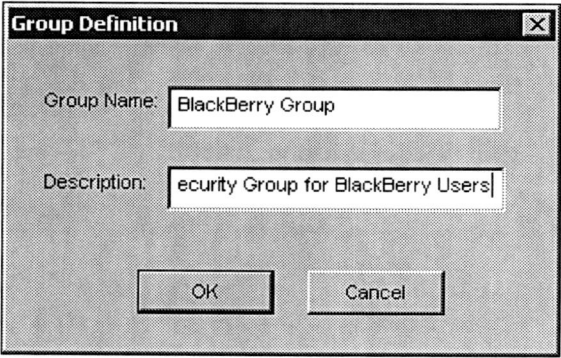

4. Enter a name in the **Group Name** field.
5. Enter a description in the **Description** field.

6. Click **OK**.

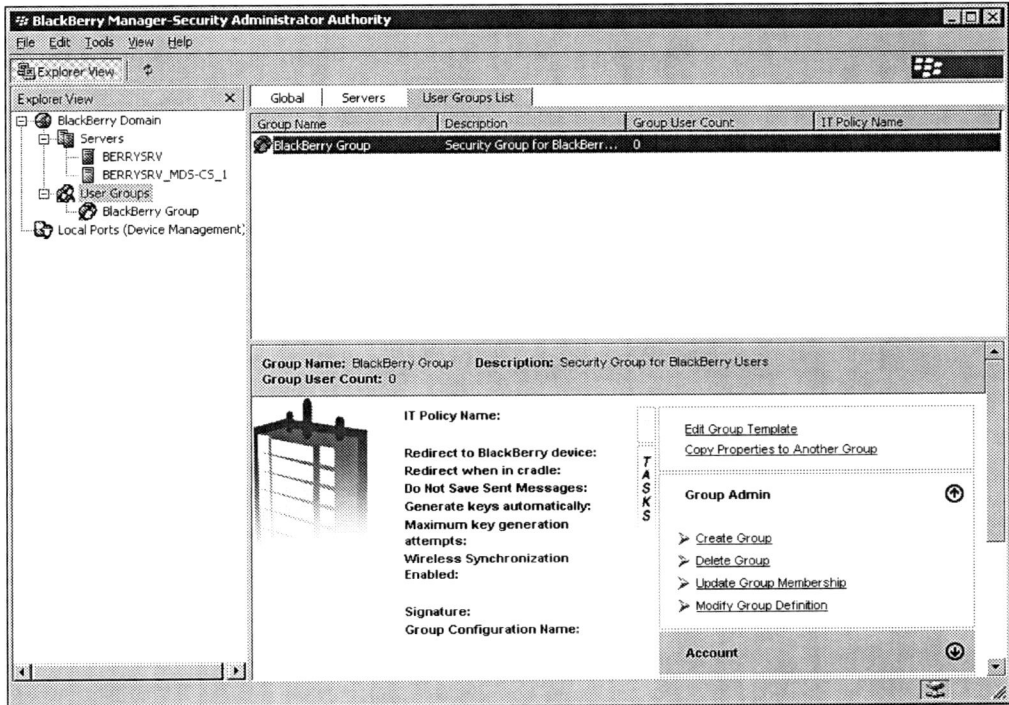

7. Select the **Edit Group Template** option.

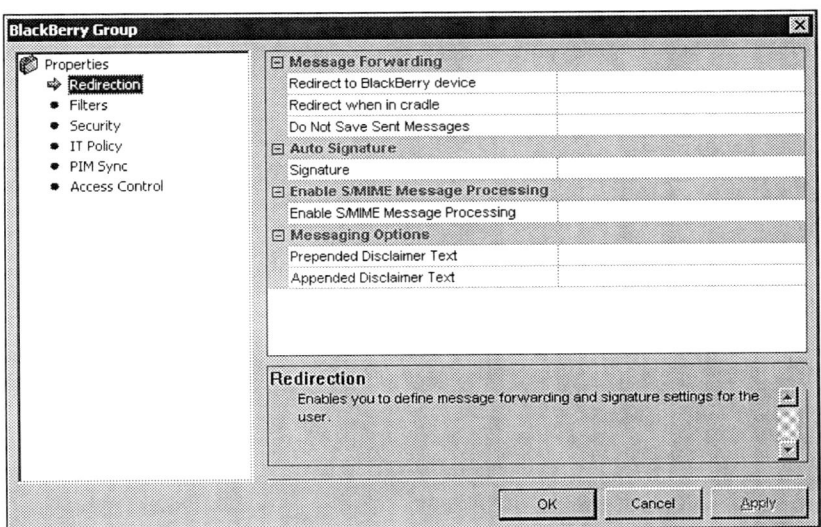

8. Select the desired settings for the group that you've created and click **OK**.

9. Select your BlackBerry Enterprise Server from the left-hand window.

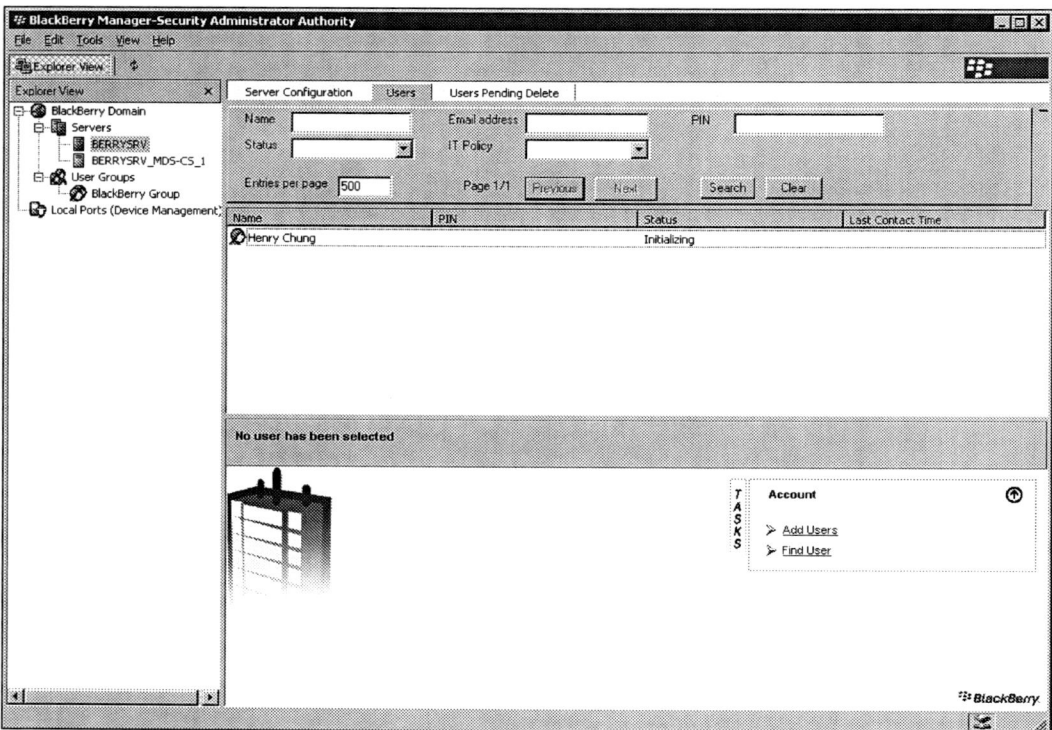

10. Select the **Users** tab and select the user account that you want to add to the group.

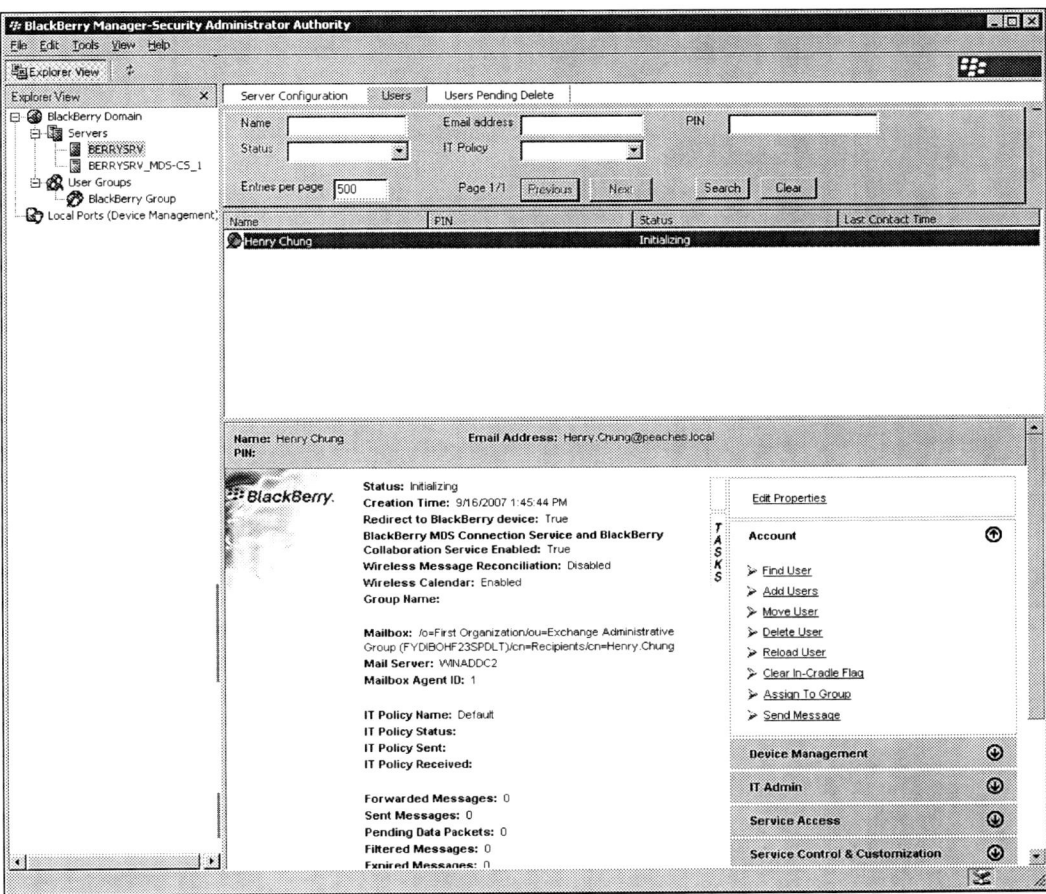

11. Select the **Account** group and select the **Assign To Group** option.

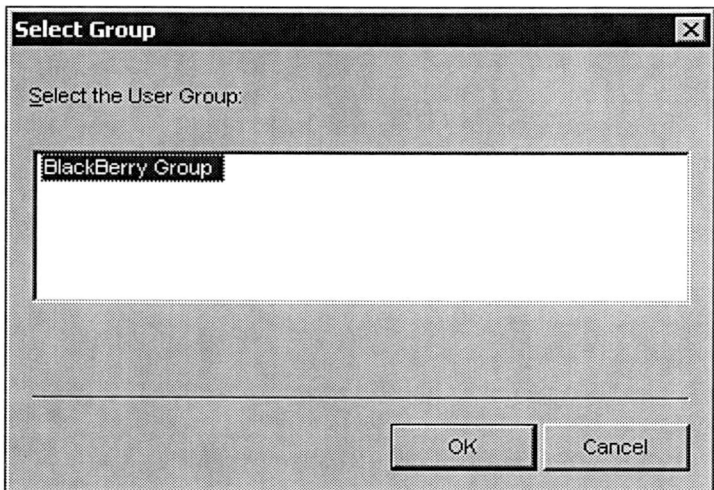

12. Select the group name and click **OK**.

Configuring Organizer Synchronization

There are a number of settings within BlackBerry Enterprise Server related to the synchronization of organizer data, also referred to as **PIM sync**. The following list details the settings that can be configured for organizer data synchronization.

- Enable or disable synchronization for specific organizer data (i.e. message filters and settings, tasks, memos, and address books). Synchronization is enabled for all data by default.

- Determine how organizer data will be synchronized, either from the device to the server, the server to the device, or both.

- Identify the data source to be used in case of conflicts, either the device or the server.

The organizer data synchronization settings may be configured globally for all users or for individual users. For information on how to configure these settings, refer to the BlackBerry Enterprise Server for Microsoft Exchange Administration Guide.

Provisioning Devices

Once you have set your users up with access to the BlackBerry Enterprise Server, you are ready to provision the BlackBerry devices to access BES. There are three methods for setting up devices within a BES environment — through BlackBerry Manager, through Wireless Enterprise Activation, or BlackBerry Desktop Manager. We will focus on configuring devices through BlackBerry Manager and through Enterprise Activation as these are the most common methods.

BlackBerry Manager Device Provisioning

The BlackBerry Manager provisioning method, referred to as cradled provisioning, provides a high level of control over the devices that are associated with your BlackBerry Enterprise Server. This method is more labor-intensive than wireless provisioning and must be performed by a user with a role of Security Administrator, Enterprise Administrator, or Device Administrator. It requires no user interaction, though, which may reduce the burden on the help desk if you're conducting a large device deployment. The following steps detail the process for provisioning a BlackBerry device and assigning it to a user account.

1. Connect the device to a workstation with the BlackBerry Manager installed.

2. Click **Start | Programs | BlackBerry Enterprise Server | BlackBerry Manager**.

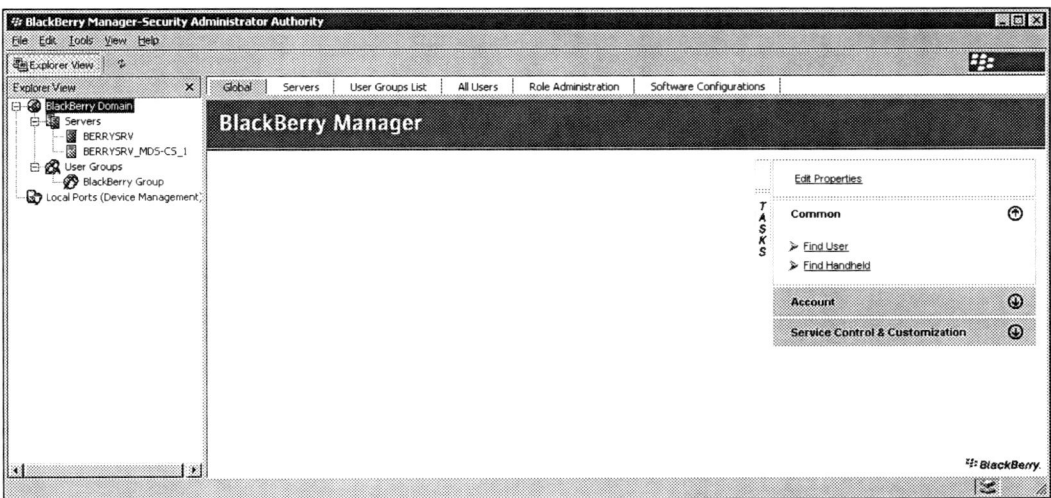

3. Select your BlackBerry Enterprise Server from the left-hand window.

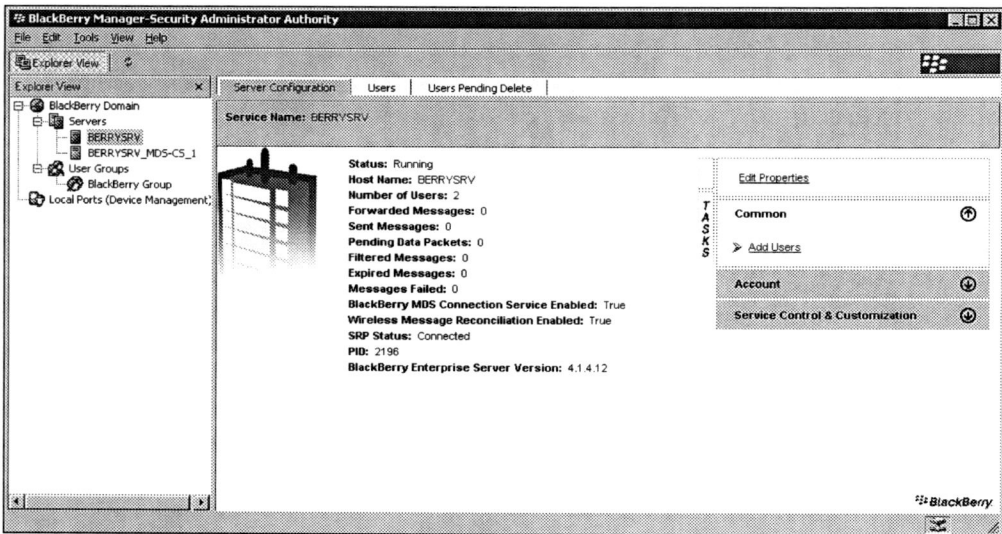

4. Select the **Users** tab and select the user account that you want to assign to the device.

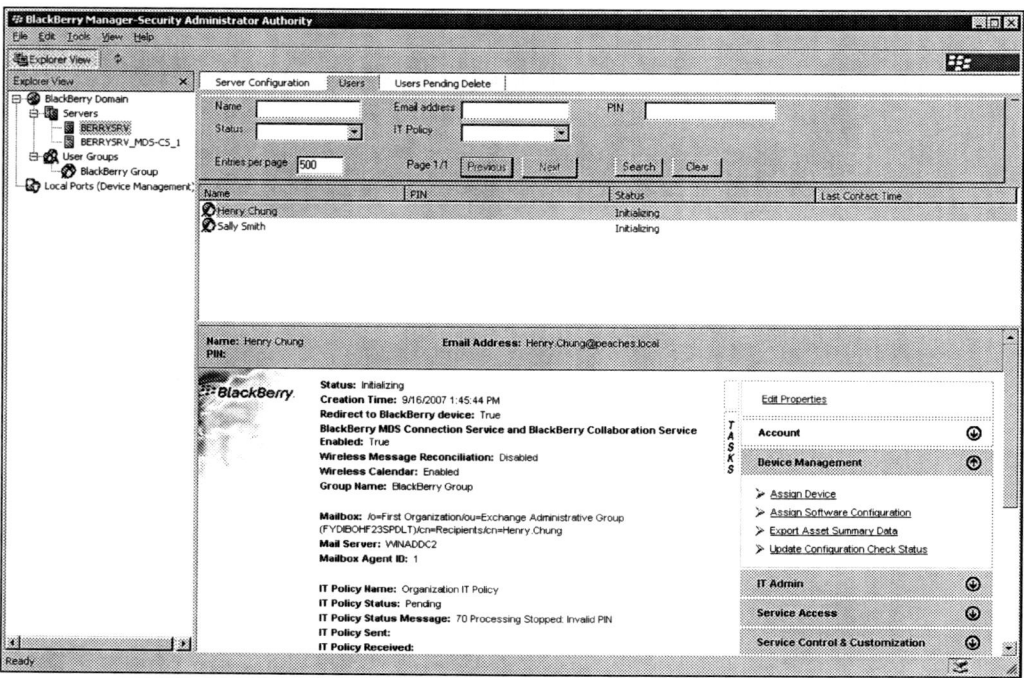

5. Select the **Device Management** group and click the **Assign Device** button.

6. Select the BlackBerry device that is connected to the workstation and click **OK**.

Wireless Device Provisioning

The wireless enterprise activation method allows a BlackBerry handheld to be associated with a user and provisioned to access the BES without connecting the device to your network. Using this method, the administrator provides the user with an activation password that they enter, along with their email address, into the Enterprise Activation program that is available on BlackBerry devices. The BES associated with the email address authenticates the activation information and automatically provisions the device for use with the user account.

The wireless activation password is created for an individual user account. It is a single-use password, meaning that once the password has been used to activate a device it is no longer valid. The password is only valid for 48 hours by default and is invalidated if the user unsuccessfully attempts to activate a device with the password five times.

The password is created by an administrator and may be communicated to the user through an automated email or over the telephone. This password should be safeguarded by the user and the administrator; if intercepted, the password could be used to activate a BlackBerry and gain access to the user's email and organizer data.

Customizing Enterprise Activation Options

There are several options that are specific to the generation of enterprise activation passwords that you may wish to configure. BES allows you to configure the email message that is sent when generating wireless activation passwords, the default password length, the type of password that is generated and the default lifespan. The password type option is very useful, especially if you're deploying devices without full QWERTY keyboards, such as the BlackBerry Pearl or the 7100 series, as you can specify passwords that are easy to enter using SureType keyboards. The following steps detail the process for customizing the enterprise activation password options.

1. On a workstation with BlackBerry Manager installed, click **Start | Programs | BlackBerry Enterprise Server | BlackBerry Manager**.

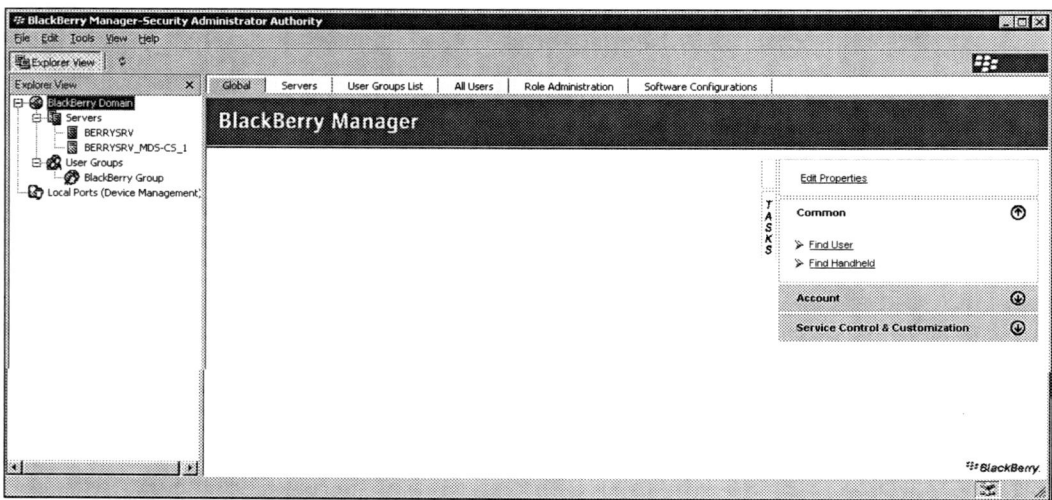

2. Select **BlackBerry Domain** from the left-hand window.

3. Select the **Global** tab and click **Edit Properties**.

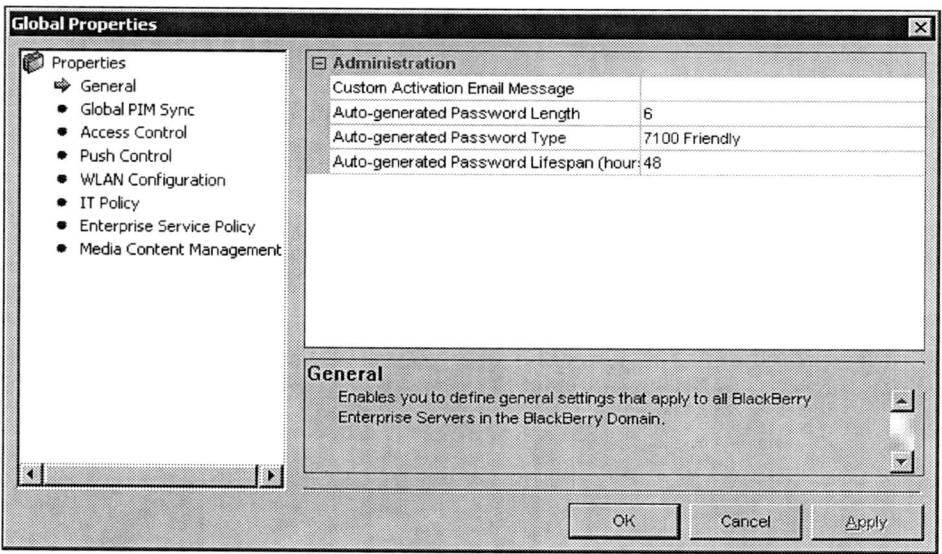

4. Select the **General** option.

5. Set the desired options in the **Administration** section.

   a. Change the auto-generated email message using the **Custom Activation Email Message** option.

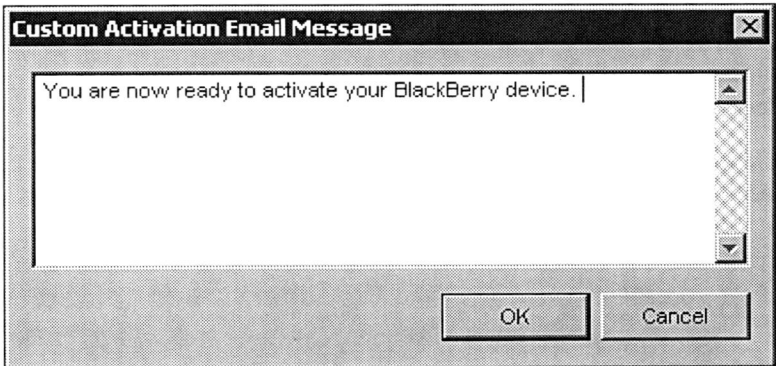

   b. Change the password length using the **Auto-generated Password Length** option.

   c. Change the password type using the **Auto-generated Password Type** option.

   d. Change the default lifespan of the password using the **Auto-generated Password Lifespan** option.

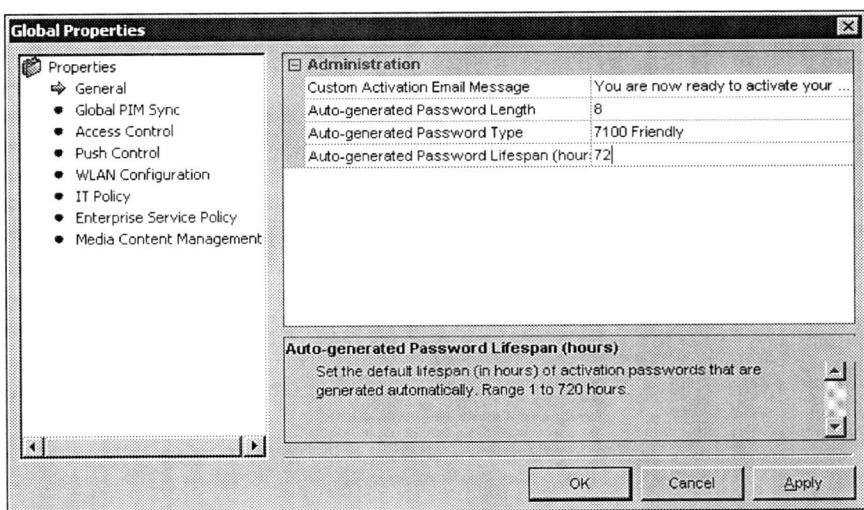

6. Click **OK**.

Setting Wireless Enterprise Activation Passwords

Activation passwords can be set individually for a single user or for a group of users. If the password is being set for an individual user, it can either be automatically generated by BES and emailed to the user or set by the administrator and given to the user in person or over the phone. If the password is being set for a group of users, a unique password is automatically generated and emailed to each user.

The following steps detail the process for setting the password for an individual user.

1. On a workstation with BlackBerry Manager installed, click **Start | Programs | BlackBerry Enterprise Server | BlackBerry Manager**.

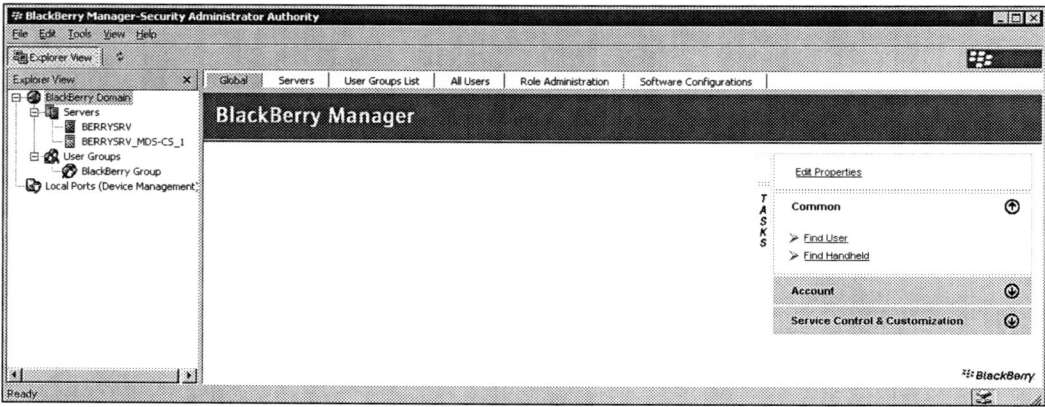

3. Select your BlackBerry Enterprise Server from the left-hand window.

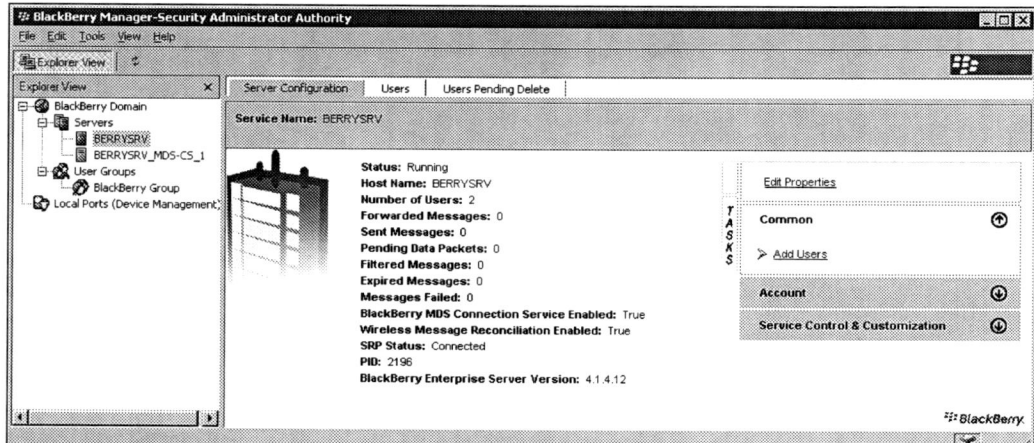

4. Select the **Users** tab and select the user account for which you want to set a password.

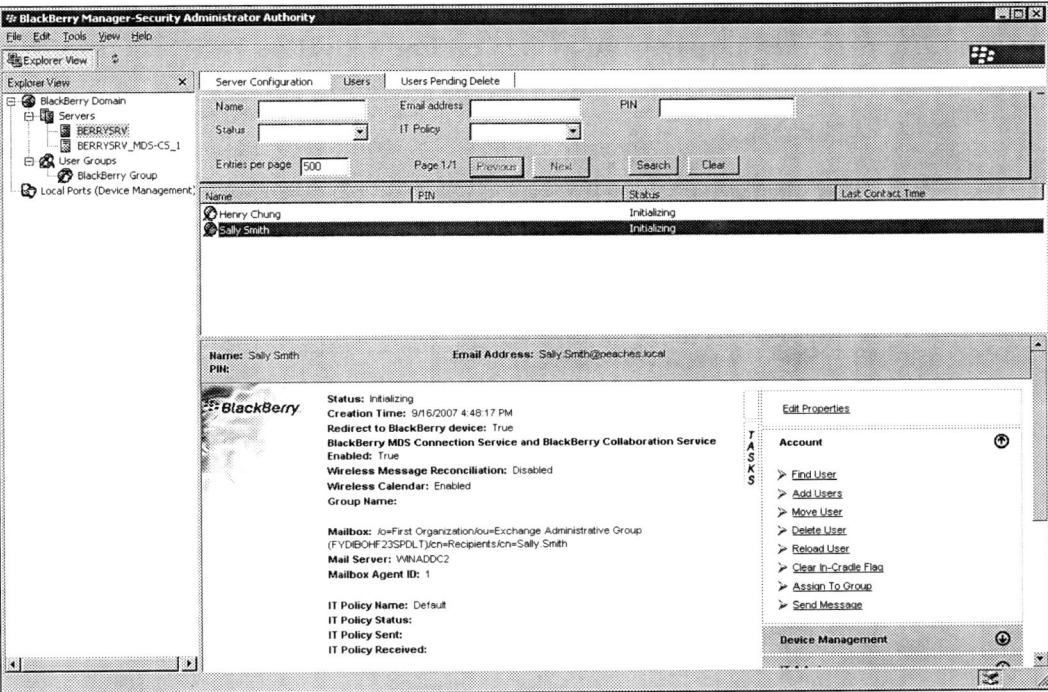

5. Select the **Service Access** group.

6. To automatically generate and email the password, select the **Generate and Email Activation Password** option. Click **OK** on the confirmation dialog box.

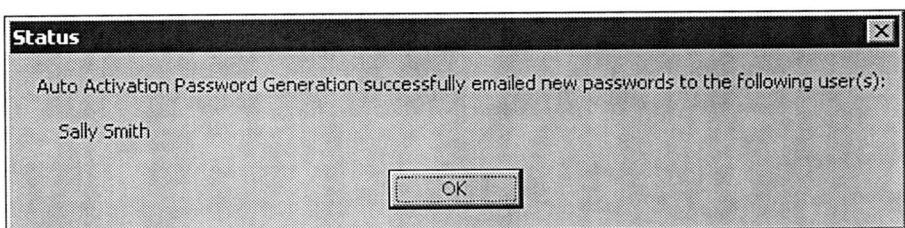

7. To manually set the activation password, select the **Set Activation Password** option.

    a. Enter the password in the **Activation Password** field.

    b. Re-enter the password in the **Confirm Activation Password** field.

    c. Enter the expiration time from the **Password Expires in** field.

    d. Click **OK**.

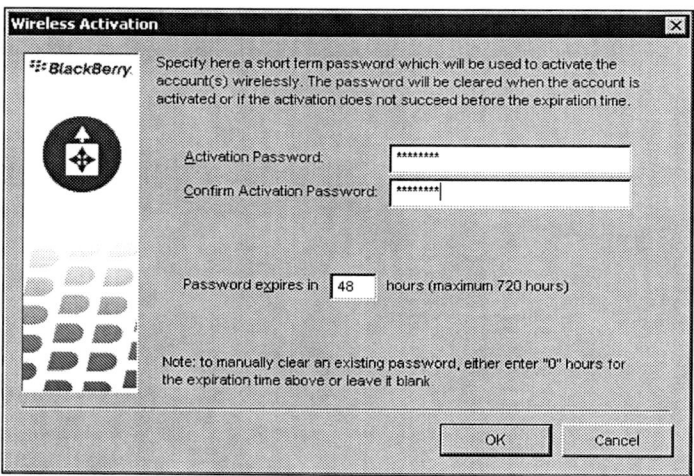

The following steps detail the process for setting activation passwords for a group of users.

1. On a workstation with BlackBerry Manager installed, click **Start | Programs | BlackBerry Enterprise Server | BlackBerry Manager**.

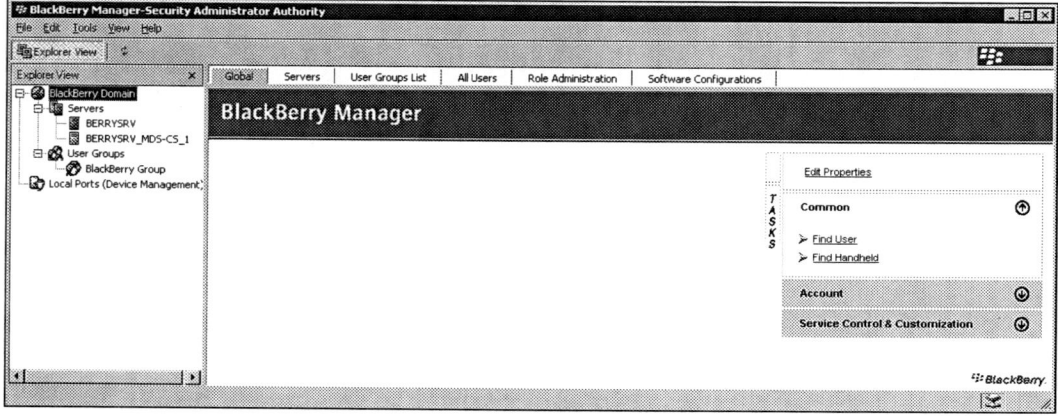

2. Select **User Groups** from the left-hand window.

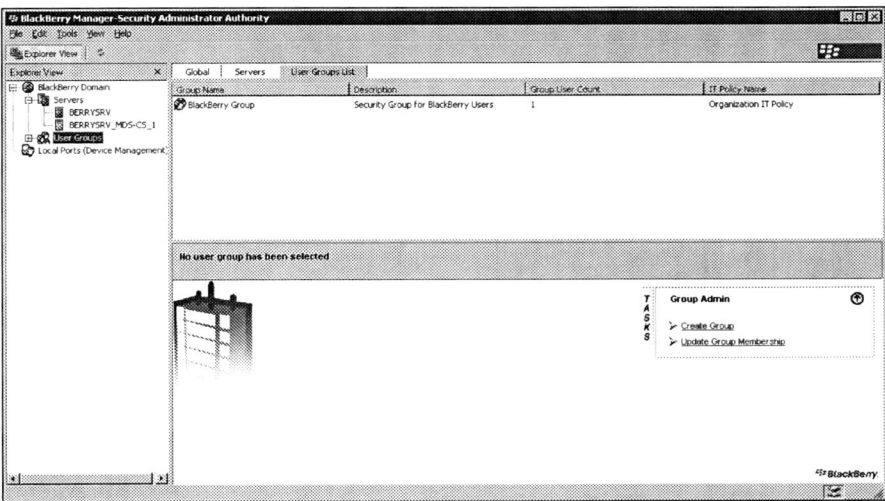

3. Select the **User Groups List** tab and select the user group for which you want to generate a password.

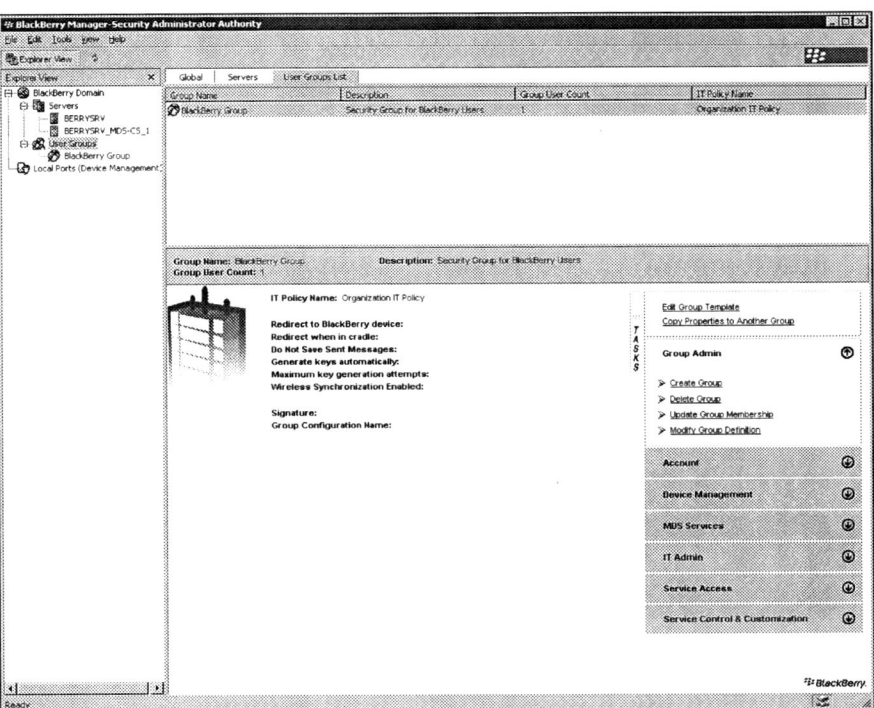

4. Select the **Service Access** group.

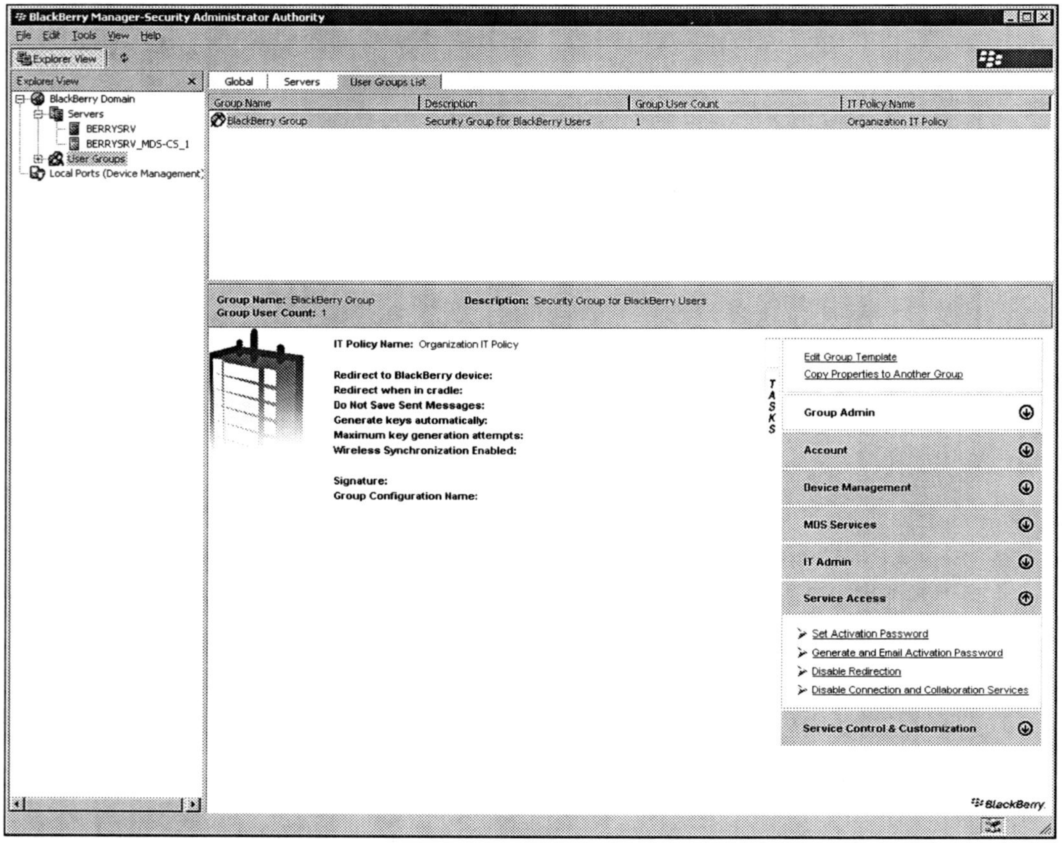

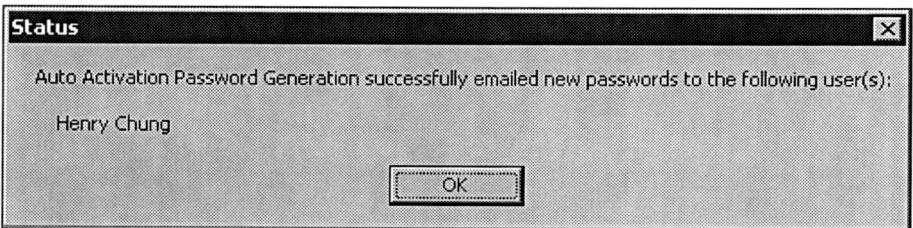

5. Select the **Generate and Email Activation Password** option.

6. Click **OK** on the confirmation dialog box.

Now that you have set the activation password, either manually or through automatic generation, the user can activate their device using the Enterprise Activation program that is found in the Main Menu of the BlackBerry device.

Summary

In this chapter, we have examined the role-based administration capabilities of the BlackBerry Enterprise Server. We have walked through the process of provisioning users to access BES and have examined the methods that may be used to activate devices for use with BES. In the next chapter, we will review the IT policy capability of BlackBerry Enterprise Server that can be used to enforce application and device configurations and rules.

6

Creating and Enforcing Policies

In the previous chapter, we covered the steps required to provision users and devices within the BlackBerry Enterprise Server environment. As administrators, we want to see users interacting with their devices in accordance with organizational policies. In this chapter, we are going to explore the capabilities provided by BES to configure and enforce a variety of policies for device settings. Administrators have the ability to set and enforce granular policies for BlackBerry software and hardware, known as IT policies, and the ability to specify both device software versions and third-party software to be deployed on handhelds. This chapter describes these capabilities and how to implement them.

IT Policies

IT policies are used to control the behavior of BlackBerry devices and BlackBerry Desktop Software within your organization. These policies, comprised of individual IT policy rules that enforce specific behaviors for applications or devices, may be assigned to individual users or to user groups within BES. BES contains over two hundred policy rules that can be configured to govern BlackBerry devices and BlackBerry Desktop Software. When a device is activated on the BlackBerry Enterprise Server a default IT policy is pushed out to the device. Many administrators will want to modify the default policy or create a new set of policies to apply within their organization.

IT policy rules are grouped based on the type of behavior that is modified, such as password policies or Bluetooth settings. Rule enforcement is determined based on the rule setting, which is set through pre-defined options (e.g., True/False/Default for the Allow Peer-to-Peer Messages rule, etc.) or with a string value (e.g., 6 for the Minimum Password Length rule, `http://www.blackberry.com` for the Home Page Address rule, etc.). In order to configure the IT policy rules for your organization, you may either modify the default IT policy or create a new policy. The following sections describe the process of creating a new IT policy and applying it to users and groups within our organization.

Creating a New IT Policy

On a workstation with BlackBerry Manager installed, click **Start | Programs | BlackBerry Enterprise Server | BlackBerry Manager**.

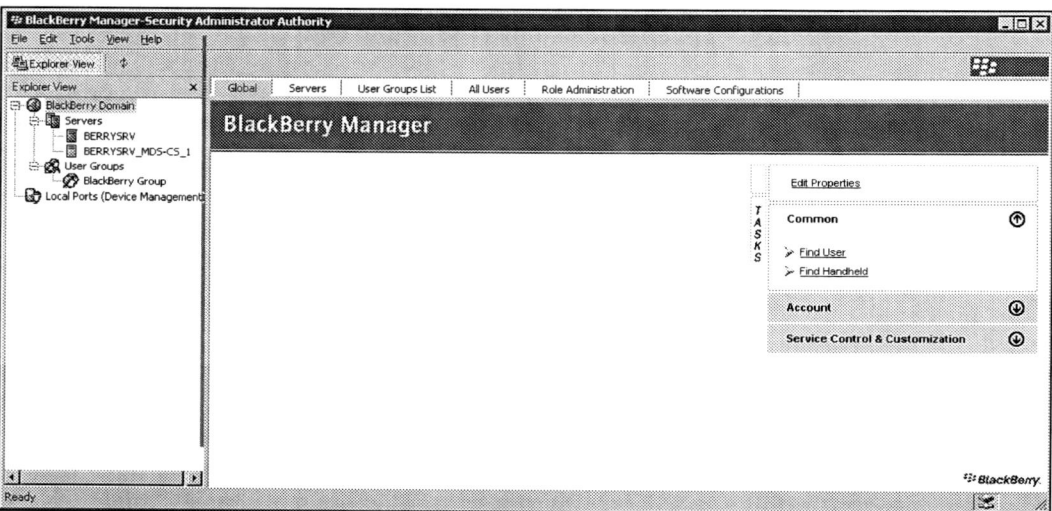

1. Select **BlackBerry Domain** from the left-hand window.

2. Select the **Global** tab and click **Edit Properties**.

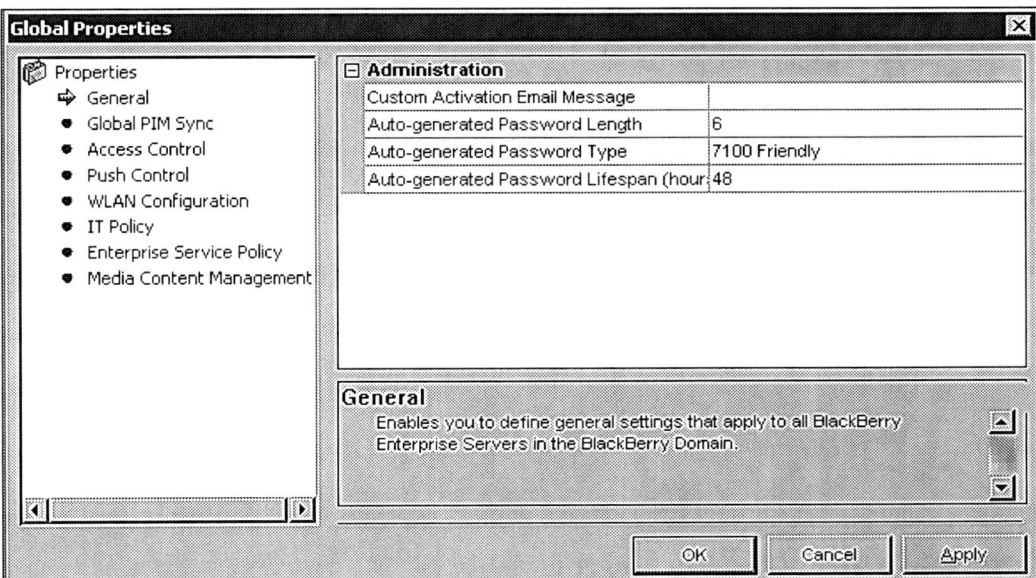

3. Select **IT Policy** from the left-hand pane under **Properties**.

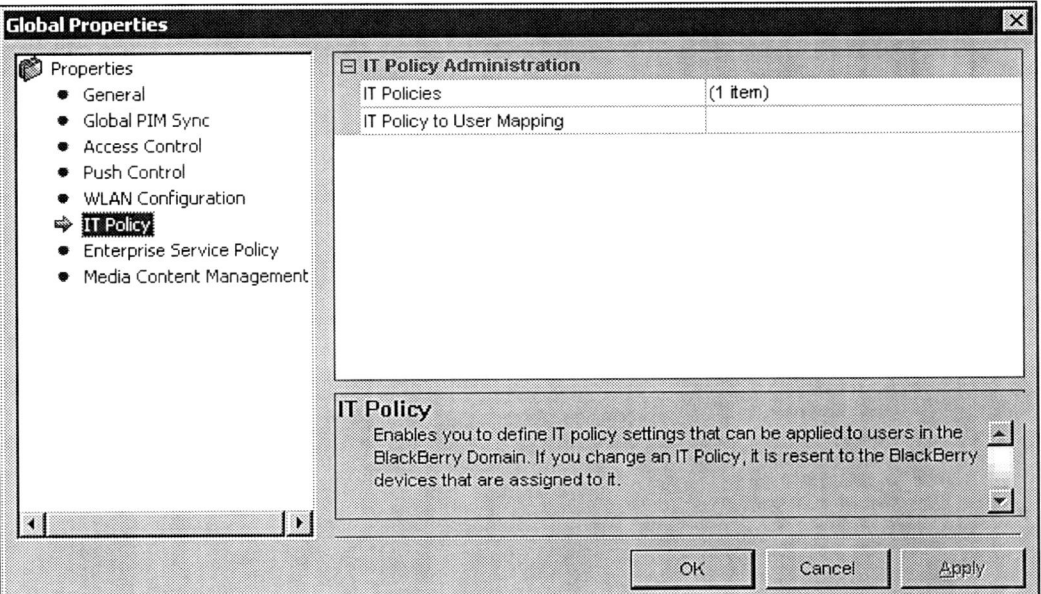

4. Select the **IT Policies** value under **IT Policy Administration**.

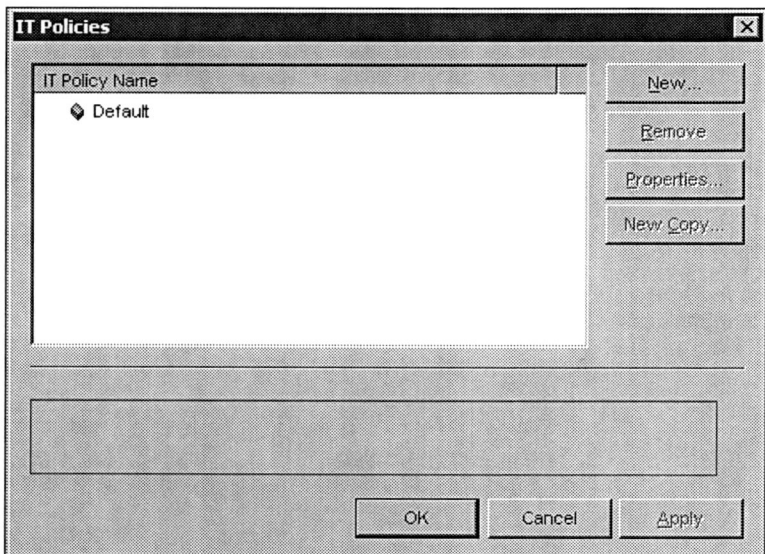

5. Click **New...** to create a new IT Policy.

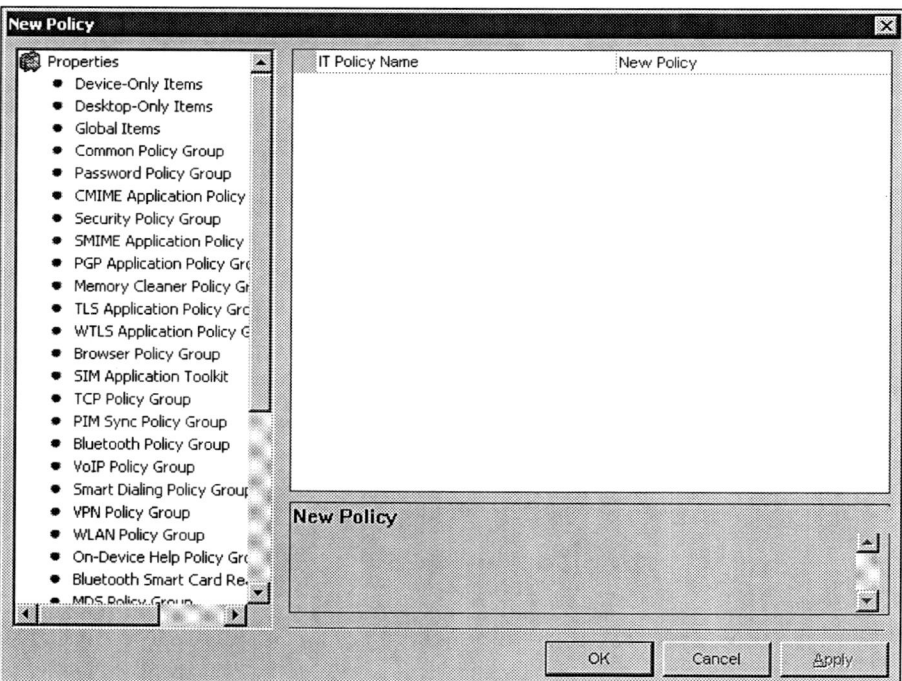

6. Enter the policy name in the **IT Policy Name** value.

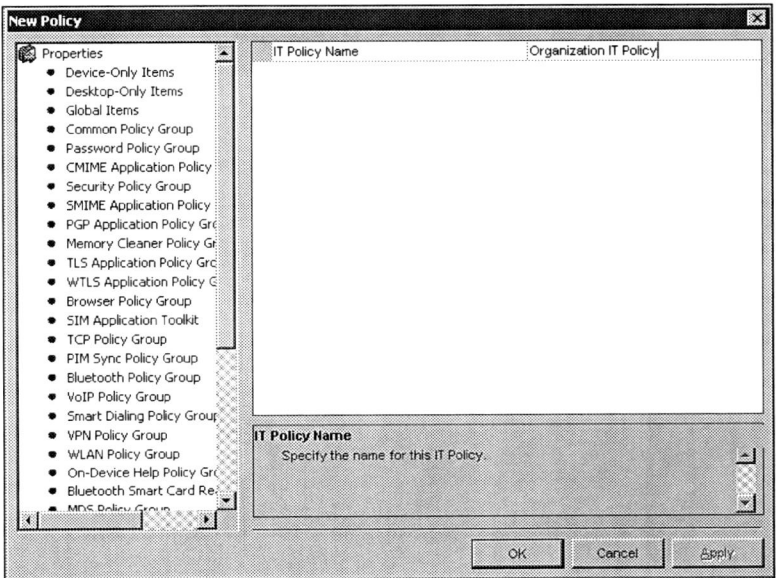

7. Select or enter the values for the IT policy rules that you want to configure in each policy group. Leave the field blank to set the default value.

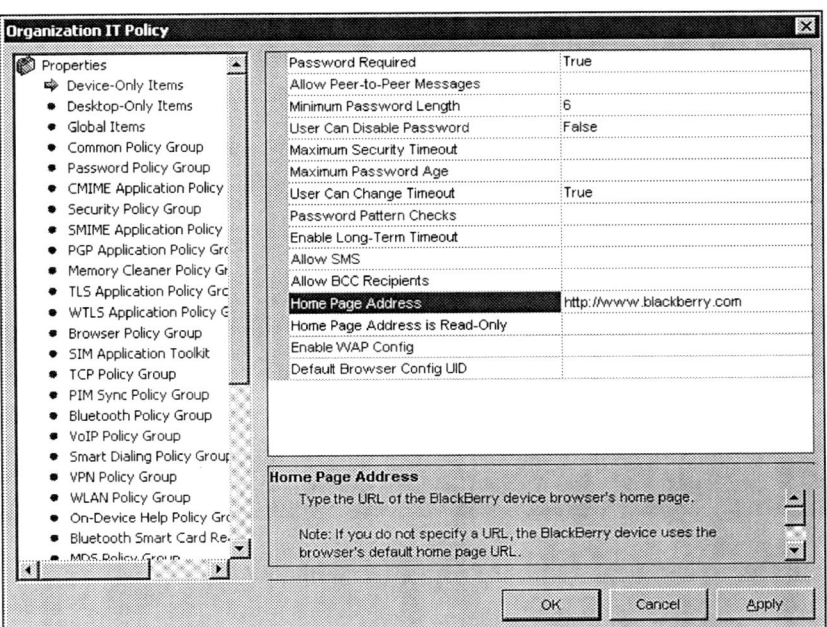

8. Click **OK** to save the IT policy settings that you have configured.

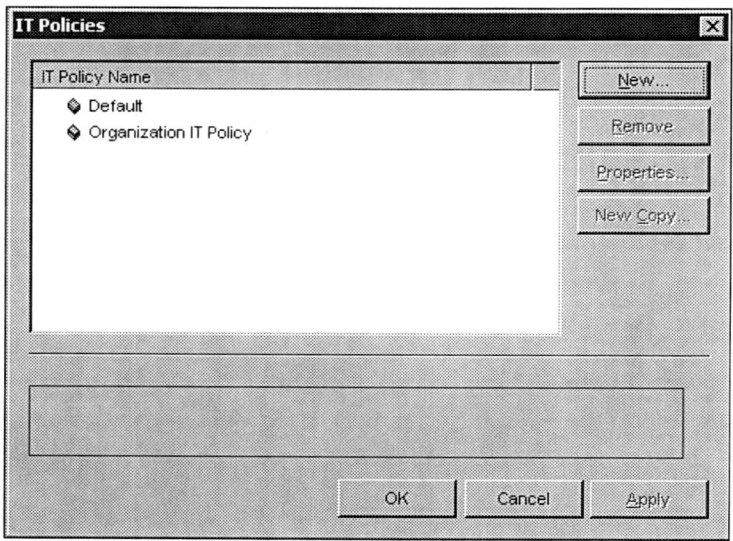

9. Click **OK** to close the **IT Policies** window.

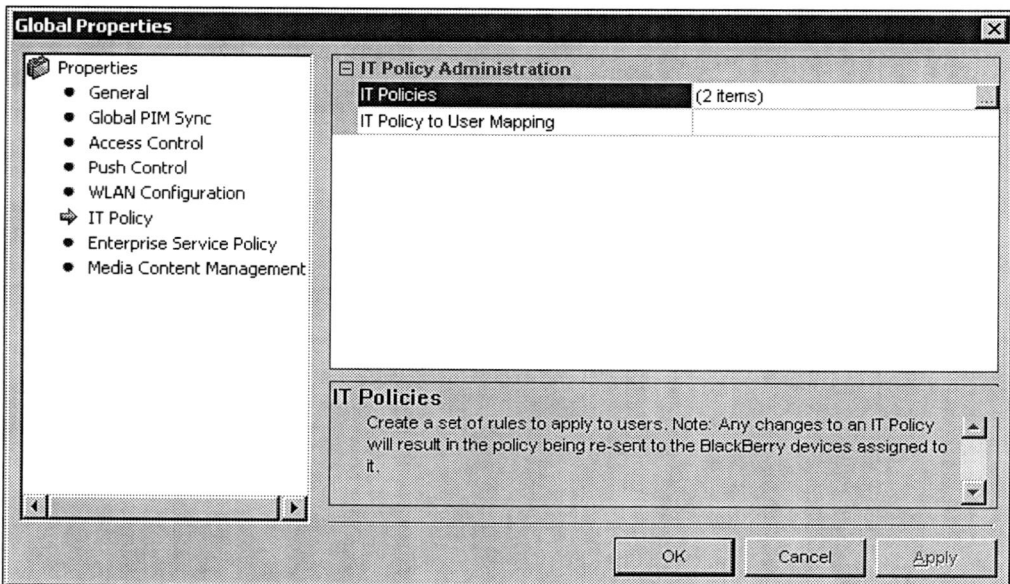

10. Click **OK** to close the **Global Properties** window.

Assigning an IT Policy

Now that we have created our IT policy, we need to apply it to make it effective. As mentioned previously, IT policies can be applied to users or to user groups. The following instructions describe the process for applying our newly-created policy to an individual user and to a user group.

1. On a workstation with BlackBerry Manager installed, click **Start | Programs | BlackBerry Enterprise Server | BlackBerry Manager**.

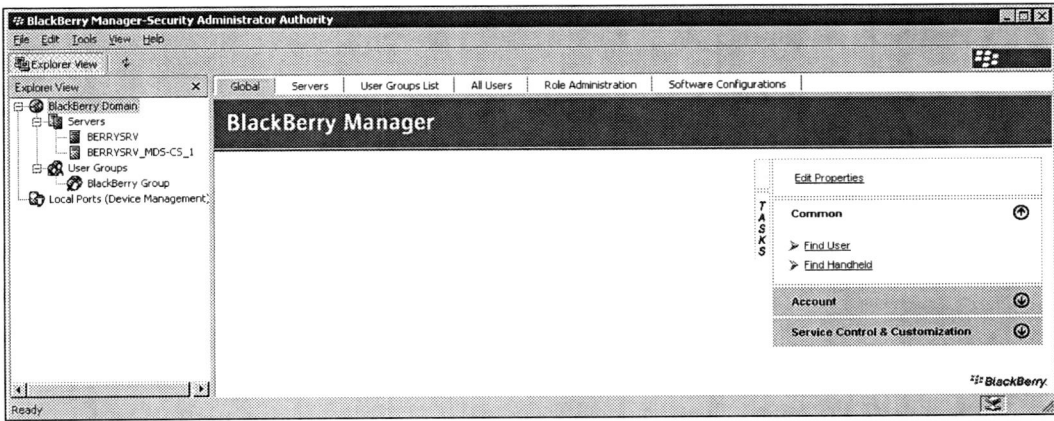

2. To assign a policy to an individual user, select **BlackBerry Domain** from the left-hand window.

3. Select the **Global** tab and click **Edit Properties**.

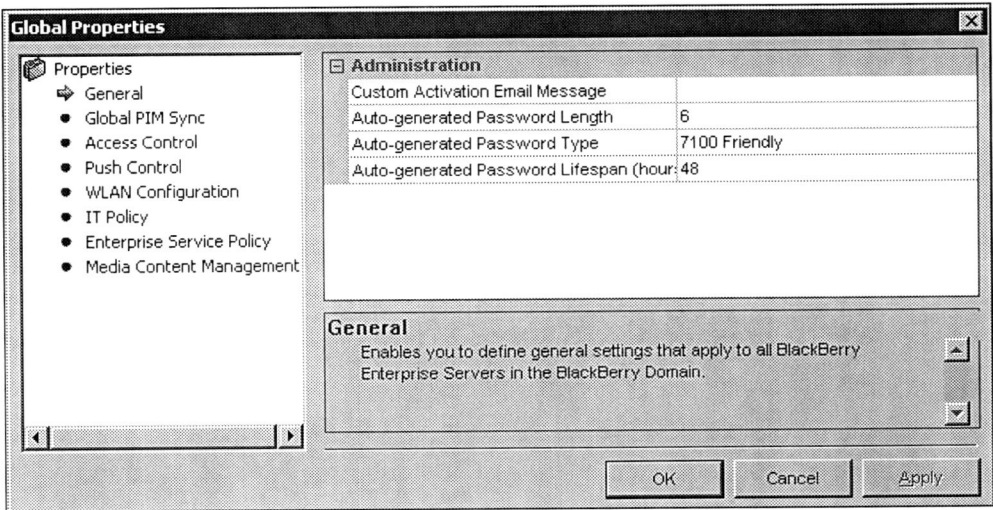

4. Select **IT Policy** from the left-hand pane under **Properties**.

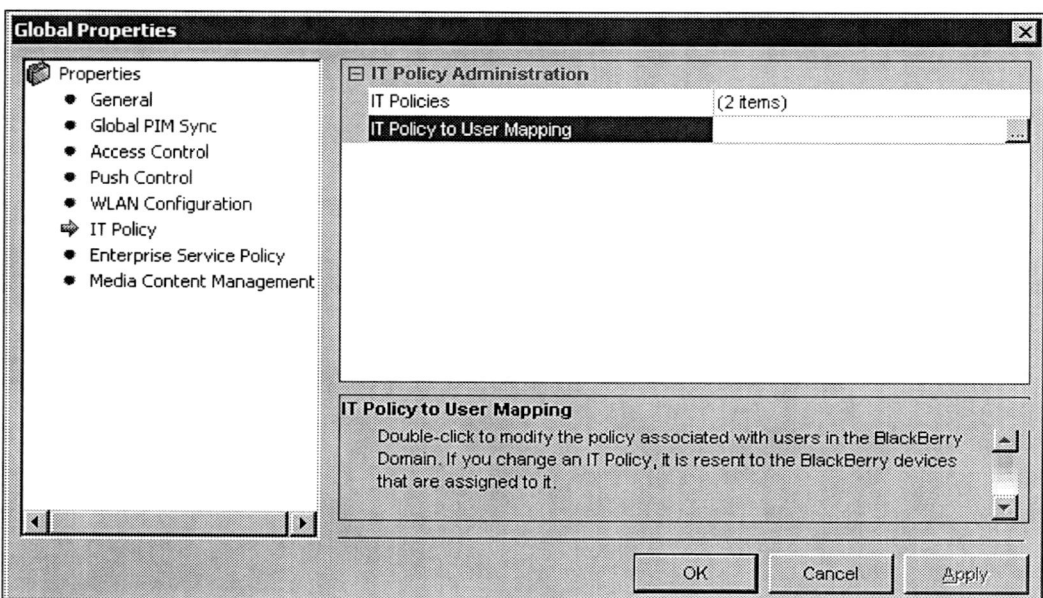

5. Select **IT Policy to User Mapping** from the **IT Policy Administration** section.

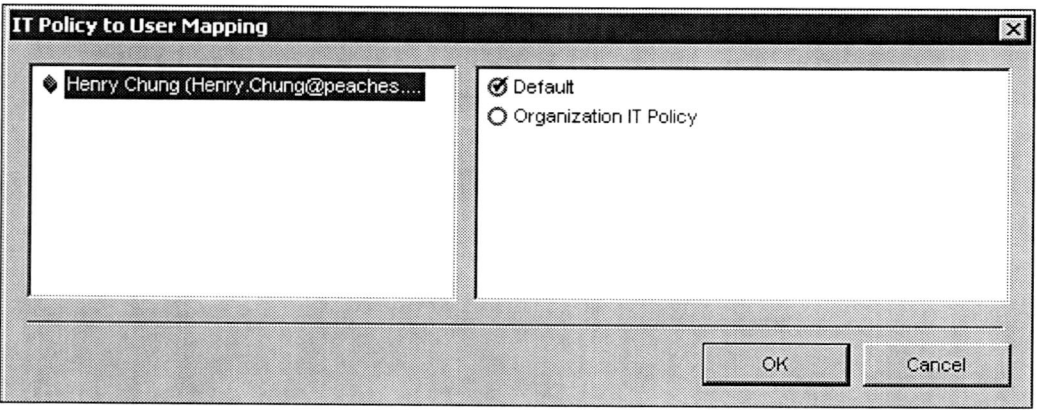

6. Select the user from the left-hand pane and select the newly-created IT policy from the right-hand pane and click **OK**.

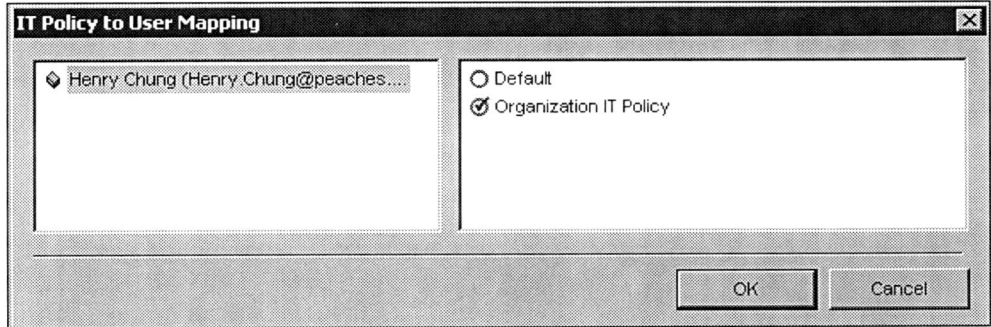

7. Click **OK** to close the **Global Properties** window.

To assign an IT policy to a user group, select **User Groups** from the left-hand pane, select a group from the **User Groups** List tab and click **Edit Group Template**.

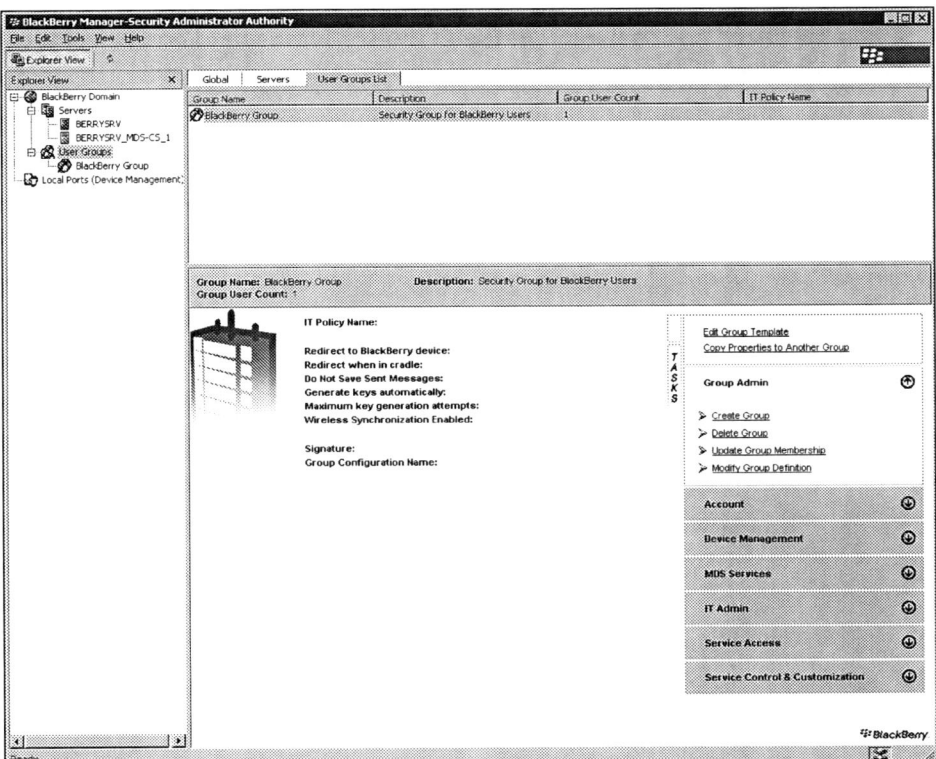

8. Select **IT Policy** from the **Properties** pane.

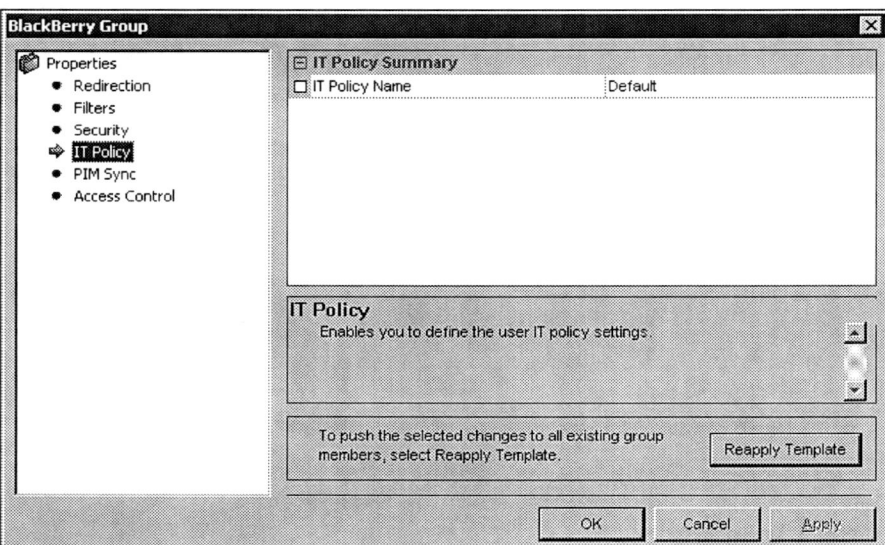

9. Click the check box to the left of the **IT Policy Name** field and select the newly-created **IT Policy** from the pull-down menu.

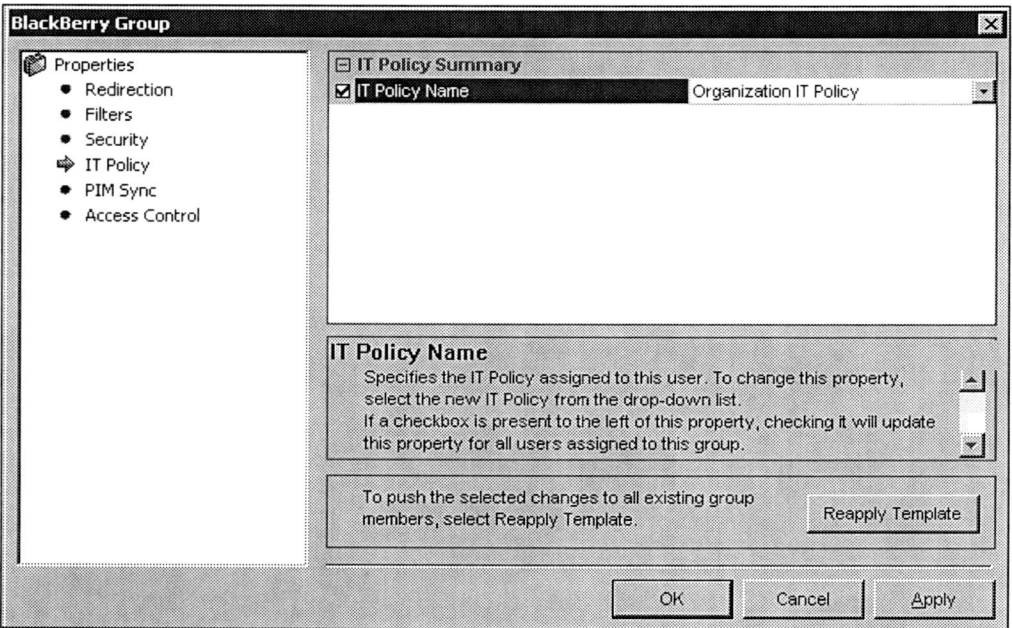

10. Click **Apply** to apply the IT policy to the selected user group.

11. Click **Reapply Template** to push the change out to users that are already members of the group.

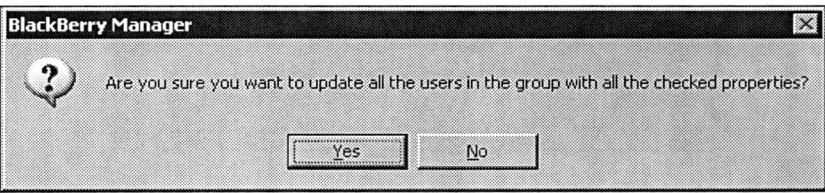

12. Click **Yes** to apply the changes to all users.

We have now successfully applied our new IT policy to both an individual user and a group of users. All users that are added to the group in the future will automatically have the IT policy settings applied and pushed to their devices.

Software Deployment

BES supports the deployment of software to BlackBerry devices, including device software and third-party applications. These deployments are effected through software configurations created within BES, controlling those applications and BlackBerry device software that should be installed and configured. Application deployments and device software upgrades may be performed wirelessly or through the LAN by connecting the device to a workstation.

In order to deploy software to our devices, we must install the device software for our BlackBerries, copy and index the third-party software, share the software on the network, and then create a software configuration; and assign it to either a user or a group. The following sections describe the steps to perform these activities.

Installing Device Software

To create software configuration, you must install the device software for your organization's device model(s) on your BES. This software is not available directly from RIM, but may be obtained from your wireless operator. The following steps describe the process for installing the device software for a BlackBerry 8700c from AT&T.

1. Download the device software from AT&T to your BES and run the Setup program.

2. Select your installation language and click **OK**.

3. Click **Next** on the Welcome screen.

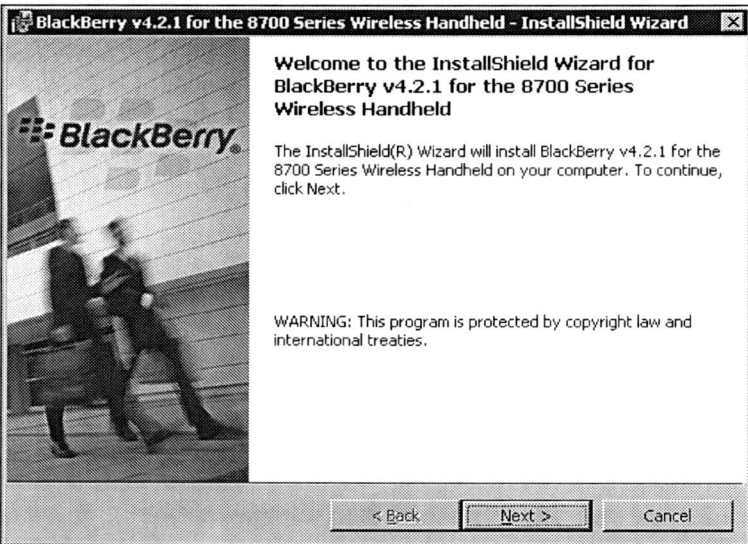

4. Select your location from the pulldown menu.

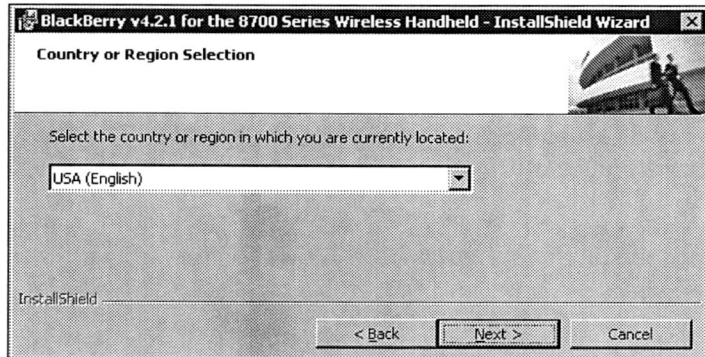

5. Select the **I accept the terms in the license agreement** radio button and click **Next**.

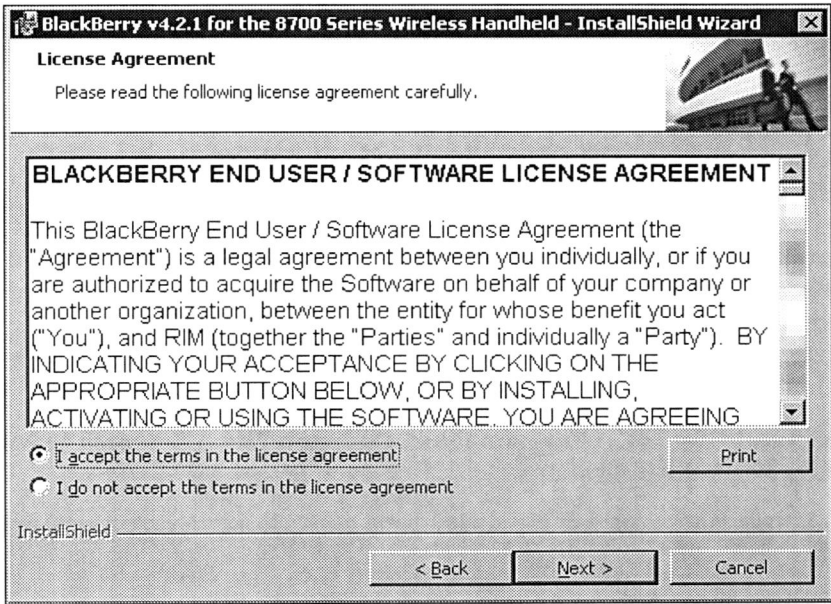

6. Click **Finish** when the installation process is complete.

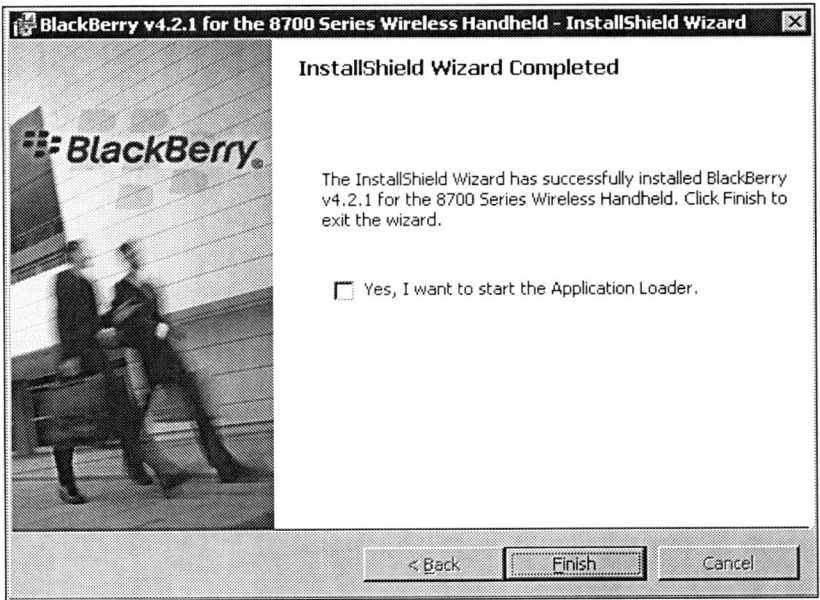

7. The software should now be successfully installed at `C:\Program Files\ Common Files\Research in Motion\Shared\Loader` Files.

Third-Party Applications

RIM provides the ability to deploy third-party applications through software configurations. These applications can be anything from enterprise instant messaging clients to Customer Relationship Management applications. These applications are typically distributed as `.alx`, `.cod`, and `.dll` files. The application files are copied to a shared location on the BES and indexed in order to be included in a software configuration. The indexing process creates two files (`specification.pkg` and `PkgDBCache.xml`) in each application directory, providing the software configuration and the Application Loader tool with information on each application. The following steps describe the process for preparing a third-party instant messaging client for deployment.

1. Create a folder in **C:\Program Files\Common Files\Research in Motion\ Shared** called Applications.

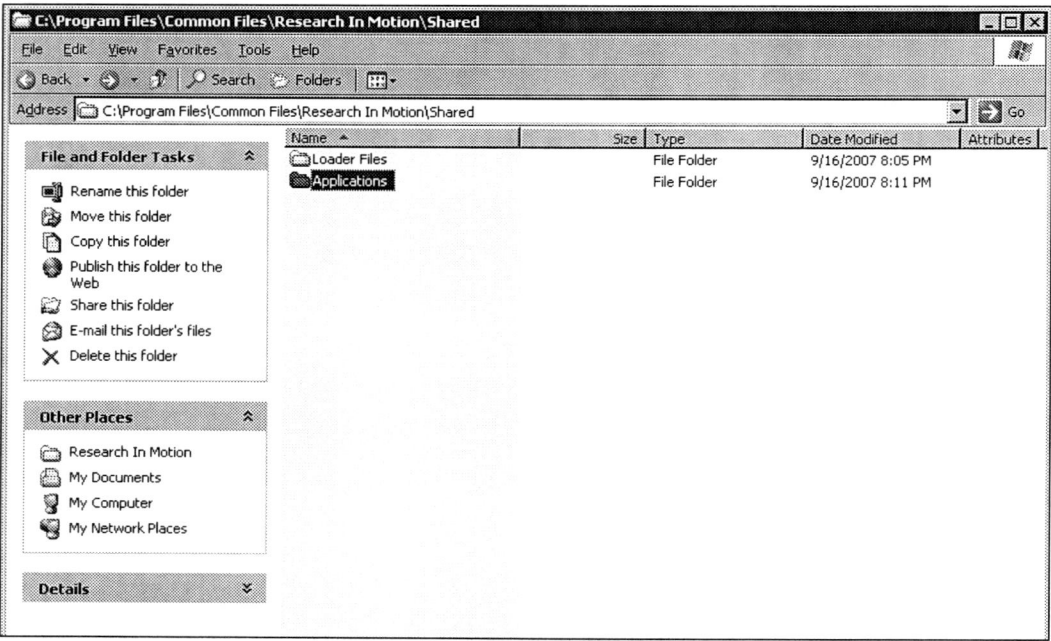

2. Create a sub-folder under **Applications** for the third-party application. Each third-party application should have its own sub-folder.

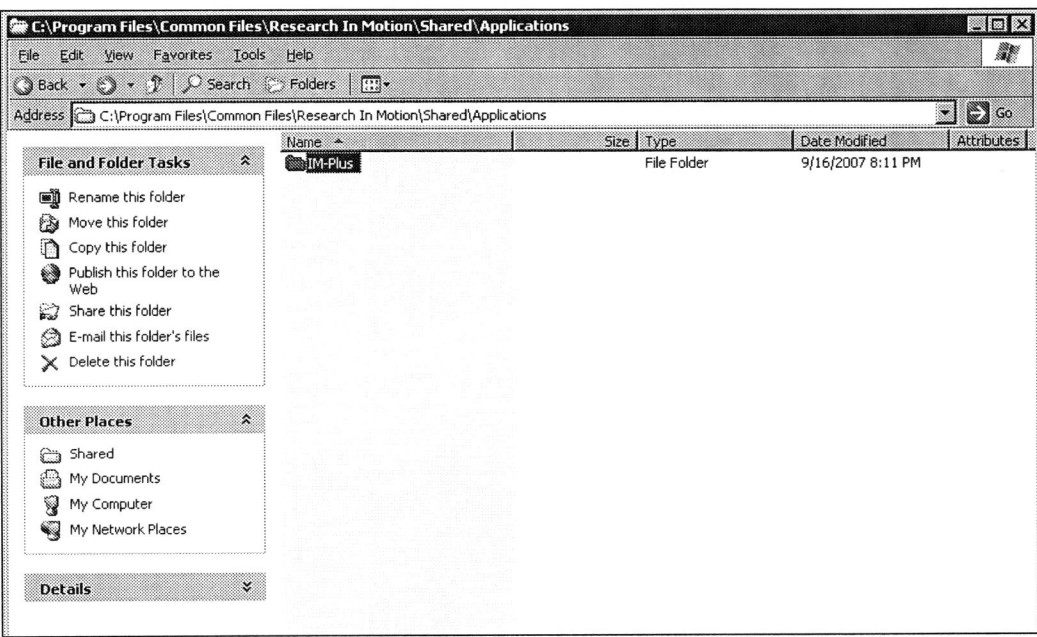

3. Copy any `.alx`, `.cod`, and `.dll` files for the application into the sub-folder created in the previous step.

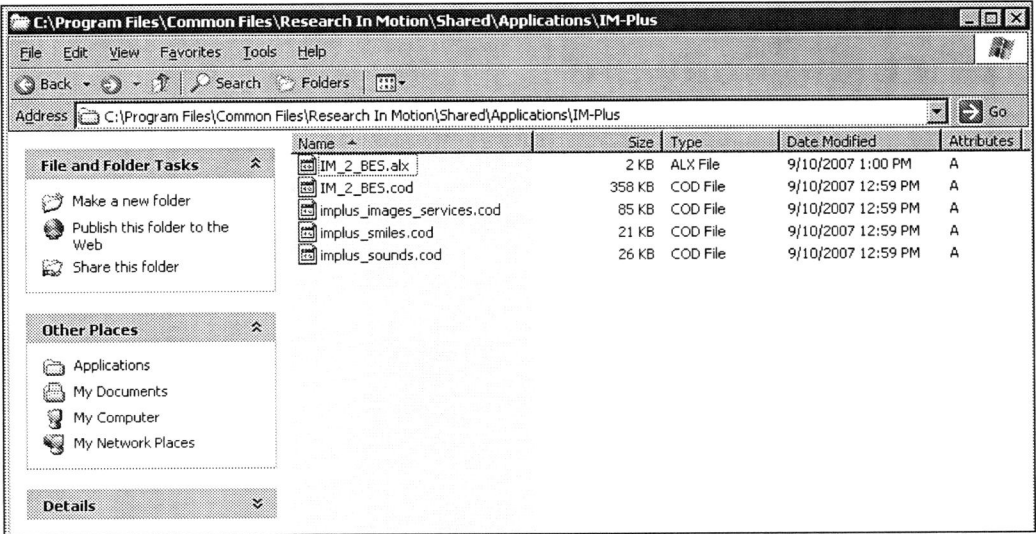

4. Open a command prompt and type **cd \Program Files\Common Files\ Research in Motion\Shared\Applications** and hit <Enter>.

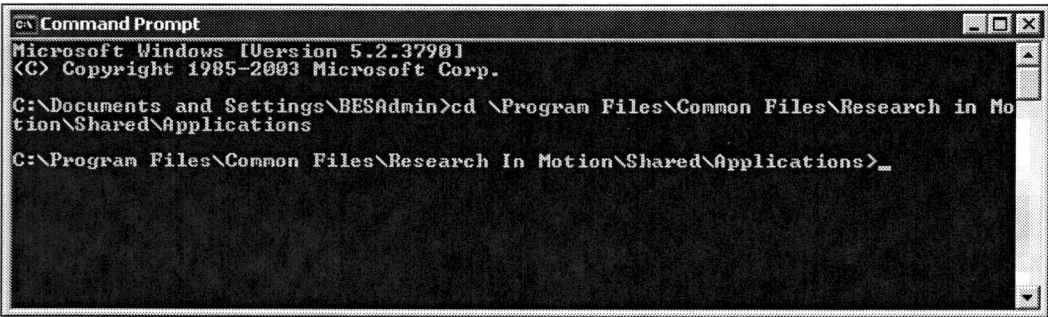

5. Type **"C:\Program Files\Common Files\Research in Motion\AppLoader\ loader.exe" /index** and hit <Enter>.

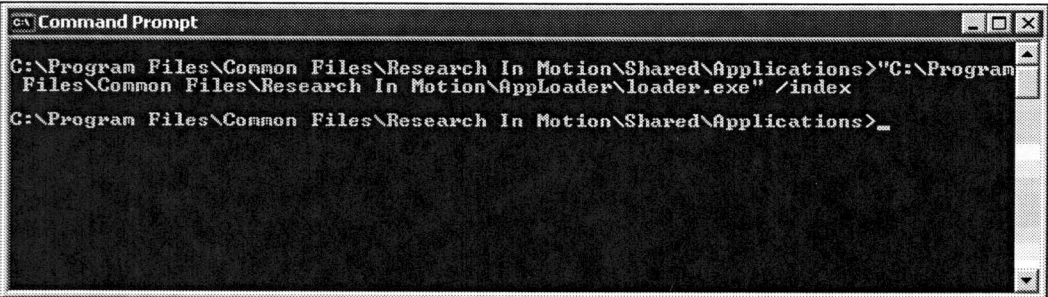

Sharing the Software

The device software and the third-party software must be shared on the network in order to create a software configuration, as any software that is deployed through the LAN must be accessible to the workstations on the network. Technically, this means that you can install the device software and third-party software on a separate file server, but we have opted to store them on the BES for the sake of simplicity. The following steps describe the process of sharing this software.

1. Using Windows Explorer, navigate to **C:\Program Files\Common Files**.

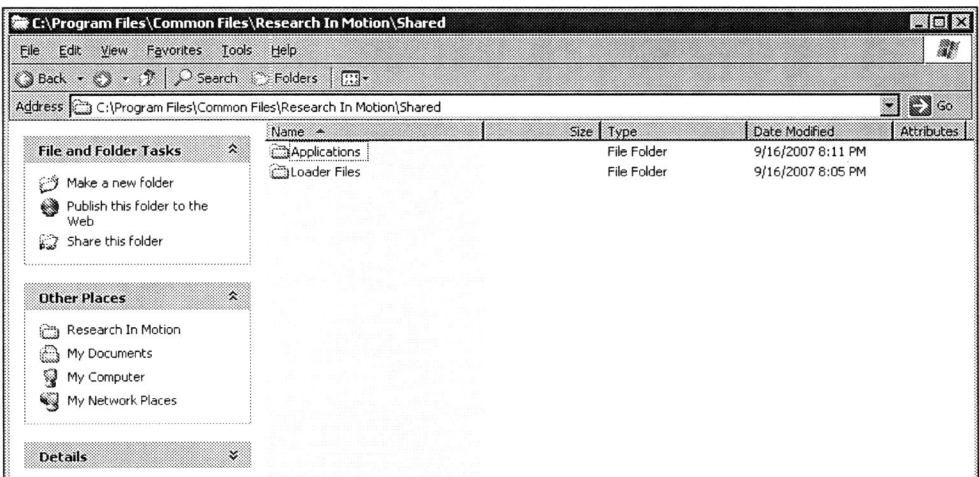

2. Right-click on the **Research in Motion** folder and select **Sharing and Security**.

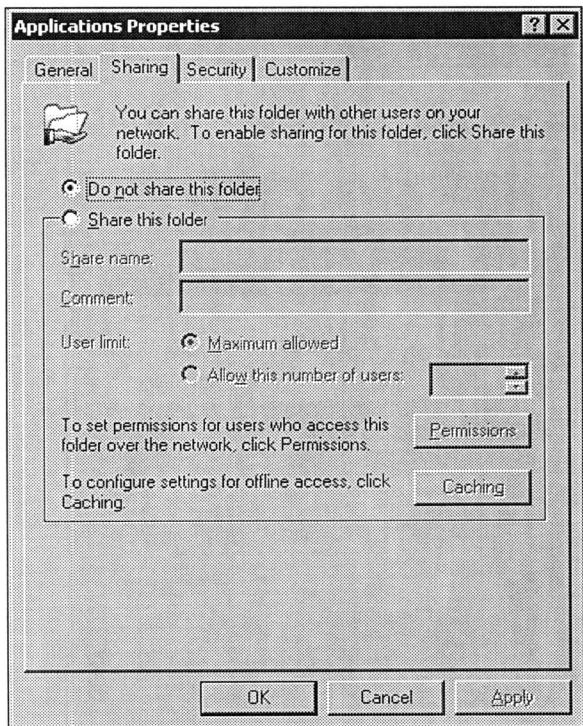

3. Select the **Share this folder** radio button, enter the desired name in the **Share name:** field and click the **Permissions** button.

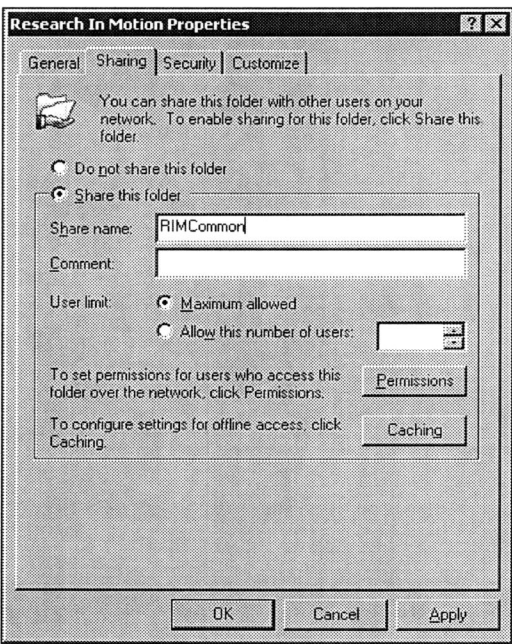

4. Ensure that the **Everyone** group has **Read** permissions and click **OK**.

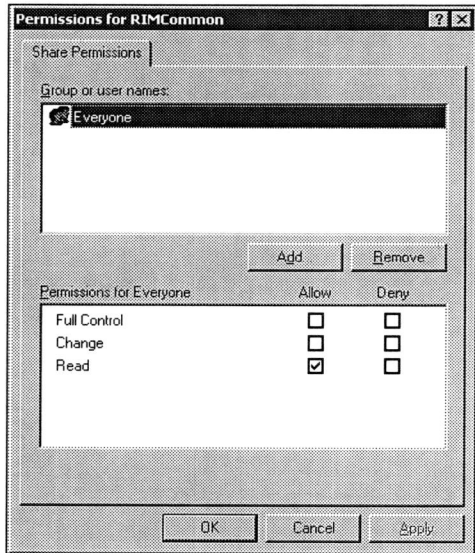

5. Click **OK** to start sharing the folder.

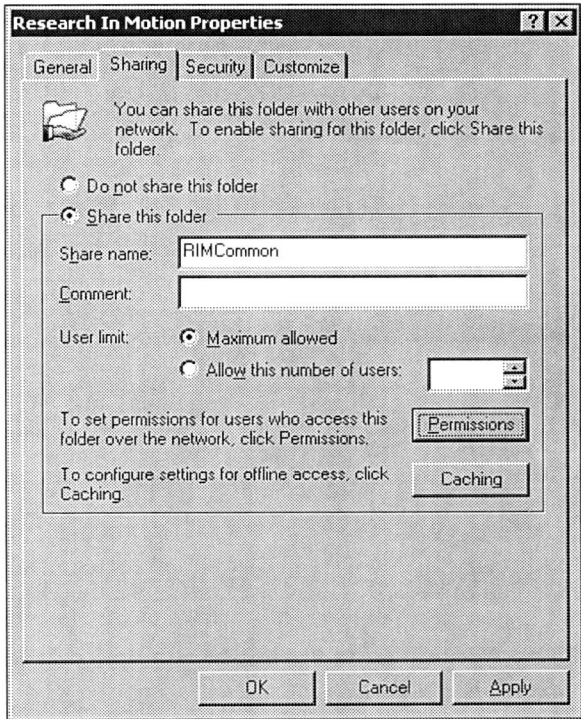

Creating and Assigning a Software Configuration

Now that we have shared the software, we are ready to start creating our software configuration and assigning them to the users or groups. Software configurations must be created individually for each different BlackBerry model in the organization and you must have the device software for the model installed in order to create a software configuration. The following steps describe the process of creating and assigning software configurations.

1. On a workstation with BlackBerry Manager installed, click **Start | Programs | BlackBerry Enterprise Server | BlackBerry Manager**.

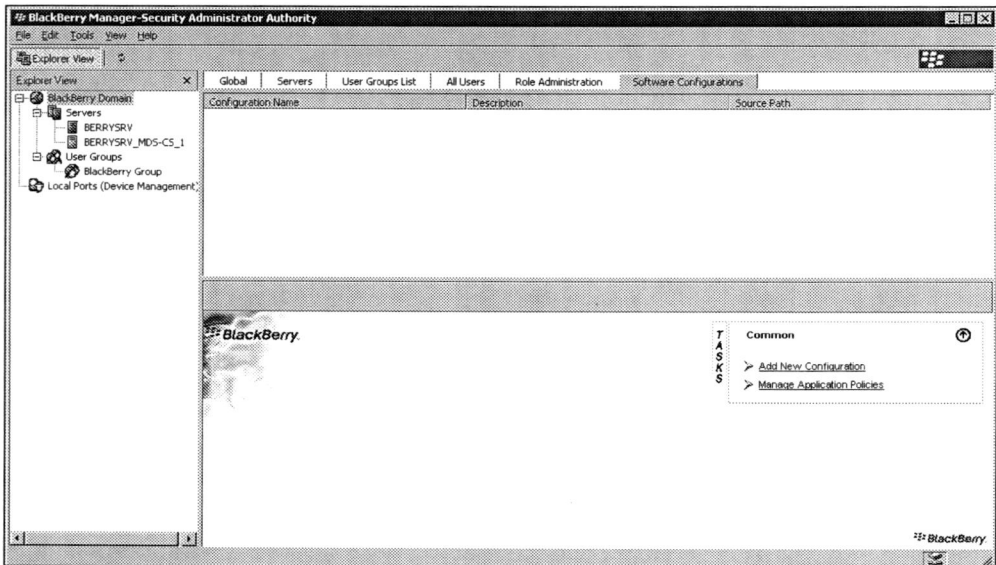

2. Select **BlackBerry Domain** from the left-hand window and select the **Software Configurations** tab.

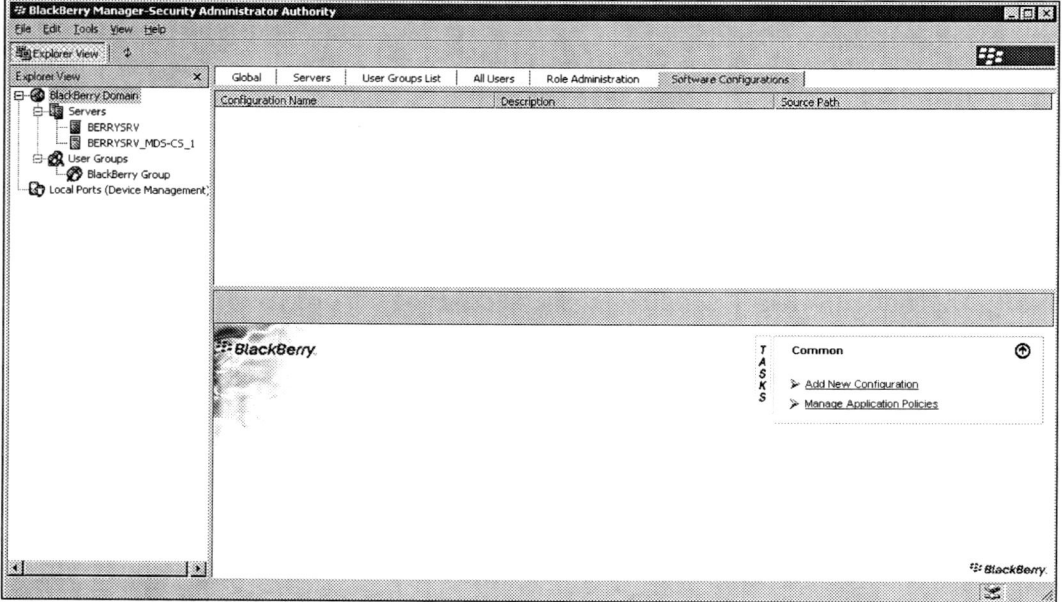

3. Click **Add New Configuration**.

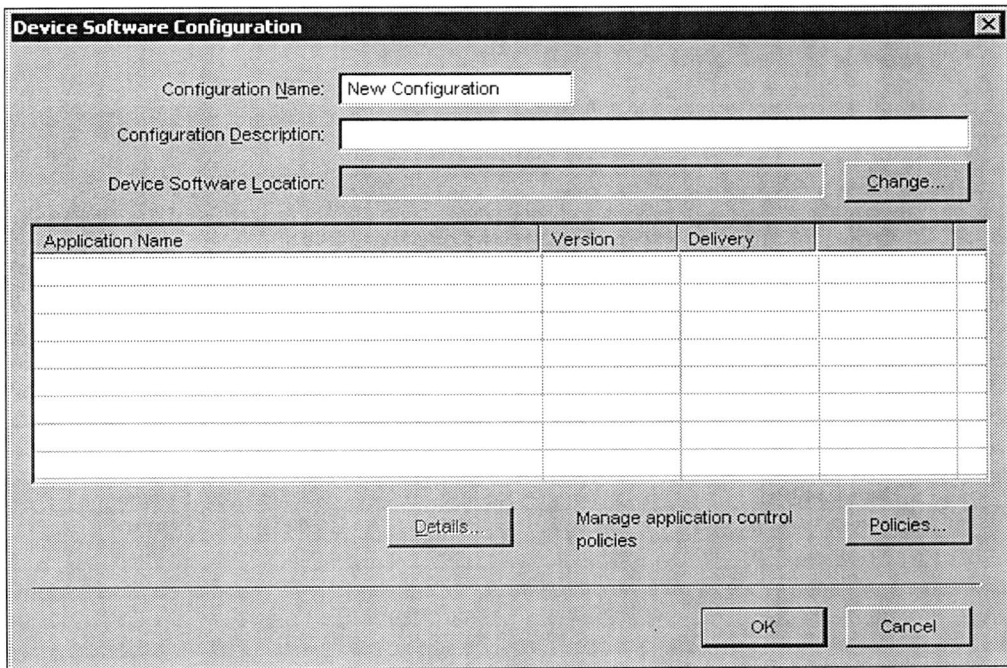

4. Enter a name in the **Configuration Name:** field and a description in the **Configuration Description:** field and click the **Change...** button to the right of the **Device Software Location:** field.

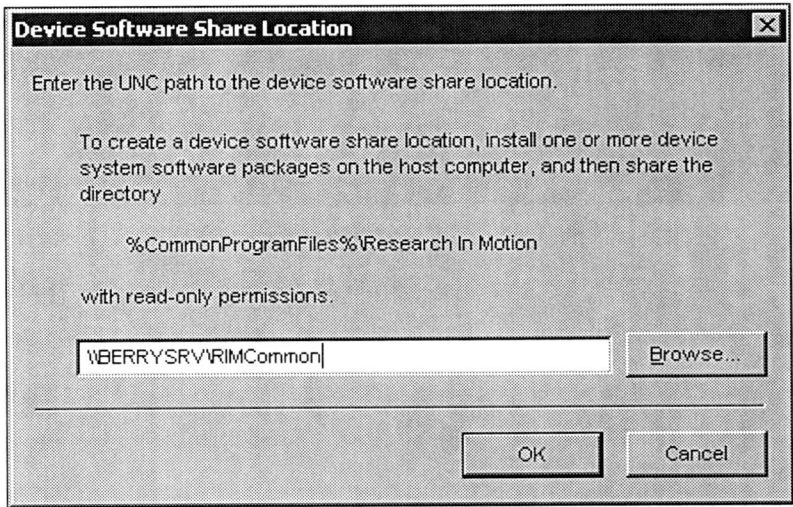

5. Enter the UNC share path to the share that was created in the previous section in the field and click OK. The **Device Software Configuration** screen should display details for the device software and third-party software available in that location.

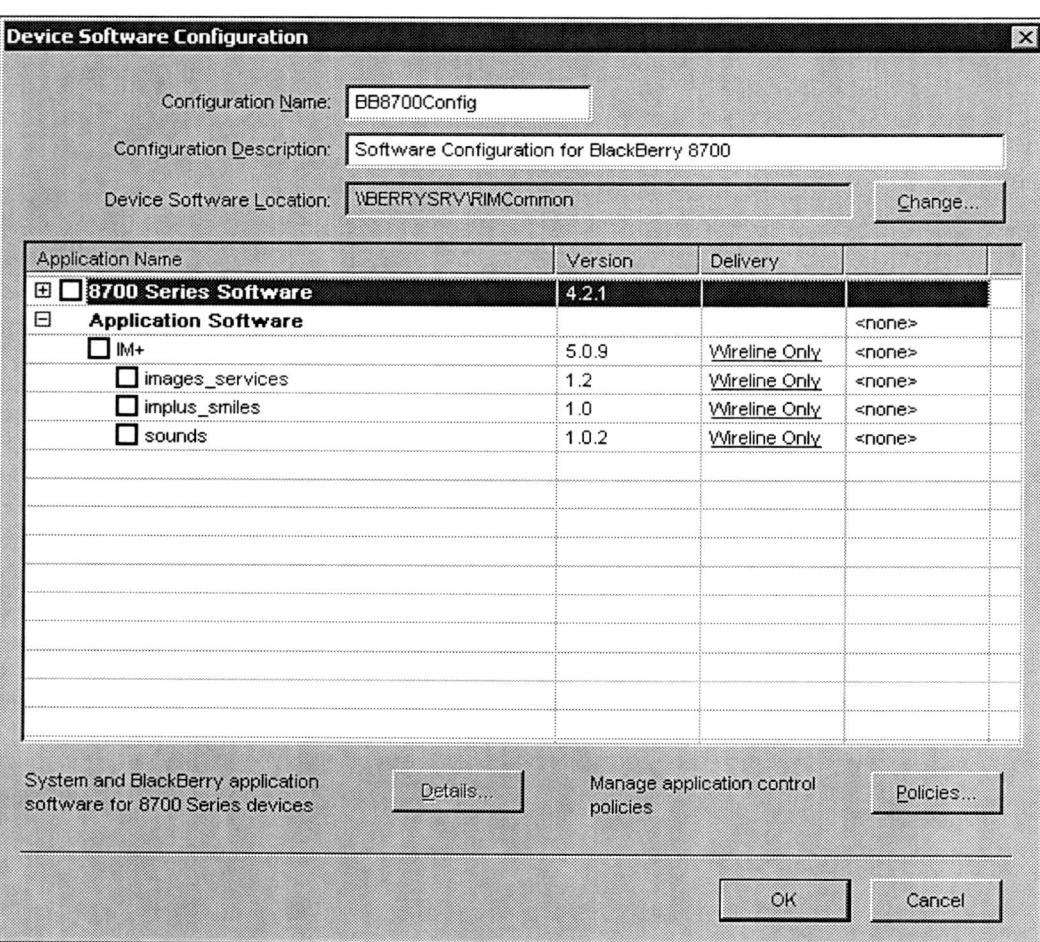

6. Select the software that you want to add to the configuration and, if desired, change the **Delivery** method to **Wireless**. This option is not available for all applications or devices, but, where available, provides the capability to distribute applications over-the-air.

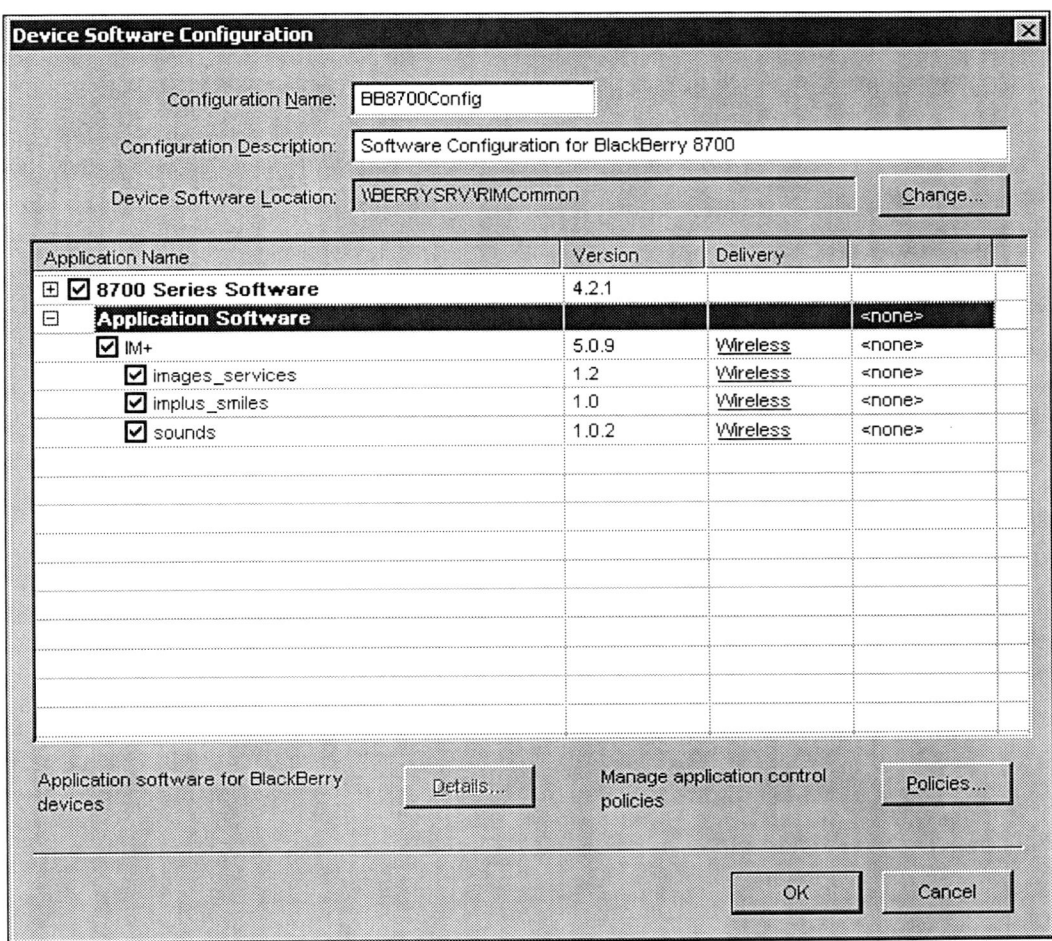

7. Click **OK** to finalize creation of the software configuration.

Now that we have created the software configuration, we should create an application control policy to define the rules for the software. There are a variety of rules that can be configured, such as whether the software is required or optional and what applications, networks, and data the software is allowed to access. The following steps describe the process of creating an application control policy and assigning it to a software configuration.

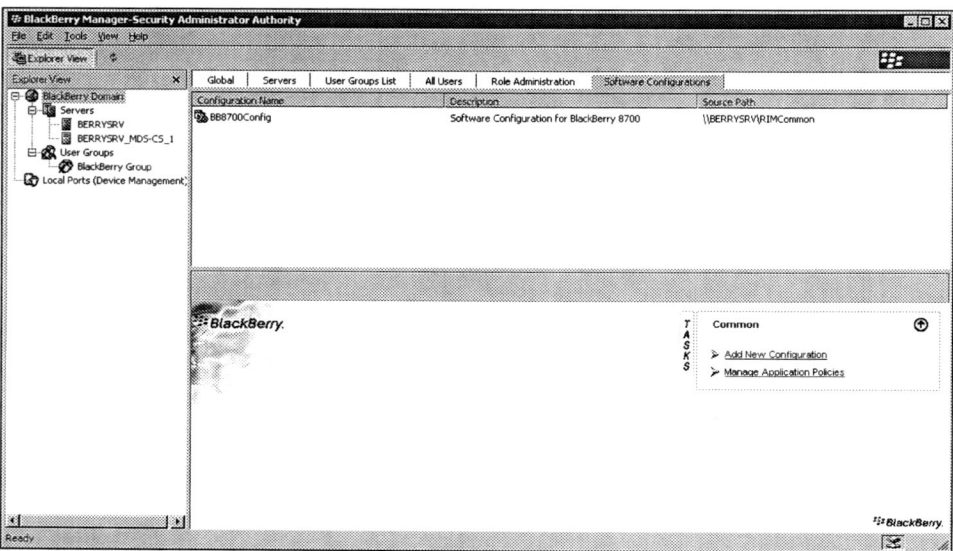

1. Click **Manage Application Policies** on the **Software Configurations** tab.

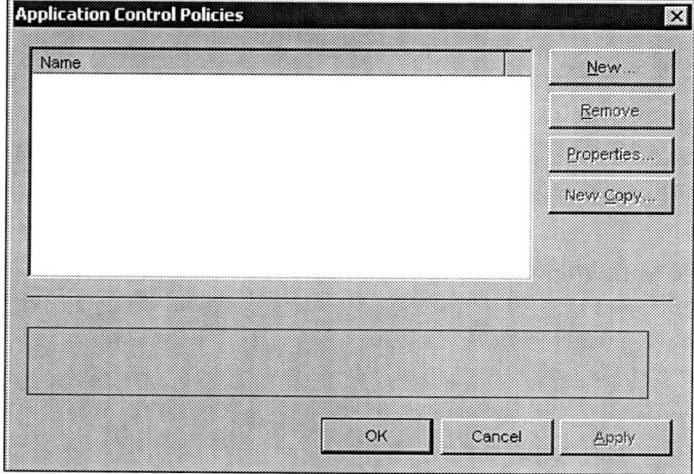

2. Click the **New...** button.

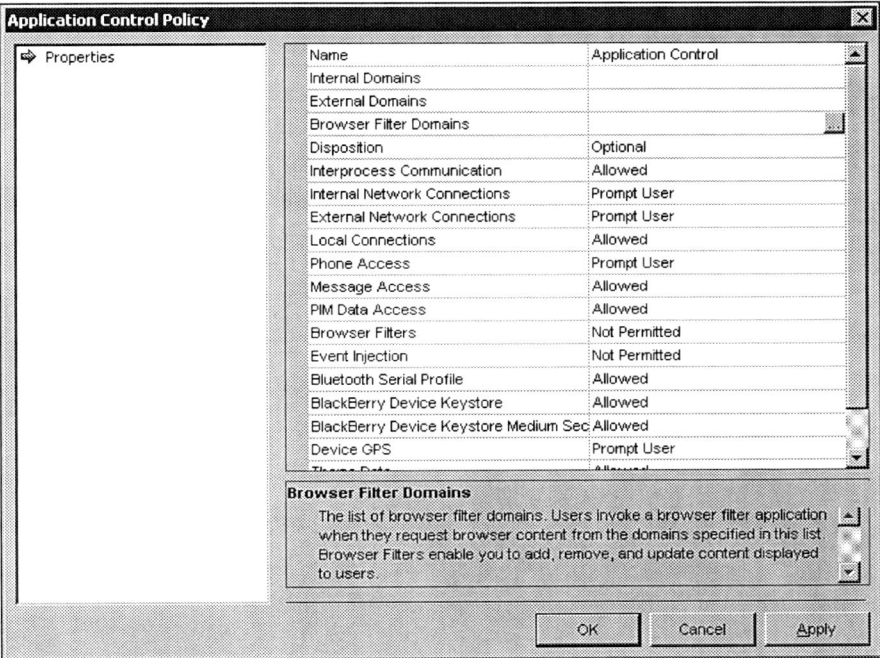

3. Enter the name in the **Name** field, select the desired policy options from the list and click **OK**.

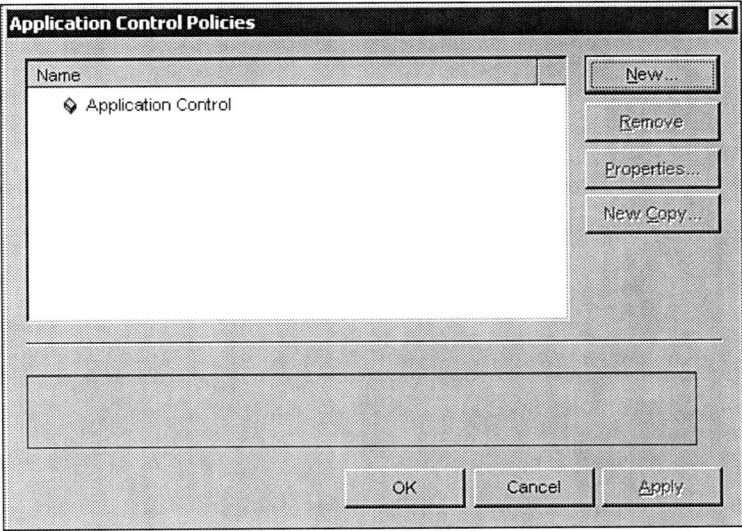

4   Click **OK** to close the **Application Control Policies** window.

5.   Select the software configuration created in the previous section from the **Software Configurations** tab.

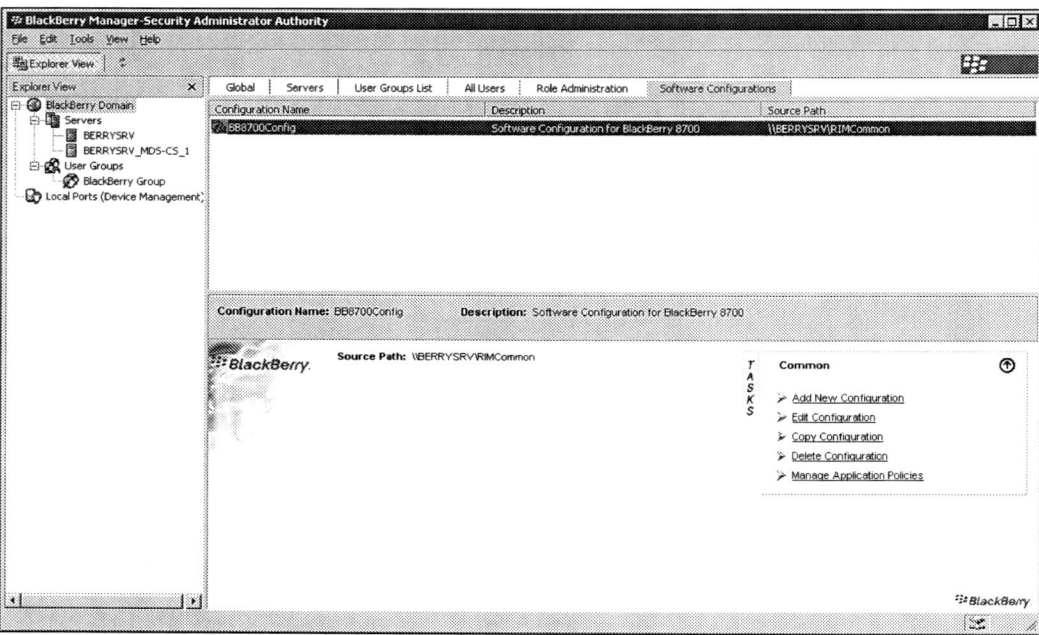

6.   Click **Edit Configuration**.

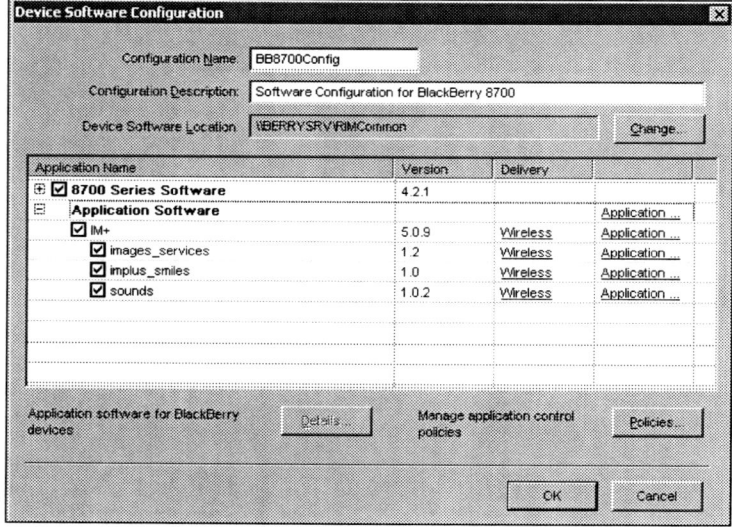

7. Select the policy that was created from the pulldown menu to the right of the **Delivery** column.

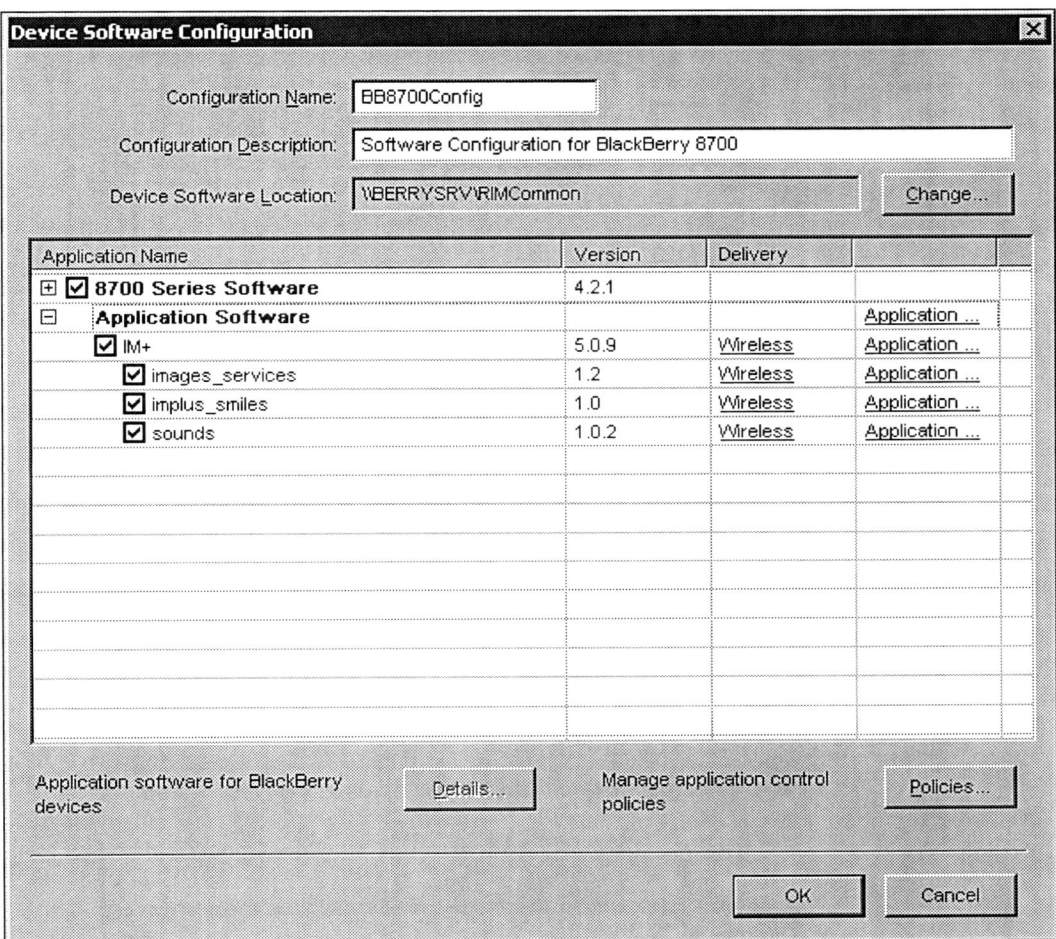

8. Click **OK** to close the **Device Software Configuration** window.

Now that we have assigned an application control policy to our software configuration, we are ready to start applying the software configuration. Software configurations may be applied to individual users or to user groups. The following steps describe both methods.

1. Select the BlackBerry Enterprise Server from the left-hand pane in the **BlackBerry Manager** and click the **Users** tab.

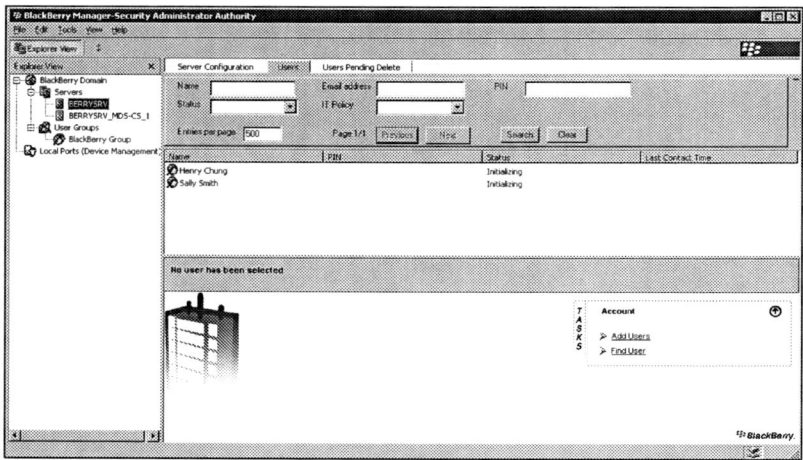

2. Select a user from the user list and expand the **Device Management** tasks group.

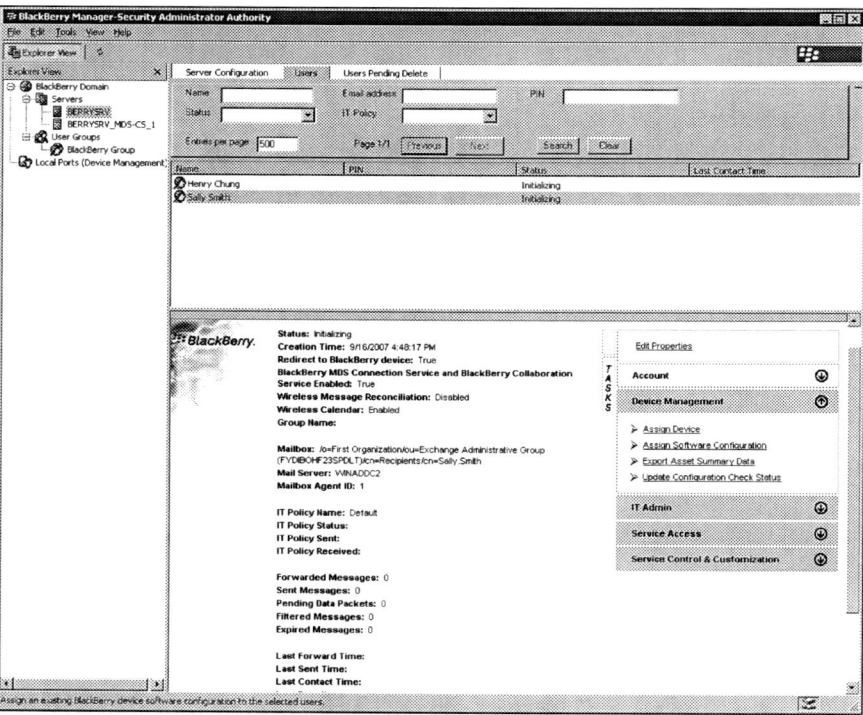

3. Click **Assign Software Configuration**.

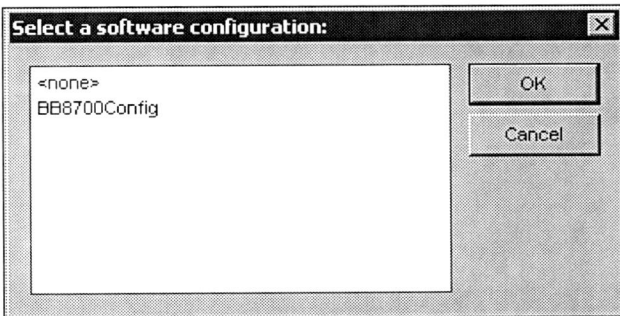

4. Select the desired software configuration from the list and click **OK** to assign the software configuration to the selected user.

5. Select **User Groups** from the left-hand pane and select the desired group from the list.

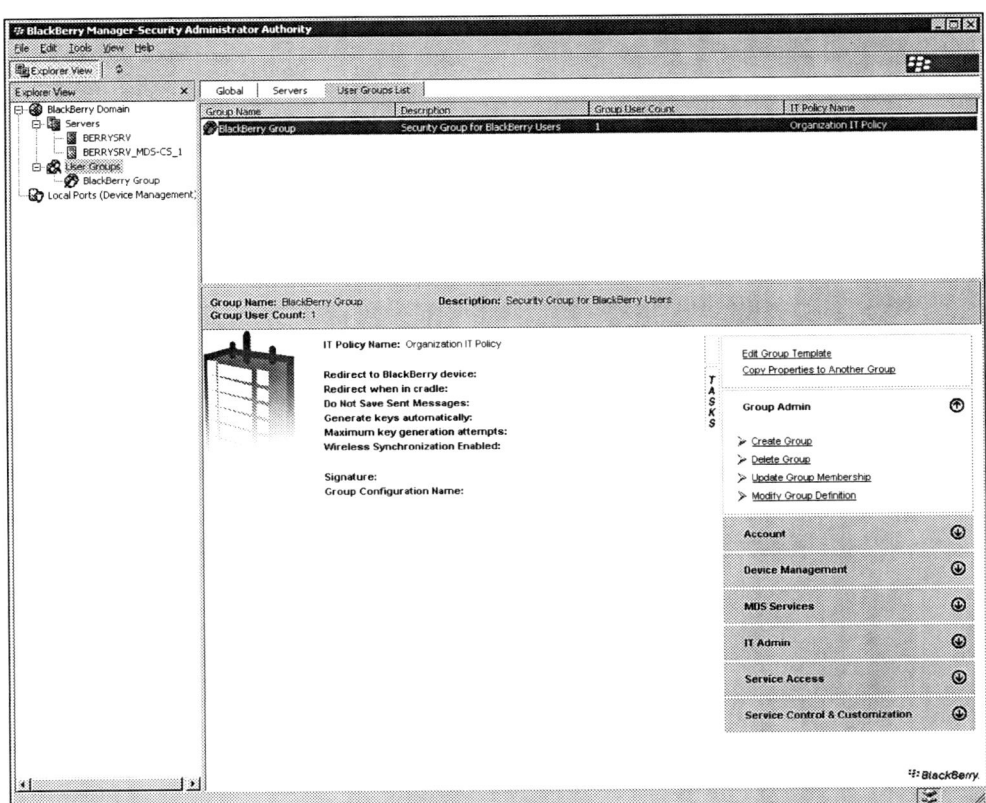

6. Select **Device Management** from the **Tasks** group.

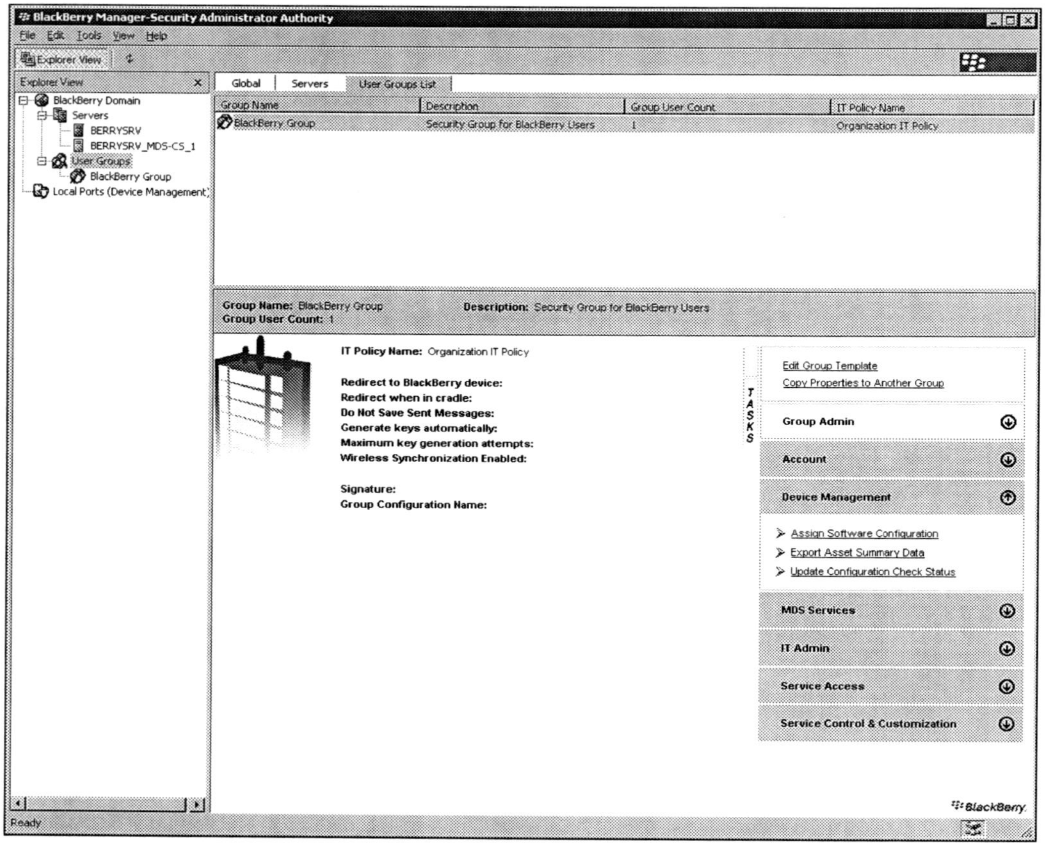

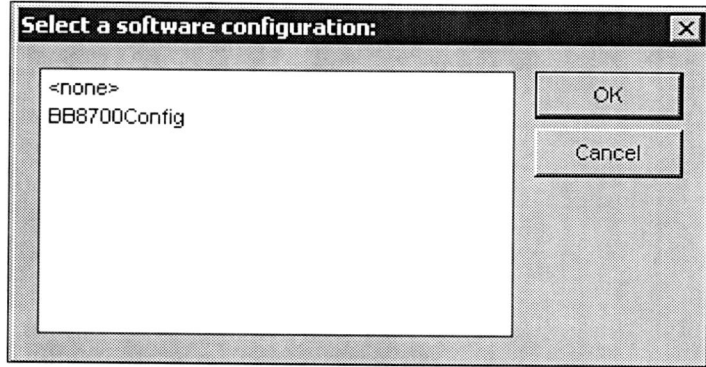

7. Click **Assign Software Configuration**.

8   Select the desired software configuration from the list and click **OK** to assign the software configuration to the selected group. You have now successfully assigned the software to an individual user and to a user group.

Summary

In this chapter, we have examined the controls available to administrators to enforce specific application and device policies, as well as the ability to create software configurations for device software and third-party applications. These capabilities facilitate administration and ensure that BlackBerry device usage is in accordance with organizational policies. In the next chapter, we will explore additional configurations and capabilities to help you get the most out of your BlackBerry Enterprise Server.

Getting the Most Out of Your BES

We have already covered the basics of getting a BlackBerry Enterprise Server up and running, provisioning users and devices, and deploying applications and IT policies. In truth, however, we have barely scratched the surface of the capabilities of BlackBerry Enterprise Server. There are numerous capabilities and configuration settings to govern the interaction of users, devices, and applications with BES. This chapter highlights the ways in which the BES can be configured and used to provide maximum value for your organization.

Multi-Tiered Administration

The administration of BlackBerry Enterprise Server implementations can be managed at several hierarchical levels. Implementations can be managed at the BlackBerry Domain level, where they will affect all BlackBerry Enterprise Servers within the domain or at the BlackBerry Enterprise Server level, where they will affect all users managed by the server. Additionally, you can administer individual users, specific to a single server, or user groups, which span across BlackBerry Enterprise Servers. There are settings that can be applied at each of these levels, as well as administrative tasks that are specific to each level. These settings and tasks are managed through the BlackBerry Manager application. The following sections describe the properties and administrative tasks specific to each level in the hierarchy.

User and Group Template Properties

We have already touched upon some of the properties that can be configured on an individual user or user group basis for IT policies and other settings. The User Properties and Group Template settings screens provide a number of additional capabilities that can be configured for either individual users or groups; such as message filters, organization synchronization settings, or basic security settings. For individual users, these settings can be accessed by selecting the user account within BlackBerry Manager and clicking the **Edit Properties** task. For user groups, these settings can be accessed by selecting the user group within BlackBerry Manager and clicking the **Edit Group Template** task. The settings are organized into functional groups—Redirection, Filters, Security, IT Policy, WLAN Configuration, PIM Sync, Advanced, and Access Control. These functional groups are described in detail in the following sections.

Redirection

The Redirection settings group contains settings specific to message forwarding, signatures and message disclaimers.

- **Message Forwarding**: These settings specify whether incoming messages are forwarded to BlackBerry devices, how messages are handled when the device is in a cradle connected to the user's computer, and whether messages sent from the BlackBerry device are saved to the user's mailbox.

- **Auto Signature**: This allows you to specify a default signature that is included on all messages sent from the BlackBerry device.

- **Enable S/MIME Message Processing**: This enables or disables S/MIME message processing for the user or group.

- **Messaging Options**: These settings allow you to specify disclaimer text that is prepended or appended to the signature for messages sent from the BlackBerry device.

Filters

The Filters settings group allows you to specify rules to filter messages, which are delivered to the BlackBerry device. These rules, similar to the rules that can be created in Microsoft Outlook, allow you to filter based on sender, recipient, message subject and body, recipient type (i.e., To:, CC:, BCC:), importance, and sensitivity. Administrators can specify whether messages that meet the specified criteria are to be forwarded or not.

Security

The Security settings group contains settings for security key generation, providing the ability to enable automatic or manual key generation. In addition, you can find out how many times key generation may be attempted.

IT Policy

The IT Policy settings group is where IT policies are assigned, as has been covered in a previous chapter. In addition, the IT Policy group for User Properties contains additional settings for VoIP, VPN, and WLAN settings.

- **VoIP Policy Group**: These settings specify the SIP username, password, and display name to use when connecting to a SIP server.

- **VPN Policy Group**: These settings define the username and password to use when connecting to a VPN in a WLAN implementation.

- **WLAN Policy Group**: These settings are used to provide the username and password for authentication in Protected Extensible Authentication Protocol (PEAP) and Lightweight Extensible Authentication Protocol (LEAP) WLAN implementations.

WLAN Configuration

The WLAN Configuration settings group is specific to user properties and is used to apply pre-defined configurations for WLAN, VPN, and VoIP to the user account. It also provides the ability to manage software tokens.

PIM Sync

The PIM Sync settings group contains settings for the synchronization of organizer data, including Message Filters, Tasks, Message Settings, Memos, Certificate Summary Data, and Address Book data. For each type of data, administrators can specify whether it should be synced to the BlackBerry device, the type of synchronization (i.e., Server to Device, Device to Server, or Bidirectional), and whether to use the data from the server or the device in case of conflicts.

Advanced

The Advanced settings group is specific to user properties and contains settings for the Mailbox Agent that is used to monitor the user mailbox. These settings are typically only changed to address network latency issues contact a Microsoft Exchange server and may have an impact on the hardware resources of BES.

Access Control

The Access Control settings group is specific to groups and is used to define rule sets for BlackBerry MDS Connection Service. These settings are only available if you are using BlackBerry MDS Services.

Server Properties

Similar to the properties that may be configured for individual users or user groups; there are a number of settings for the BlackBerry Enterprise Server. Many of these settings are duplicates of the user and group settings, but will enforce those settings for all users on the BES. These settings can be accessed by selecting the BlackBerry Enterprise Server within BlackBerry Manager and clicking the **Edit Properties** task. The settings are organized into functional groups – General, Messaging, IT Admin, Global Filters, Sync Server, BES Alert and MDS Services. These functional groups are described in detail in the following sections.

General

The General settings group provides access to the settings that control connection to the BlackBerry Infrastructure, including SRP identifiers, authentication keys, and host information. This is also where administrators define the encryption algorithms to be used (i.e., 3DES, AES, or both).

Messaging

The Messaging settings group is used to set a number of server-wide options for messaging settings.

- **Messaging Options**: These define a number of messaging options. Some of these are similar to the settings provided in the user and group Redirection settings group, such as the disclaimer text that may be appended or prepended to the signature. This is also where an auto-BCC address is specified, for organizations that want to audit all messages sent through BlackBerry devices. These options also provide the configuration options for wireless message and hard delete reconciliation, reconciling read, and unread marks and message moves as well as messages that are hard-deleted (i.e. Shift+DEL in Outlook) from the desktop email program. This is also where users set attachment options, such as maximum individual size and total size.

- **Message Prepopulation**: This allows administrators to define how messages are populated when a device is activated, including how many days are populated and the total number of messages to be populated.

- **Performance:** This manages the performance of the BES with regard to message storage, defining the size of the message database.

- **Secure Messages**, These settings are used to manage the S/MIME options for messages.

IT Admin

The IT Admin settings group defines server settings related to IT policies, including the time interval for re-sending IT policies and whether to disable users that have unapplied IT policies.

Global Filters

The Global Filters settings group is used to manage message filters for messages that are sent through the BES, similar to the Filters settings group for users and user groups. These settings should be applied carefully, as they will affect all users that send and receive messages on this server.

Sync Server

The Sync Server settings group provides the ability to define the audit root folder where SMS, PIN, and messages that are subject to auditing are stored.

BES Alert

The BES Alert settings group enables BES error messages to be sent to specified email addresses or consoles if an error message reaches a specified error level (e.g., Critical, Error, Warning, and Informational). Different levels can be enabled for different users, as defined in this settings group.

MDS Services

The MDS Services settings group is used to set the MDS Connection Server URL for this BES.

 Many of the Server Properties settings changes required a restart of the BlackBerry Enterprise Server in order to make the change effective.

BlackBerry Domain Properties

There are a number of properties that are configured at the BlackBerry Domain level, meaning that these settings will be applied globally to all objects within the domain, including servers, users, and user groups. These settings can be accessed by selecting the BlackBerry Domain within BlackBerry Manager and clicking the **Edit Properties** task. The settings are organized into functional groups—General, Global PIM Sync, Access Control, Push Control, WLAN Configuration, IT Policy, Enterprise Service Policy, and Media Content Management. These functional groups are described in detail in the following sections.

General

The General settings group provides access to administration settings related to the generation and email of device activation passwords. Administrators can create a custom email message for activation and specify the policies for auto-generated passwords, including length, type (i.e., 7100 Friendly, Lowercase only, all alpha-numeric characters), and password lifespan.

Global PIM Sync

The Global PIM Sync settings group provides similar options to the PIM Sync group for users and user groups, except that these settings are applied to all users within the BlackBerry Domain.

Access Control

The Access Control settings group is used to define access controls for the BlackBerry MDS Connection Service, including push and pull data controls.

Push Control

The Push Control settings group is where push configuration settings are defined for the BlackBerry MDS Connection Service, such as maximum stored push messages and maximum message age.

WLAN Configuration

The WLAN Configuration settings group is used to create the Configuration Sets for the WLAN, VPN, and VoIP that are assigned to users in the WLAN Configuration settings group under each user account.

IT Policies

The IT Policies settings group provides the ability to define IT policy sets, as we did in Chapter 6. It also provides the ability to view and modify the policies that are assigned to an individual user.

Enterprise Service Policy

The Enterprise Service Policy settings group is used to modify Enterprise Service Policy settings, which define the BlackBerry devices that are allowed to access servers in the Domain.

Media Content Management

The Media Content Management settings group provides the ability to restrict the type of data that is transmitted using BlackBerry MDS.

User Tasks

In addition to the User Properties, BES provides access to a number of user administration tasks through BlackBerry Manager. These tasks are arranged into several groups—Account, Device Management, IT Admin, Service Access, and Service Control & Customization. We have already explored some of the individual tasks in previous chapters, but all of the tasks are described in greater detail in the following sections.

Account

Account tasks are used to administer user accounts, performing activities such as adding and deleting users or managing group members.

- **Find User** provides the ability to find users within the BlackBerry Domain. This is useful for deployments with large numbers of users.

- **Add Users** is used to add new users to the BES, as we did in Chapter 5.

- **Move User** is for assigning a user to be managed by a different BES within the BlackBerry Domain.

- **Delete User** provides the ability to remove a user from BES.

- **Reload User** is a troubleshooting tool that reloads user information and restarts the messaging communications between the device and the server.

- **Clear In-Cradle Flag** is used to re-set the status of the connection between a device and the user's computer.

- **Assign to Group** is used to add users to a group, as described in Chapter 5.

- **Remove from Group** provides the ability to remove a user from membership in a group.

- **Send Message** enables administrators to send PIN and email messages to selected users.

Device Management

Device Management tasks are for device administration, including assigning devices and managing software configurations.

- **Assign Device** is used to provision a locally-connected device and assign it to a specified user.

- **Assign Software Configuration** provides the ability to assign specific software configurations, as we did in Chapter 6.

- **Export Asset Summary Data** creates a comma-separated values file containing asset information for the selected users, such as PIN, BlackBerry model, phone number, serial number, etc.

- **Update Configuration Check Status** is used to initiate a comparison of the device software against the software configuration assigned to the device.

IT Admin

IT Admin tasks provide IT administrative capabilities, such as IT policy assignment, application deployment and owner information.

- **Resend IT Policy** is used to manually push out the assigned IT policy.

- **Assign IT Policy** is for assigning a pre-defined IT policy to the user, as described in Chapter 6.

- **Resend Peer-to-Peer Key** provides the ability to resend the current peer-to-peer encryption key out to the selected user.

- **Resend Service Book** is used to redeploy the service book that controls wireless data synchronization to the device.

- **Deploy Applications** initiates the deployment of specified applications to the user device. Application deployment can take several hours, so this can be used to accelerate the process for a single user.

- **Set Password and Lock Device** is one of the two critical tasks for lost or stolen devices, providing the ability to set a new password and automatically lock a device, preventing access by unauthorized users. This also provides the ability to set owner information on the device.

- **Set Owner Information** is used to define the owner information on the specified user's device.

- **Erase Data and Disable Handheld** is the other critical task, providing the ability to erase the data that is stored on the handheld and disable it. This will remove all data previously stored and will not allow the handheld to communicate with the BES.

Service Access

Service Access tasks are used to provision devices or modify access to BES services.

- **Set Activation Password** is used to manually define the activation password for a user, as described in Chapter 5.

- **Generate and Email Activation Password** provides the ability to automatically generate and email activation passwords for users, as described in Chapter 5.

- **Disable/Enable Redirection** is used to disable or enable message redirection to a user's BlackBerry device.

- **Choose Folders for Redirection** allows the administrator to choose the mailbox folders that will be redirected to the user's device.

- **Disable/Enable Connection and Collaboration Services** provide the ability to disable or enable MDS Connection Services and BlackBerry Collaboration Services for a user.

Service Control & Customization

Service Control & Customization tasks provide the ability to modify service configuration settings, including organizer data field mappings, statistics, and message filters.

- **Edit PIM Sync Field Mapping** is used to re-define the field mapping between Microsoft Outlook fields and BlackBerry device fields.

- **Reset PIM Sync Field Mapping** is used to restore the default PIM sync field mappings.

- **Clear PIM Sync Backup Data** provides the ability to remove any wireless backups that have been conducted for organizer data.

- **Purge Pending Data Packets** is a troubleshooting tool used to remove any data that is queued to be sent to the user's device.

- **Clear Statistics** removes the statistics that are currently stored for user, such as messages sent and received.

- **Export Stats to File** creates a tab-delimited text file with user statistics and, if desired, clears the statistics for the selected user.

- **Export Filters to File** is used to save the user's message filter settings to an XML file that can be imported on another BES.

- **Import Filters from File** is used to import an XML file containing message filters.

Group Tasks

Much like the user administration tasks, BES provides a set of tasks for managing groups. The majorities of the task groups are the same as those for user administration, but deliver a sub-set of actions that are specifically for groups. There are two task groups that are specific to user groups—Group Admin and MDS Services.

Group Admin

Group Admin tasks are used for group administration, including adding and removing groups, and managing membership.

- **Create Group** is used to create a new user group.
- **Delete Group** provides the ability to delete previously-created user groups.
- **Update Group Membership** returns administrators to the list of users in the BlackBerry domain in order to add them to a group.
- **Modify Group Definition** is used to change the name and description of a user group.

MDS Services

MDS Services tasks are for managing BlackBerry MDS policies related to MDS Studio applications.

- **Assign Device Policy** is used to assign BlackBerry MDS application policies to a user group.
- **Install on Device** provides the ability to deploy MDS Studio applications to the devices for the selected user group.
- **Uninstall on Device** removes MDS Studio applications from the devices of user group.

BlackBerry Domain Tasks

There are several administrative tasks available under the BlackBerry Domain, similar to those for users and user groups. Some of the tasks are the same as those for users and groups, but they apply to all global users and groups within the domain settings rather than the user groups or users on an individual server, while others are unique to the BlackBerry Domain. The following sections describe the tasks specific to BlackBerry Domains.

Account

There is one Account task that is unique to BlackBerry Domains, which is specific to the task of managing licenses for BlackBerry Enterprise Servers.

Service Control & Customization

Many of the Service Control & Customization tasks are similar to those contained in the task group for users, but they are applied on a global basis. In addition, there are several unique tasks.

- **Enable Enterprise Service Policy** is used to enable Enterprise Service Policy, which defines a white list of BlackBerry devices that can access servers within the domain based on PIN or model number.

- **Update Peer-to-Peer Encryption Key** sets or removes corporate peer-to-peer encryption keys for use by BlackBerries within your organization.

- **Import IT Policy Definitions** provides the ability to import IT policy files from other BlackBerry Domains to be used within your domain.

- **MDS CS to BES Mapping** defines the mapping between BlackBerry MDS Connection Service servers and BlackBerry Enterprise Servers.

- **IM to BES Mapping** is used to map corporate IM servers and BlackBerry Enterprise Servers.

- **Delete MDS Service** provides the ability to delete MDS server listings that are not currently serving any BlackBerry Enterprise Servers.

- **Delete MDS Connection Service** is used to delete MDS Connection Service servers that aren't in use.

- **Delete IM Service** provides the ability to delete corporate IM server listings that are not being used within the BlackBerry Domain.

Summary

In this chapter, we have reviewed many of the configuration settings and administration tasks that can be performed on BlackBerry Enterprise Server, including those that are specific to individual users, user groups, individual servers, and an entire BlackBerry Domain. These settings should provide you with a good understanding of the flexibility and configurability of your BES implementation. In the next chapter, we will focus on the security and disaster recovery aspects of the BES.

8

Security & Disaster Recovery

As with any critical network service, you're going to look forward towards the security and disaster recovery capabilities of your BlackBerry Enterprise Server. This chapter explores the security mechanisms built into BES, including encryption of messages and device contents, as well as device authorization. Additionally, we will review the capabilities provided by BES with regard to continuity of operations and improving availability during a disaster with a focus on improving availability for both the BlackBerry Enterprise Server and the Configuration Database.

Security

We have briefly touched upon some of the security features of BES in previous chapters. There are multiple aspects of securing the BES implementation including encryption methods, device content protection, email, PIN message protection, and device authorization. The following sections describe each of these aspects in greater detail.

Encryption

When talking about wireless data, the question on everyone's mind, from the Chief Executive Officer to the network administrator, is how secure *is* the data flying through the air and across the Internet? RIM has developed a solid answer to that question, with strong encryption protecting your data as it traverses through the BlackBerry world.

From the moment a user sends a message from their Blackberry until it arrives on the Blackberry Enterprise Server, the data is encrypted using symmetric key algorithms in the form of either Triple Data Encryption Standard (3DES) or Advanced Encryption Standard (AES). 3DES, with its 112-bit key, provide a strong minimum level of protection. AES encryption uses 256-bit keys, providing stronger protection and better prevention from brute force attacks, as well as enhanced performance.

This protection comes at a price, however. If AES is chosen as the encryption method, your organization must be using Blackberry Desktop Software version 4.0 or higher and your BlackBerry devices must have operating software at version 4.0 or higher. The Blackberry Enterprise Server must be 4.0 or later as well. BES does support a mixed software environment, allowing 3DES for older devices and desktop software and AES for more current installations and devices.

Setting the Encryption Method

The encryption method, 3DES, or AES may be set on a server-by-server basis. The following instructions describe how to set the desired encryption method for a BES.

1. On a workstation with BlackBerry Manager installed, click **Start | Programs | BlackBerry Enterprise Server | BlackBerry Manager**.

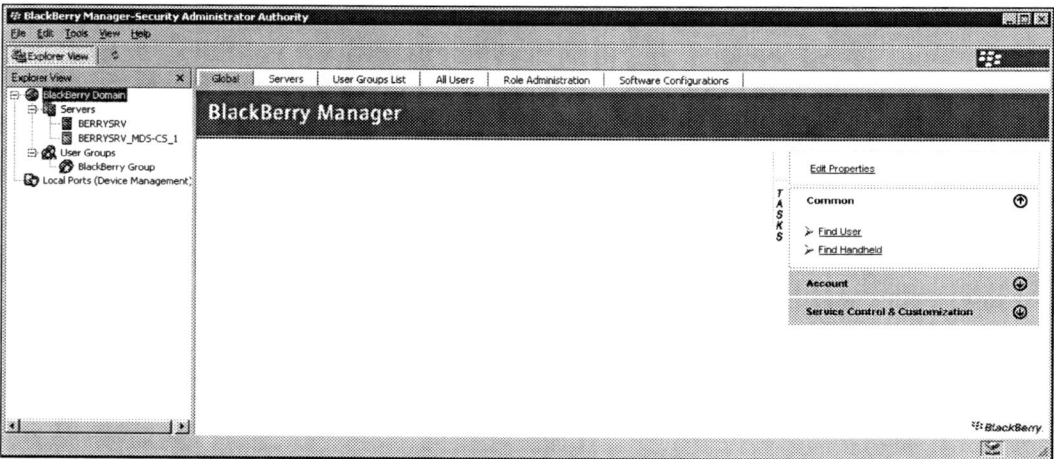

2. Select **BlackBerry Domain** from the left-hand window.

3. Select the **Servers** tab and select your server from the list.

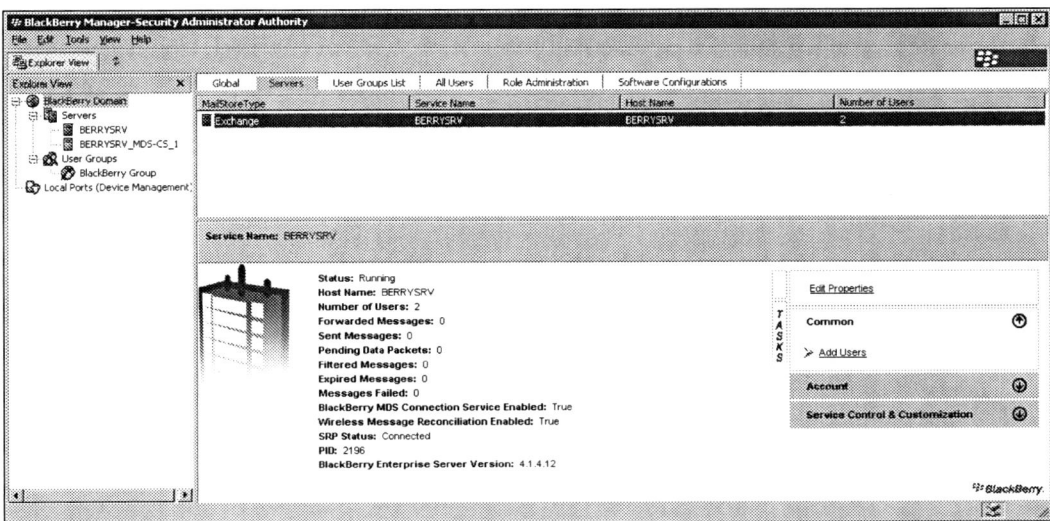

4. Click the **Edit Properties** task.

5. Select your desired **Encryption Algorithm** from **Security** section of the **General** section and click **OK**.

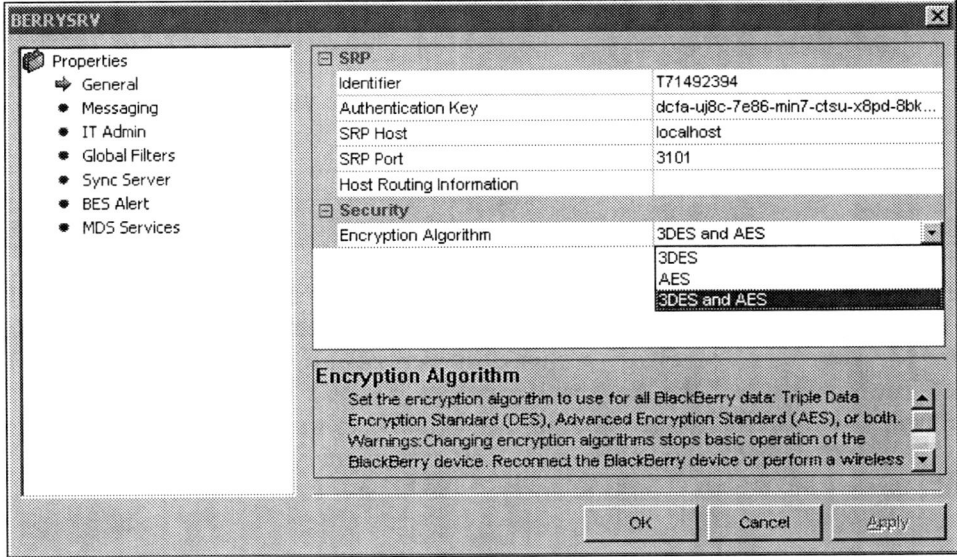

Content Protection

Content protection is a mechanism that protects the data on BlackBerry devices when the device is locked. If a device has content protection enabled, it will encrypt specific data stored on the device using 256-bit AES encryption and a public Elliptical Curve Cryptography (ECC) key to encrypt data that is received while the device is locked. Specifically, content protection is used to encrypt sensitive email, calendar, memo, task, and contact data; as well as AutoText entries and BlackBerry Browser data, including data that is pushed or saved to the device and the browser cache.

Content protection can be enabled by the user directly on the device or by the BlackBerry administrator using IT policy rules. The following IT policy rules, located in the Security Policy Group, govern content protection settings.

- **Content Protection Strength** — this rule enables content protection and determines the strength of the content protection.
  - **Default** — by default, content protection is turned off.
  - **Strong** — Strong protection uses a 160-bit ECC key to protect data.
  - **Stronger** — Stronger, uses a 283-bit ECC key; RIM recommends enforcing a minimum 12 character device password to maximize the encryption strength.
  - **Strongest** — This setting uses a 571-bit ECC key, which is bolstered by enforcing a minimum 21 character password on the device.

- **Force Content Protection of Master Keys** — This rule protects the Master Encryption Key by encrypting it using a Grand Master Key when the device is locked.

Blackberry Encryption Keys

BlackBerry Enterprise Server uses multiple encryption keys to protect different kinds of data. Two encryption keys are generated by default — the Master Encryption Key and the Message Key. These keys are used to encrypt and decrypt all traffic between the BES components and the Blackberry devices. It is also possible to enable the BlackBerry device to manually generate two other keys to protect data when the device is locked — the Content Protection Key, which encrypts user data, and the Grand Master Key, which is used to encrypt the Master Encryption Key.

Master Encryption Key

The Master Encryption Key is unique to each BlackBerry device and is used by devices to encrypt messages before transmission and to decrypt received messages. Messages are sent using symmetrical encryption, which means that the Master Encryption Keys must match in order for the message to be decrypted. The Master Encryption Key is stored in the three places, listed below.

1. Within the user's mailbox on the Microsoft Exchange Server
2. On the BlackBerry device, within a key store database on flash memory
3. On the BlackBerry Enterprise Server within the BlackBerry Configuration Database

Message Key

The BlackBerry Enterprise Server also generates a session key, called the Message Key, which further protects the data that is sent and received by the BlackBerry device. Each message sent or received by the device is first encrypted using the Message Key and then the Master Encryption Key. While the Master Encryption Key protects the integrity by verifying the sender of the message, the Message Key protects the confidentiality of the data by using a randomized key to encrypt the message. These session keys are not stored, so once the key is used to decrypt the message it is deleted and the memory associated with the key is freed up.

Content Protection Key

When content protection is enabled on a BlackBerry device, a Content Protection Key and an ECC asymmetric public key are generated to encrypt and decrypt all of the user's data on the device when the BlackBerry is locked and unlocked.

Grand Master Key

If content protection is enabled, the BlackBerry device can protect the Master Encryption Key with a Grand Master Key. This is used to encrypt the Master Encryption Key that is stored in flash memory on the BlackBerry device. The Grand Master Key is used to decrypt the Master Encryption Key if the device receives data while it is locked.

Additional Message Encryption

In addition to the encryption mechanisms described above, BlackBerry Enterprise Server supports the use of S/MIME and PGP technology to provide extra security for email messages. When using the standard encryption mechanisms provided by BES, messages are encrypted between BES and the BlackBerry device, but they are not encrypted when they are sent to the Microsoft Exchange Server and beyond. S/MIME and PGP provide sender-to-recipient security in the form of digital signatures and encryption. Both methods require additional support packages and configurations. For more information on implementing these capabilities, refer to the white papers published by RIM.

PIN-to-PIN Messages

BlackBerry devices allow you to send messages between devices via the PIN function, which is similar to text messaging; every BlackBerry device is given a unique PIN at the time of manufacturing that identifies the device on the RIM wireless network. All BlackBerry devices have a common global peer-to-peer encryption key by default. This means that BlackBerry devices on your corporate network can send PIN messages to any BlackBerry device. As there is a common peer-to-peer encryption key, the message can be decrypted by any BlackBerry device. If you wish to limit PIN messages to devices within your organization, you can generate a corporate peer-to-peer encryption key that is only available to devices within your BlackBerry Domain. If necessary, you can update this key if you think that the current key has been compromised.

Regardless of the type of peer-to-peer key that is used, either global or corporate, PIN messages are scrambled, not encrypted, which means that anyone with access to the peer-to-peer key would be able to read the message. This is better than sending messages in clear text, but PIN messages should not be used for sensitive information, due to their relative insecurity compared to other BlackBerry communications.

Creating a Corporate Peer-to-Peer Key

The following directions describe the process for creating or updating a corporate peer-to-peer key for PIN scrambling.

1. On a workstation with BlackBerry Manager installed, click **Start | Programs | BlackBerry Enterprise Server | BlackBerry Manager**.

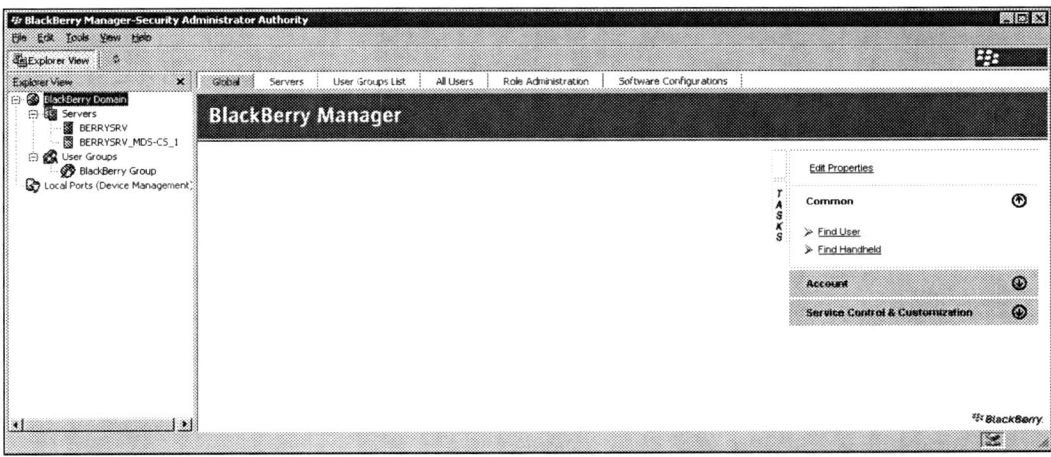

2. Select **BlackBerry Domain** from the left-hand window and select the **Service Control & Customization** task group from the **Global** tab.

3. Select **Update Peer-to-Peer Encryption Key**.

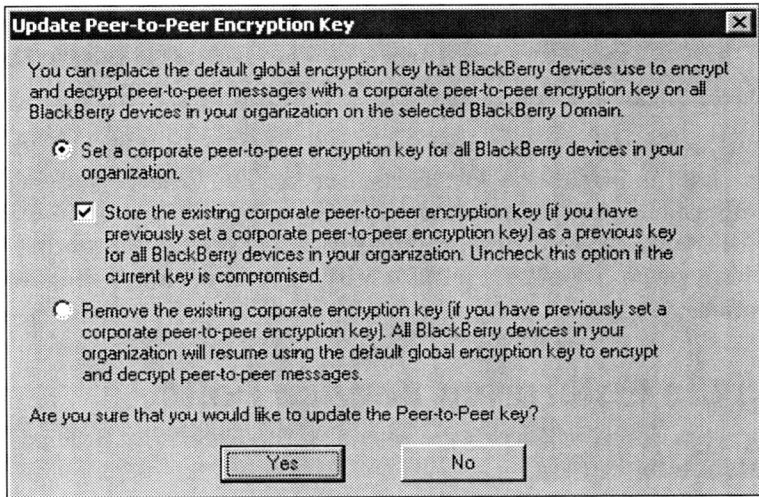

4. Click **Yes** to update the key or create a new key. If you think that the current key has been compromised, uncheck the box labeled **Store the existing corporate peer-to-peer encryption key**.

BlackBerry Device Authorization

The BlackBerry Enterprise Server has the ability to govern which devices are allowed to activate and join the BES environment. This ability is provided through the Enterprise Service Policy, which provides a white-list ("approval list") of device characteristics; if a BlackBerry device does not meet the characteristics, then it will not be allowed to complete Enterprise Activation. Administrators can specify four different types of characteristics, described in the table below.

White List	Description
Personal Identification Numbers (PIN)	Administrators may specify individual PINs that are authorized to access services on the Blackberry Enterprise Server, similar to filtering on MAC addresses on network hardware.
PIN Range	It is possible to specify one or more PIN ranges for devices that are authorized to access the BlackBerry Enterprise Server
Manufacturer	You may also specify device manufacturer, disallowing connections from devices that are manufactured by companies that are not on the list.
Model	Access may be restricted to specific BlackBerry device models.

If a device being activated meets any of the specified criteria, it will be allowed to activate and access the BlackBerry Enterprise Server. The Enterprise Service Policy is flexible though, as it is possible to allow specific user accounts to override the policies. The following sections describe the process of enabling Enterprise Service Policy, specifying white-list criteria and identifying user accounts that are allowed to override the policy.

Enabling the Enterprise Service Policy

The following steps describe the process to enable the Enterprise Service Policy and to specify the white-list criteria.

1. On a workstation with BlackBerry Manager installed, click **Start | Programs | BlackBerry Enterprise Server | BlackBerry Manager**.

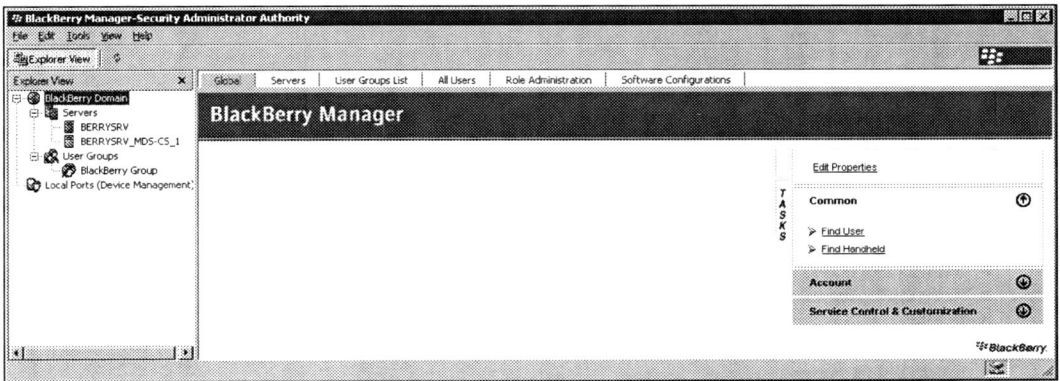

2. Select **BlackBerry Domain** from the left-hand window and select the **Service Control & Customization** task group from the **Global** tab.

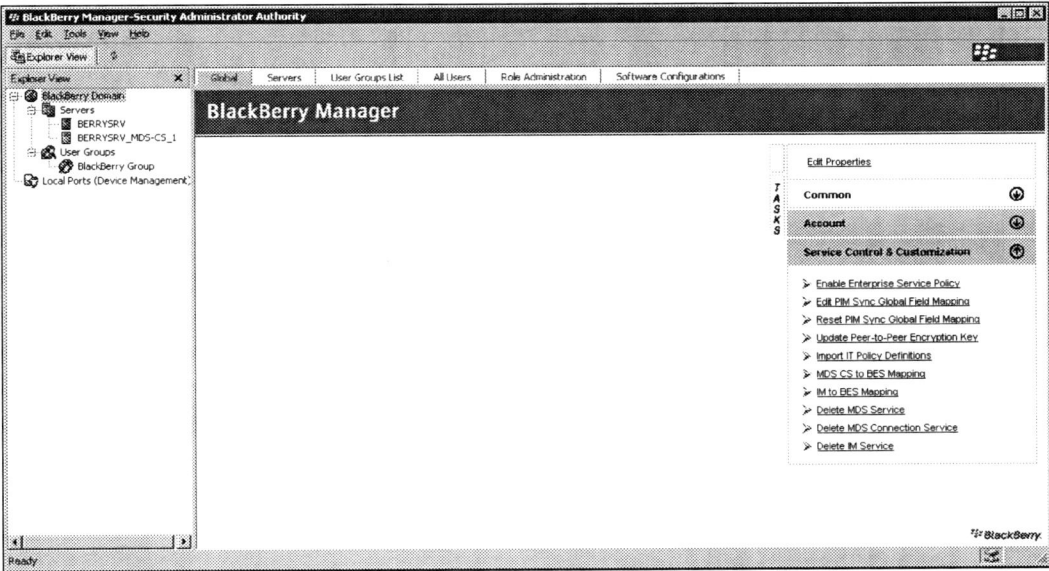

3. Select **Enable Enterprise Service Policy**.

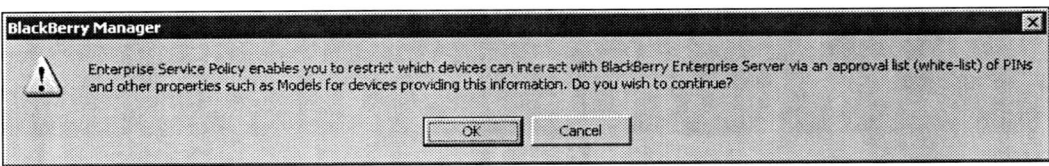

4. Click **OK** to enable Enterprise Service Policy.

5. Click **Edit Properties**.

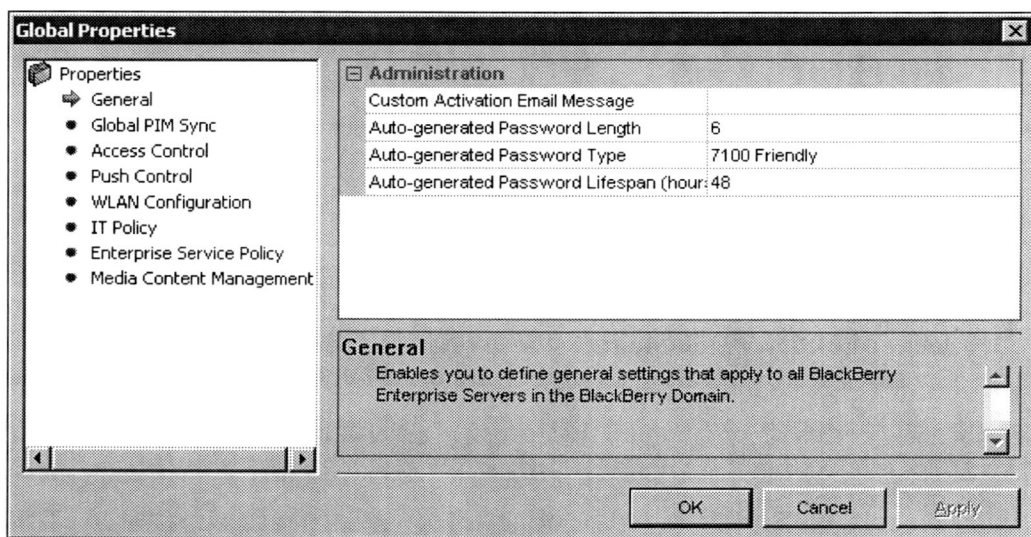

6. Select **Enterprise Service Policy** from the left-hand window.

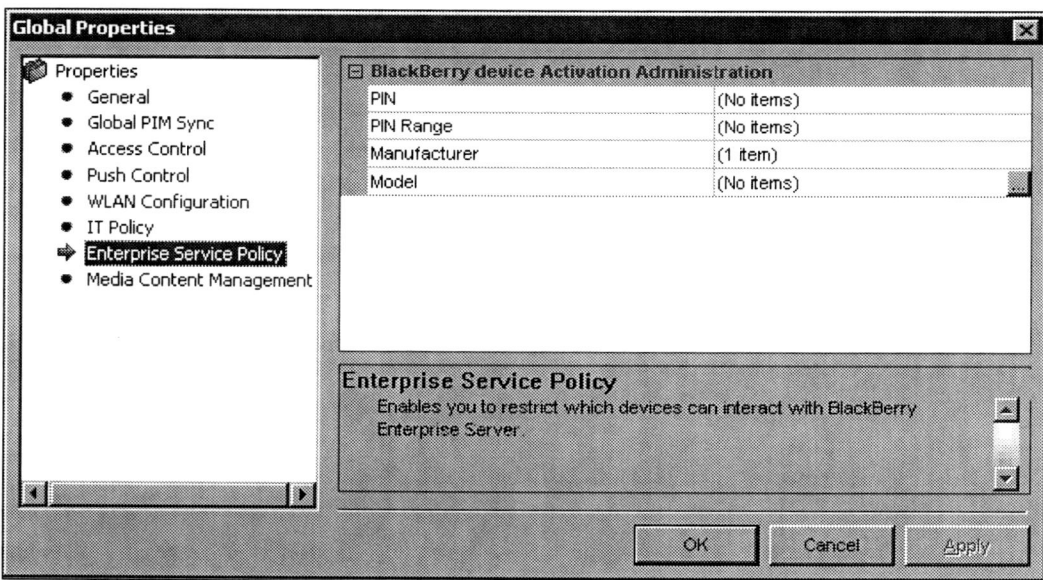

7. Select the desired criteria and click **OK**.

Allowing Users to Override the Enterprise Service Policy

The following steps describe the process to allow a specific user to override the Enterprise Service Policy.

1. On a workstation with BlackBerry Manager installed, click **Start | Programs | BlackBerry Enterprise Server | BlackBerry Manager**.

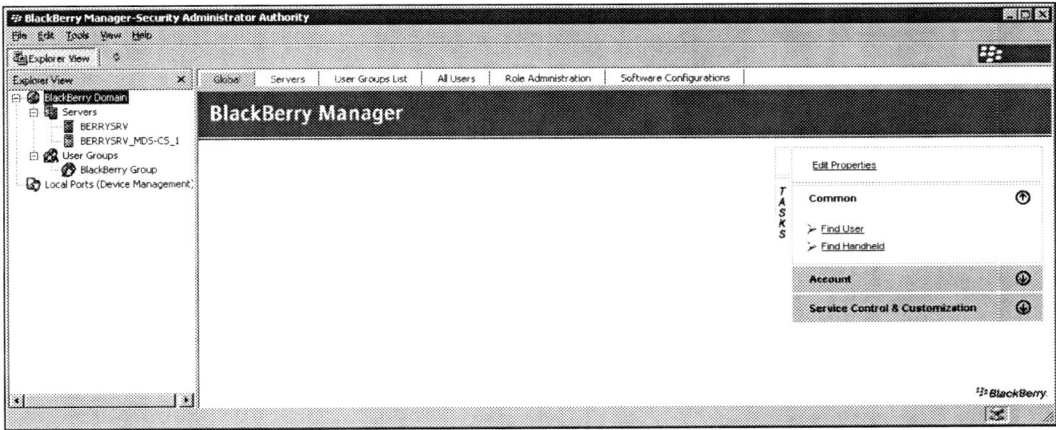

2. Select your BlackBerry Enterprise Server from the left-hand window.

3. Select the **Users** tab and select the user that you want to allow.

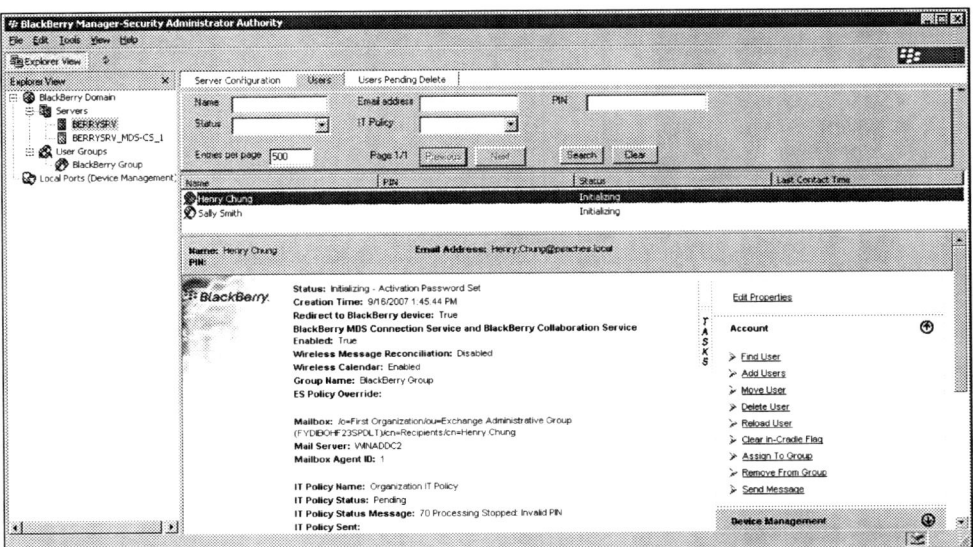

4. Select **Edit Properties**.

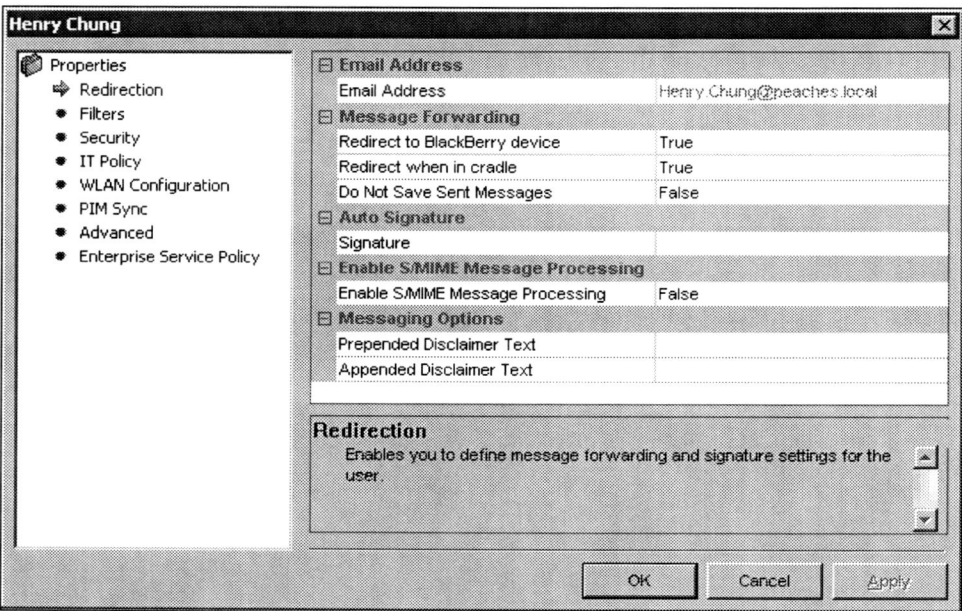

5. Select **Enterprise Service Policy** from the **Properties** pane.

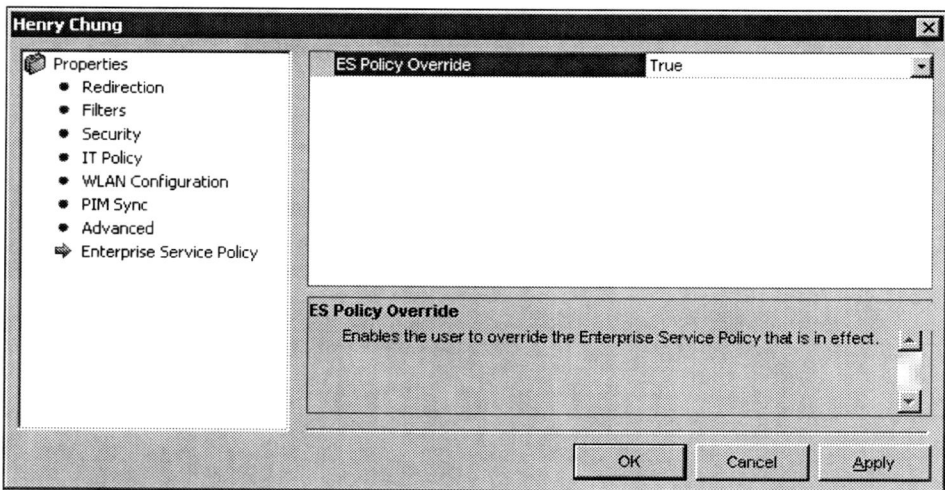

6. Set **ES Policy Override** to **True** and click **OK**.

Disaster Recovery

As with any important application service, it is essential to evaluate and formulate disaster recovery plans for your BlackBerry Enterprise Server implementation. Luckily, BES provides the flexibility and scalability to support solid disaster recovery and continuity of operations. Aside from planning for network failover and other typical disaster recovery mechanisms, there are two elements of the BlackBerry solution that we need to address—the BlackBerry Enterprise Server itself and the database instance that hosts the BlackBerry Configuration Database. The following sections describe approaches to disaster recovery for each of these elements.

Blackberry Enterprise Server Disaster Recovery

The BlackBerry Enterprise Server is a potential point of failure during a disaster scenario, especially if you only have one BES in your BlackBerry Domain. However, it is possible to configure a standby instance of BES, perhaps located at a different site, to take over for your primary server in case of disaster. If the primary instance becomes unavailable, as a result of a hardware failure, a local network interruption, or a local disaster; you can immediately switch to the standby instance.

This standby instance is configured to use the same credentials as your primary server, making it appear to the BlackBerry Infrastructure and your BlackBerry devices that they are the same server. The standby instance should not be brought online at the same time as the primary server, as no two BlackBerry Enterprise Servers can use the same SRP credentials simultaneously. Ideally, you should prepare this standby instance before a disaster actually occurs, as it's easier to ensure that you've properly created, replicated the primary instance by comparing the settings between the two. However, it is possible to create a new instance after a disaster occurs, provided that the BlackBerry Configuration Database is still available.

Creating the Standby Instance

The process for creating a standby instance is similar to the process for installing BlackBerry Enterprise Server. The goal is to duplicate the primary instance, right down to the version, service packs, and hot fixes. When you update your primary BES, it is important to install the same patches on your standby instance. The following instructions describe the important points of installation and post-install configuration.

1. The BlackBerry Enterprise Server Name should be identical to the name for the primary instance. The server name is configured on the **Installation Info** screen.

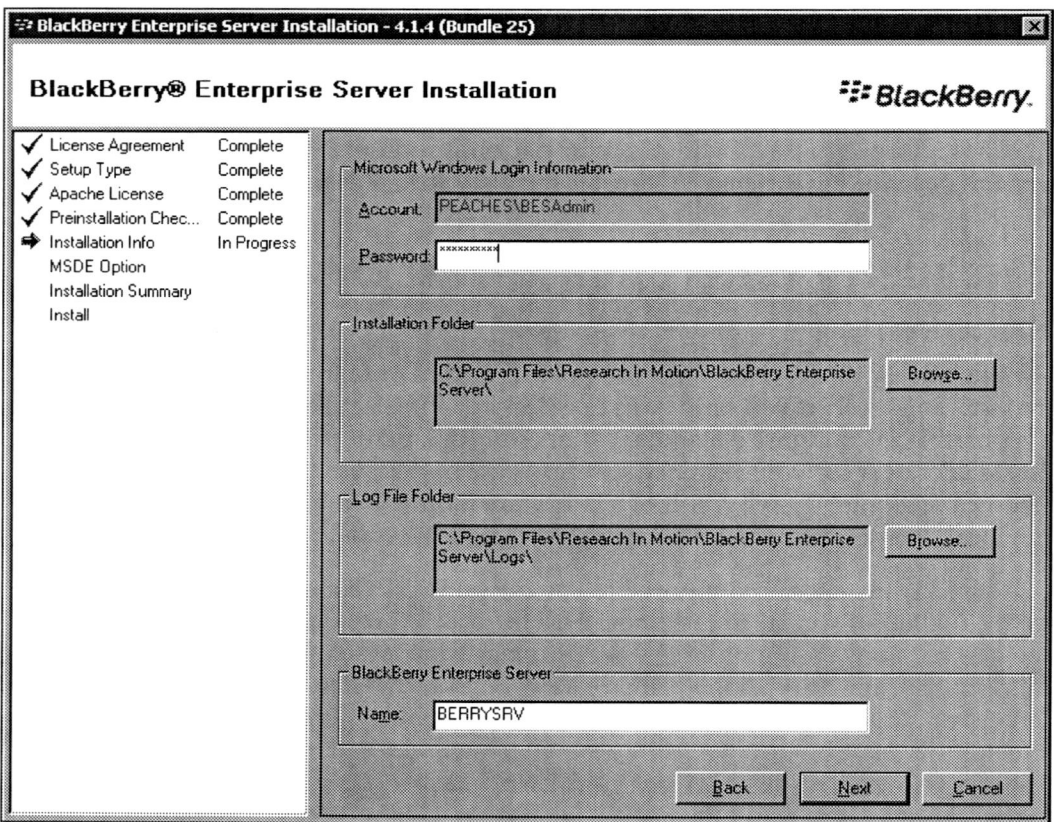

2. The BlackBerry Configuration Database Name should be the same, although the server it's hosted on may differ. The database name is configured on the **Database Settings** screen.

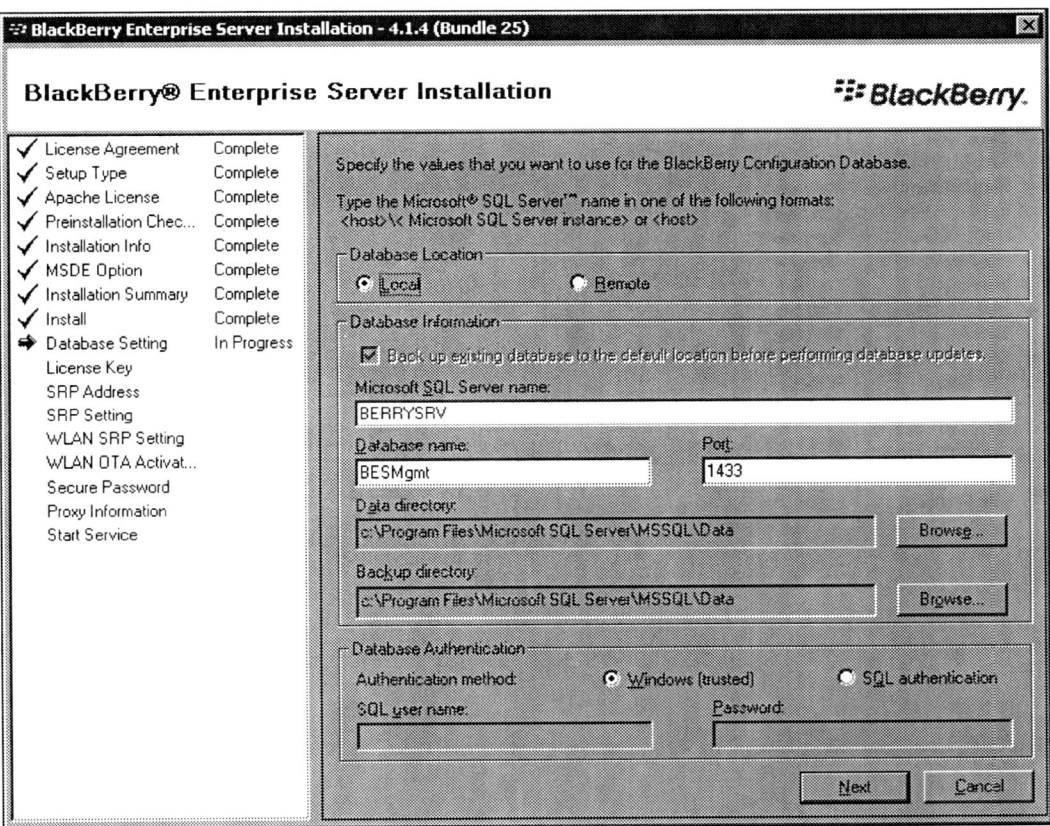

3. The SRP Identifier and SRP Authentication Key should be the same. These are configured on the **SRP Setting** screen.

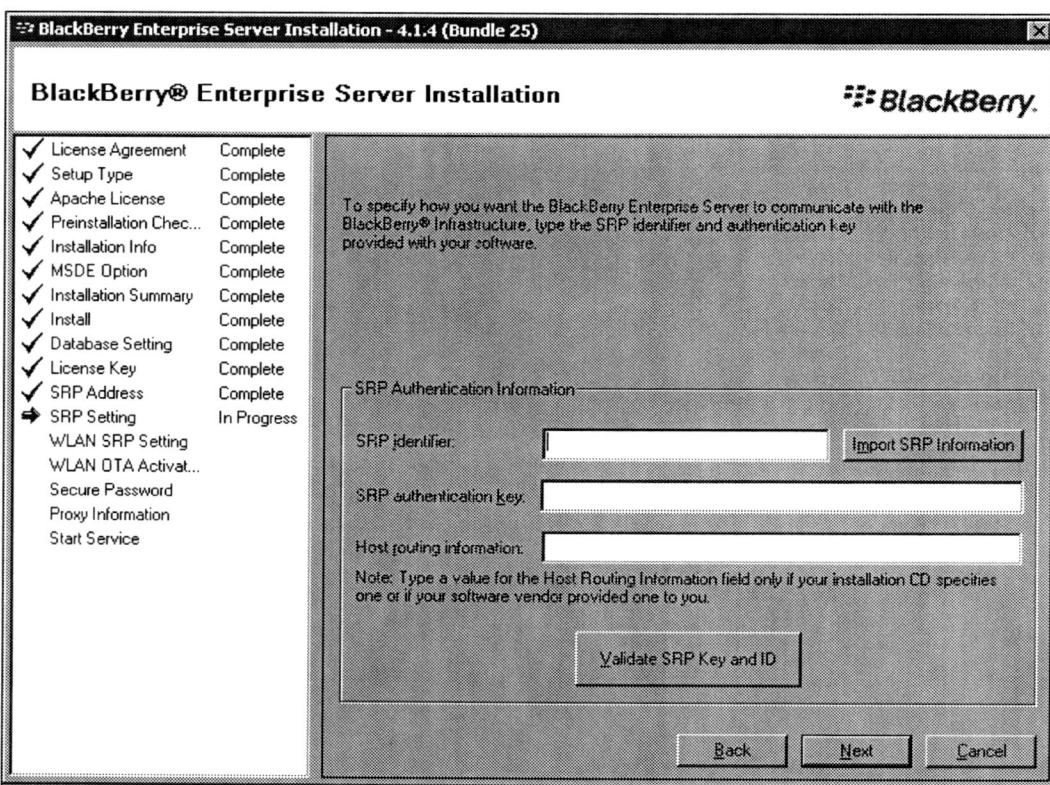

4. At the end of the installation process, on the **Start Service** screen, you should un-check the **Start Service** check box so that the BlackBerry Enterprise Server services are not started.

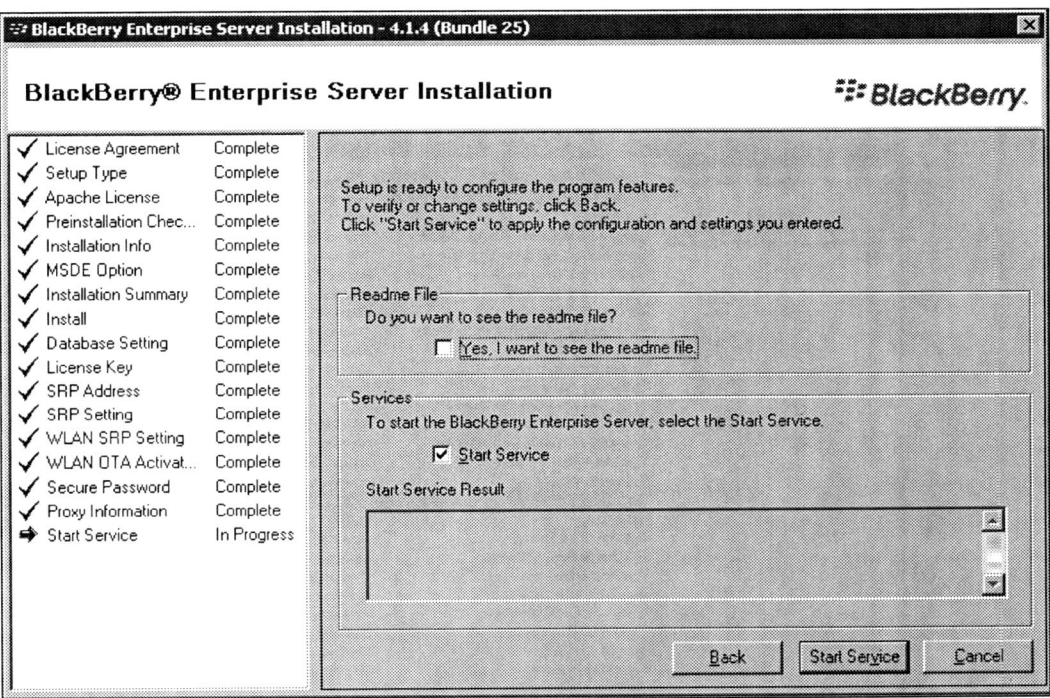

5. Disable the BlackBerry Enterprise Server services to keep them from starting automatically. On the standby instance server, click **Start | Control Panels | Administrative Tools | Services**. Set the startup type for all of the BlackBerry services to Disabled.

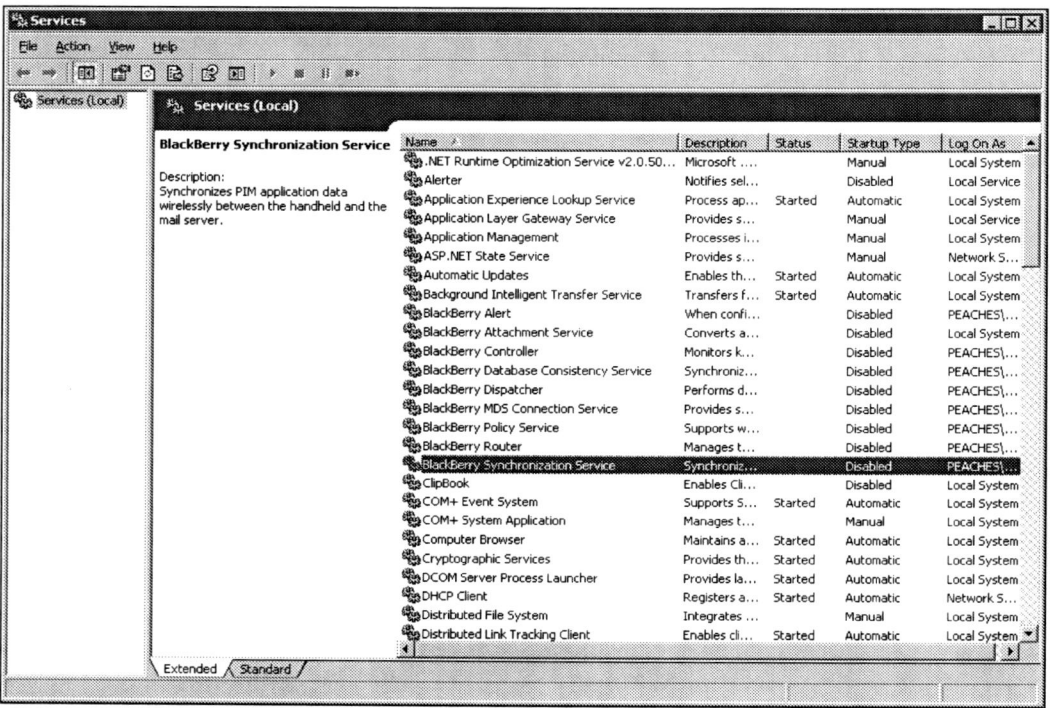

Responding to Disaster Scenarios

If you have prepared everything properly, the process of enabling your standby instance during a disaster response should be simple and straightforward. Basically, all you need to do is start the services, configure, and test the connection to the BlackBerry Infrastructure. The following steps describe the process for enabling a standby instance.

Ensure that you do not bring the standby instance online at the same time as the primary instance; RIM does not allow connections from multiple servers with the same SRP credentials and it may result in a loss of connectivity for both servers.

1. On the standby instance server, click **Start | Control Panels | Administrative Tools | Services**. Set the startup type for all of the BlackBerry services to Automatic. Start the BlackBerry services in the following order.

   a. BlackBerry Controller

   b. BlackBerry Router

   c. BlackBerry Dispatcher

   d. Remaining services

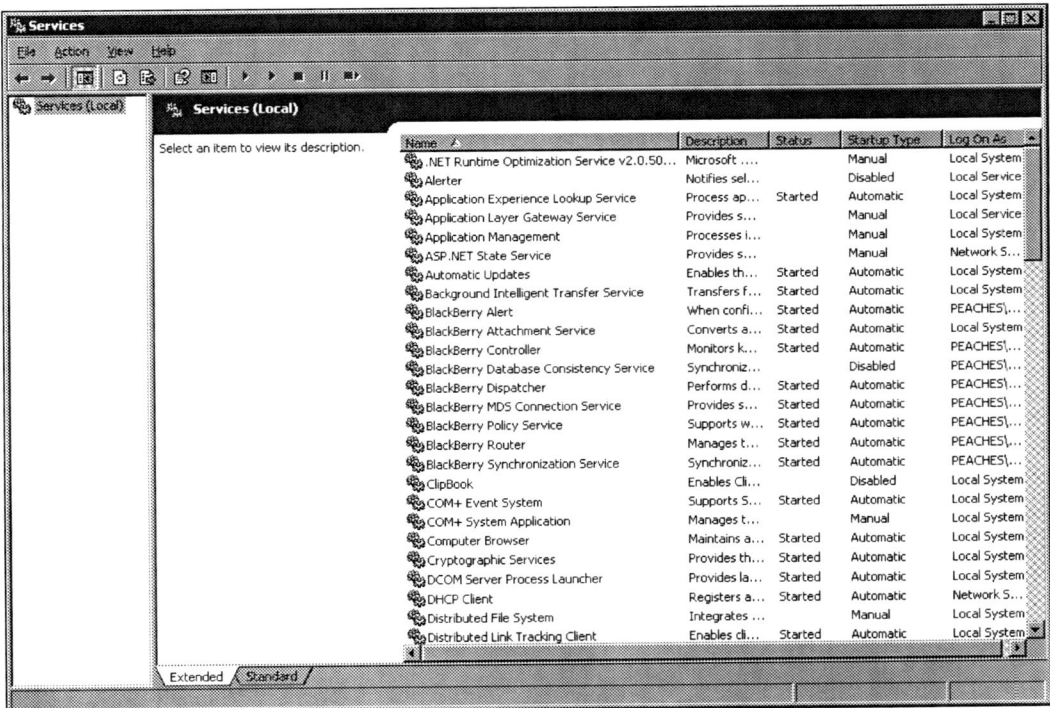

2. Click **Start | Programs | BlackBerry Enterprise Server | BlackBerry Server Configuration**.

3. To test the connection with the Configuration Database, click **Test SQL Server Connection** on the **Database Connectivity** tab. Click **OK** on the confirmation dialog box.

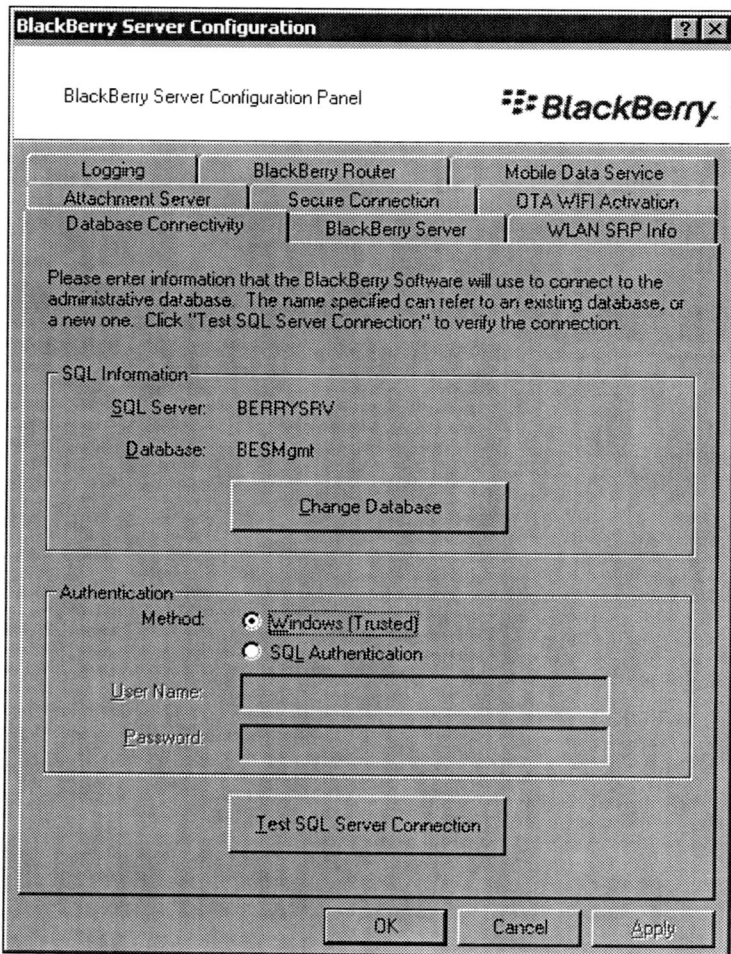

4. To validate the connection with the BlackBerry Infrastructure, click the **BlackBerry Server** tab and click **Validate SRP Key and ID**. Click **OK** on the confirmation dialog box.

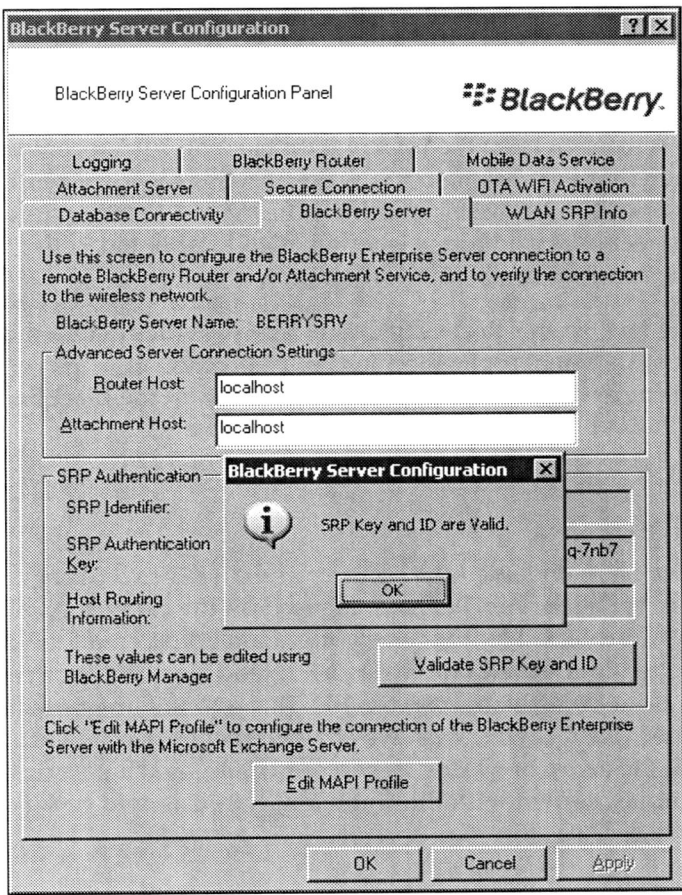

5. Click **OK** to close the BlackBerry Server Configuration application.

Blackberry Configuration Database Disaster Recovery

Planning for the disaster recovery of our BlackBerry Configuration Database is more involving than the process to setup a standby BES instance and is heavily dependent upon the database server that is used. The MSDE does not support extensive disaster recovery capabilities and is reliant upon regular backups from the primary Configuration Database to keep the information current. RIM recommends a disaster recovery approach that uses Microsoft SQL Servers transactional replication. Using this process, the primary database publishes information to the secondary database, ensuring that the secondary database is automatically updated with the latest BlackBerry Configuration Database information.

RIM has published a Disaster Recovery Guide that provides detailed instructions on configuring transactional replication for both Microsoft SQL Server 2000 and SQL Server 2005 environments. This guide is available on the BlackBerry Technical Solution Center at `http://www.blackberry.com/btsc`.

Summary

In this chapter, we have reviewed the security and disaster recovery capabilities of BlackBerry Enterprise Server. We have focused on the encryption algorithms and the data that is protected by that encryption, including email messages, PIN messages, and other data stored on the device. In addition, we have reviewed the capability to limit device activation on the BES through the implementation of an Enterprise Service Policy. Lastly, we have covered the disaster recovery capabilities of BES, including the setup of a standby server instance and a description of database replication technique. Armed with this knowledge, you should be able to secure and protect BlackBerry services for your organization.

Index

updating 150

D

database server
  enabling, to communicate with BES 36
demilitarized zone. *See* **DMZ**
device software
  about 111
  installing 111
disaster recovery
  about 157
  BlackBerry Configuration Database 166
  BlackBerry Enterprise Server 157
  disaster scenarios, responding to 162
disaster scenarios
  about 162
  responding 162
DMZ 17

E

encryption
  3DES 9
  about 9, 145
  advanced encryption standard 9
  AES 9
  algorithms 9
  BlackBerry device authorization 152
  BlackBerry encryption keys 148
  content protection 148
  content protection key 149
  Grand Master key 149
  Master encryption key 149
  message encryption 150
  Message key 149
  method, setting 146
  secure mutipurpose internet mail
     extensions 9
  triple data encryption standard 9
  Triple DES 9
enterprise activation options
  about 91
  customizing 91
Enterprise Service Policy
  enabling 152-154
  users allowing, to override 155
  white list 152

enterprise service policy settings
  about 138
  settings 138

G

group tasks
  about 142
  Group Admin 142
  MDS services tasks 142

I

IT policies
  about 102
  applying to, individual user 107-109
  applying to, user group 107-112
  assigning 107
  creating 102-106
  settings 135, 138

J

Junior Helpdesk administrator 70

M

Master encryption key
  about 149
  storing 149
MDS
  about 11
  formats supported 11
  standards supported 11
  services settings 137
  services tasks 142
media content management settings
  about 139
  settings 139
messaging settings, server properties
  about 136
  messaging options 136
  messaging prepopulation 136
  performance 136
  secure messages 136
Microsoft Exchange permissions
  assigning to, service account 26-29
  configuring for, service account 35

Thank you for buying
BlackBerry Enterprise Server for Microsoft® Exchange

About Packt Publishing

Packt, pronounced 'packed', published its first book *"Mastering phpMyAdmin for Effective MySQL Management"* in April 2004 and subsequently continued to specialize in publishing highly focused books on specific technologies and solutions.

Our books and publications share the experiences of your fellow IT professionals in adapting and customizing today's systems, applications, and frameworks. Our solution based books give you the knowledge and power to customize the software and technologies you're using to get the job done. Packt books are more specific and less general than the IT books you have seen in the past. Our unique business model allows us to bring you more focused information, giving you more of what you need to know, and less of what you don't.

Packt is a modern, yet unique publishing company, which focuses on producing quality, cutting-edge books for communities of developers, administrators, and newbies alike. For more information, please visit our website: www.packtpub.com.

Writing for Packt

We welcome all inquiries from people who are interested in authoring. Book proposals should be sent to authors@packtpub.com. If your book idea is still at an early stage and you would like to discuss it first before writing a formal book proposal, contact us; one of our commissioning editors will get in touch with you.

We're not just looking for published authors; if you have strong technical skills but no writing experience, our experienced editors can help you develop a writing career, or simply get some additional reward for your expertise.

Linux Email

ISBN: 1-904811-37-X   Paperback: 295 pages

A simple step-by-step guide to setting up a
Linux email server using the most popular free
Open Source tools

1. All the information you need to easily set up
   your own Linux email server

2. Shows how to provide web access to email,
   virus and spam protection, and more

3. Techniques to backup and protect your datas

4. Applications used include PostFix, Courier,
   SquirrelMail, SpamAssassin, ProcMail,
   and ClamAV

Zimbra

ISBN: 978-1-847192-08-0   Paperback: 220 pages

Get your organization up and running with
Zimbra, fast

1. Get your organization up and running with
   Zimbra, fast

2. Administer the Zimbra server and work with
   the Zimbra web client

3. Protect your Zimbra installation from hackers,
   spammers, and viruses

4. Access Zimbra from Microsoft Outlook

Please check **www.PacktPub.com** for information on our titles

OpenVPN

ISBN: 1-904811-85-X   Paperback: 258 pages

Learn how to build secure VPNs using this powerful Open Source application

1. Learn how to install, configure, and create tunnels with OpenVPN on Linux, Windows, and MacOSX

2. Use OpenVPN with DHCP, routers, firewall, and HTTP proxy servers

3. Advanced management of security certificates

Qmail Quickstarter

ISBN: 978-1-847191-15-1   Paperback: 152 pages

A fast-paced and easy-to-follow, step-by-step guide that gets you up and running quickly

1. Qmail Basics

2. Storing and retrieving of emails

3. Virtualisation

4. Filtering Spam

5. Hosting Multiple Domains, Encryption, and Mailing Lists

Please check **www.PacktPub.com** for information on our titles

Printed in the United Kingdom
by Lightning Source UK Ltd.
124134UK00002B/1-30/A